Praise for Jolly Lad

"[Doran] thinks he's Oliver fucking Cromwell... He's a lunatic."
Mark E Smith

"Makes *Withnail & I* look like *Little House On The Prairie.*"
Caitlin Moran

"An anti-misery memoir and alternative music celebration... full of rock star encounters and hilarious one-liners as memorably droll as you'd expect from a Fall fan. With brutal honesty it also reminds that often it's still the writers who lead lives larger and more interesting than many of their media-managed musician subjects."
★★★★ Benjamin Myers, *MOJO*

"One of the best ~~music~~ writers you'll ever come across."
Drowned In Sound

"A wonderful tale... very funny."
The Independent

"Some kind of major hellride."
Mike Watt (the Minutemen, The Stooges)

"Beautifully wrought... the work of a real writer propelled by that most vital of properties, self-doubt."
Jonathan Meades

"An honest, brilliant, hilarious memoir that touches quite a lot of nerves. A must read for anyone who needs to sort their head out! Amen." Gillian Gilbert (New Order)

"A startling guide to self-destruction... hilarious yet insightful."
Cian Traynor, *The Irish Times*

"Every page is studded with bluntly brilliant prose... Can't recommend it highly enough." David Stubbs, author of *Future Days* and *Mars By 1980*

"John's powerful words make you feel part of his harrowing trip as you turn each page. Like a modern version of a Dickens or Hogarth sketch but with its beginnings in St Helens."
Tim Burgess (The Charlatans)

"Staggeringly poetic... steeped in deep truth about what it was, and is, to be a music nut in the 80s, 90s and the now."
Simon Price

"Upon finishing *Jolly Lad*, a lyrical, endlessly compelling memoir by the music journalist John Doran, you will probably wonder how he is still alive. You will not be alone. The co-editor and co-founder of acclaimed music website The Quietus apparently has organs that could endure a nuclear firestorm."
Musa Okwonga, *The Huff Post*

"The best book I've read about recovery since John Healy's magnificently scalding *The Grass Arena*." Wyndham Wallace author of *Lee, Myself & I*

"John Doran's remarkable *Jolly Lad* channels the vitality of *Down And Out In Paris And London*. It strikes the same timeless chimes. Politicised documentary as rich and pithy as Orwell's own gives way to a deeper probe until we feel we are being given a guided tour of the inner world through the eyes of one surviving evangelist... This is a brave and vital voice, emerging." Rick Holland

"This book is one of the great first person narratives of recent times – funny, bruising and with an eye for the detail of horror. I hope invoking the spectres of Winterson, Joyce and Hunter S. Thompson is to offer fairly high praise. This is not the work of a Bright Young Thing – even by Doran's own admission – but of a true maverick."
Alexander Holbrook, *Louder Than War*

"This addiction memoir is as compelling as it is poetic... Doran weaves a story of deeply observed and brilliantly conveyed self-doubting reflection." Martin James, *Times Higher Education*

"[*Jolly Lad*] finds expression not in what [Doran] recounts but in the wit and style of his delivery... It's a bravura story and there is no Disneyesque ending to the tale of an individual who is difficult to like but who has the honesty to admit there is little that could be liked about his past life." *Irish Left Review*

"A pugnacious account of the descent into addiction." Colm McCauliffe, *The New Statesman*

"The key to the book's power and incision is Doran's calm, reflective, procedural account of the alcohol addiction that comes close to killing him." Roy Wilkinson, *Caught By The River*

"Jolly Lad is an addiction memoir, but one which deconstructs the macho bullshit, the self-pity and the outright lying that surrounds the literature of addiction... a fucked-up, horrible, brilliant, hilarious tale." C D Rose, *3AM Magazine*

First published by Strange Attractor Press 2015
This edition published 2018
© John Doran 2015 / 2018
ISBN 978-1-907222-33-7

Edited by Natasha Soobramanien
Cover art and design by Simon Fowler
Illustrations by Krent Able

Strange Attractor Press
BM SAP, London, WC1N 3XX
www.strangeattractor.co.uk

Distributed by the MIT Press, Cambridge, Massachusetts.
And London, England.
Printed and bound in Estonia by Tallinna Raamatutrükikoda.

JOLLY LAD

JOHN DORAN
Illustrated by Krent Able

For Nick Talbot

FOREWORD

This book began with a failure of the imagination.

In 2011 *VICE* magazine asked me for a weekly column. The only instruction they gave me was simple: "You can write about whatever you want but it can't be about music."

I was keen but there was a problem – I couldn't think of a single good idea. I became aware that I was wasting a great opportunity as deadlines passed by and I failed to file my inaugural column. And soon I was measuring the time that had passed since their initial offer of work in months rather than weeks. I stopped finding the well-worn Douglas Adams quote amusing. ("I love deadlines. I like the whooshing sound they make as they fly by.") He was right. It was like living in Isleworth, directly under the Heathrow flight path, such was the volume of deadlines passing overhead in tight formation.

Eventually my mind went back to a conversation I'd had with a friend during the May of 2002. Paul Gill is a computer games writer and one of the authors of the Hacienda-affiliated acid house fanzine *Freaky Dancing* and he instilled an idea into me about three quarters of the way through a 48-hour ecstasy and alcohol binge in Manchester. He laid out his idea that all worthwhile cultural production came from a clinical and unflinching gaze at the minutiae of one's own life and that was whether we were talking about the *American Splendor* comics by Harvey Pekar, the poetry of Charles Bukowski, the films of Carol Morley or the lyrics of the world's greatest rock band, The Fall.

"You have to write what you know about John!" he shouted dramatically, waving his hands over his head. He then pointed at the large ornamental brass kettle in the hearth of the lounge bar of The Bull pub nearly Piccadilly Station. "Do you think the landlord will mind if I vomit into that giant teapot? Not sure if I can make it to the toilets in time. Or if I can stand up."

"Better not Paul, it's Sunday lunch time, we're the only people in here and he's stood right there staring at us. If it was Friday at last orders, it'd be a different matter..." I cautioned.

The column ended up being called MENK – a shortened version of 'mental' used in some, but by no means all, parts of Merseyside, to mean intellectually feeble or mentally handicapped rather than mentally ill. I grew up round the corner from the largest Victorian insane asylum in Europe, Rainhill Hospital, and this harsh epithet would be shouted at me by other kids when I got off the bus after school.

So I started writing about what was happening to me, and if nothing of interest was happening to me on a given week, then I would write about something that had happened to me years previously. The first column concerned the run-down little room in a shared warehouse space that I ran the Quietus out of with my good friend and business partner, Luke Turner. I wrote about how ours was the only building in a street full of empty office blocks and factory spaces that was not currently being knocked down to make luxury flats and how our tiny space was becoming overrun with vermin. The short piece was also about how I attended Alcoholics Anonymous on my 40th birthday. The seven-day deadline came round quickly again, so I wrote about struggling with the idea of writing for *VICE* and how worrying about dressing my month-old son in heavy metal themed baby clothes was obviously a veil for a much deeper anxiety about how good a father I was going to be in the future. Then I wrote about the stress of DJing at the wedding of friends and not getting the choice of music right. And then about what it was like living in my block of flats on a housing estate in Stamford Hill, in Hackney. About the hallucinations of spiders I used to suffer when I was younger. About how I had been diagnosed as being on the bipolar spectrum. About struggling with my thirst for drink and drugs. About how my life had been scarred by lengthy bouts of mental illness.

Slowly themes started coalescing out of this slew of observation and reminiscence: the recovery from alcoholism, the joy of fatherhood, repairing the damage done by decades of habitual drug use, coping with poor mental health, friendship, growing old and obsessive behaviour – especially regarding music and art.

The column proved relatively popular – or at least no one asked me to stop writing it. By spring of 2014, after three years, I'd filed 66 chapters of MENK so decided to take a hiatus while I worked on this book.

Instead of releasing an anthology of columns however, I decided to completely rewrite the material into a narrative, which would concern my recovery from alcoholism, the attempt to cope with mental illness and becoming a father.

I was determined not to write a 'my drink and drug hell' kind of book for several reasons – the main one being that I had, for the most part, had a really good time drinking. True, a handful of pretty appalling things have happened to me and some people that I know or used to know over the years. But I have, for the most part, left them out of this book as they are not illuminating, not edifying and in some cases concern other people who aren't here to consent to their appearance. Instead this book concentrates on what you face after the drink and the drugs have gone.

In my experience, being an alcoholic is debt consolidation for your life. Drink becomes the only thing you care about – eventually to the point where you don't even care if you live or die. So when you stop drinking... well, that's when the real trouble starts. Everything you drank to avoid dealing with – which in my case included mental illness, debt, depression, the impulse to self-harm, the impulse to commit suicide, anxiety, social dysfunction, body dysmorphia, stress, anger, violent rage and hypochondria – suddenly comes back into focus the second you stop.

I started drinking when I was 13. I was drinking every day by the time I was 15. Then I stayed constantly drunk until I was 37. When I stopped I had no idea what I would be like as an adult.

And that is what this book is about.

A Few Drops Of The Vile Stuff (1984)

So, let me tell you about my first beer.

Rainhill is a village which stands just off junction 7 of the M62 motorway, some ways between Liverpool and St Helens. And after being born two miles up the road on the maternity ward of Whiston Hospital in 1971, Rainhill is where I spent the first 18 years of my life.

Approximately 140 years before this a Catholic church was commissioned by local landowner Bartholomew Bretherton, designed by his architect Joshua Dawson and constructed by local builders and stone masons. St Bartholomew's Roman Catholic Church was completed in 1840 and a bell tower was added nine years later. The impressive prostyle church – the type that immediately springs to mind if you imagine a Greek or Roman temple – was built using designs based on the Basilica di San Bartolomeo all'Isola in Rome.

I was an altar boy at St Bart's for years. It was a profession I never excelled at. I never rose up through the ranks there. I am not grudgeful though. I only had two career options in mind before the age of 13, priest and astronaut, so it was just as well in retrospect. There was one terrifying week when the deputy altar boy got stuck into the communion wine and fell about insensible on the

altar instead of ringing the bell during the service. I got promoted
to deputy in the week of panic that followed his speedy expulsion
but they soon found someone better than me – someone with
better people skills who could get along with the bad tempered
bell ringers – and busted me back down again. Even though it
was boring, I enjoyed being an altar boy when Father Mac, an old
fellow from remote rural Ireland, was the parish priest. He could
seem dour but I liked him.

Sir Nikolaus Pevsner, author of the 46-volume series of county-
by-county guides, *The Buildings Of England* (1951-74), described
St Bart's as "the noblest Catholic church in South Lancashire"
and such was its uniqueness that it gained a grade 2 listing just five
months before I was born. However it was nobler when Pevsner
wrote about it and it was nobler in the 1970s when I was a kid
– and decked out in a long black cassock tied at the waist with
ornamental, tasselled rope and topped with a plain white, square
yoke surplice – than it is now.

The St Bart's of my youth was the most imposing church I
would ever visit. Most of the structure was built from sandstone
the colour of dried arterial blood, taken from the local Pex Hill
quarry. Faithful church-goers were able to see its massive, ornate
wrought iron gates long before they reached them as they walked
up Rainhill's main thoroughfare, Warrington Road. Once inside
the gates, there was a courtyard surrounded by gravestones, then
a large flight of limestone steps up to six, massive fluted Ionic
columns supporting an imposing hexastyle portico. The steps
would take on a peculiar kind of intransigent wetness during
autumn, and I saw at least three parishioners come a cropper after
either bounding into or out of church in a hurry and then going
for a burton. The front doors were huge – the height of a two
storey house, and a bugger to open if you were only a kid – but
once you managed to swing them ajar the gloomy interior was
even more impressive, with a row of austere Corinthian columns
supporting a coffered barrel vault ceiling. The pillars led the eye
toward a generously rounded apse with closely set Doric pilasters
and a domed ceiling. The most anachronistic thing about the

structure given its setting in a small village near the Lancashire border of Merseyside was probably the tall Italian-style bell tower. While walking around in Rainhill, you could sometimes see the Roman, pyramid-roofed campanile topped with crucifix, poking above the orderly suburban rooftops. Painted along the rear interior walls of the apse were massive portraits of some of the apostles standing grimly to attention with their means of destruction clearly visible. Peter holding the keys to Heaven – his bloody wrist and foot wounds on show. James holding a sword and a bible. Bartholomew holding the scythe used to behead him. Up in the cavernous, dimly lit, domed roof above the altar, Christ In Majesty stood on a cloud against glittering constellations, A for Alpha and O for Omega at his feet.

On top of the masses on Sunday mornings, there were also special services and religious holidays altar boys had to serve at. We used to get a five pence piece for doing weddings and a ten pence piece for doing funerals. I liked the money and loved the sense of occasion but once I had to do a funeral service for the father of a girl in my year. She cried all the way through the mass and by the end I couldn't look her in the eye. Afterwards I took the ten pence piece and threw it over the high sandstone wall into the grounds of Loyola Hall, the nearby Jesuit retreat and convent. (One of the altar boys who was a few years older than me and serving at the same time was Frank Cottrell Boyce who would go on to write popular children's books and scripts for films such as *24 Hour Party People* and *A Cock And Bull Story*, though I can't remember ever talking to him or even what he looked like.) At Christmas Father Mac would hire a projector and Cine 8 reels of films like *Halloween*, *Jaws* and *Alien* which had been condensed down to their 20 most exciting and gory minutes. Everyone above the age of 14 would get tots of whiskey and a cigarette each.

On Easter Sunday there would be a procession from the church, across Warrington Road and into the grounds of the convent. Father Mac would hold the Eucharist in a magnificent gold and glass container, while four of us would struggle in the stiff spring breeze to hold a tasselled canopy on long wooden poles over his

head. Another altar boy would walk ahead swinging a thurible
on chains containing smoking incense which would dissipate
immediately into the wind. Goose-stepping behind us, spotty
representatives from the Boys Brigade, Girl Guides, the Scouts
and other quasi-military, crypto-fascist youth outfits designed to
prepare square-jawed protestant teenagers for slaughter abroad,
visiting us from the godless temple of Right Footers down the
road, carried their giant flags and pennants.

I don't know where this disdain for other faiths came from as
it wasn't encouraged by Father Mac, the nuns from Loyola Hall
or our teachers. Wherever the lack of respect originated, it ran
pretty deep though. The year I quit being an altar boy, my best
mate Stu and I went out in St Helens drinking. On the way home
we stopped at Rainhill Bridge for chips, mushrooms and gravy.
Then, for reasons that now escape me, we climbed up the side of
Saint James Methodist Church and sat on the apex of the roof to
eat them. After a while of pissing about and a thwarted attempt
to climb the steeple, a police car drove past. We took the only
option open to us and pretended to be gargoyles. The police car
didn't stop. We cheered and got back to eating. After about three
or four minutes another police car drove past so we did exactly
the same thing. This happened about six times. "We're invisible!"
Stu roared. Eventually we grew bored and climbed down where
we were immediately monstered by the dibble. They frog marched
us out to a squad car and put Stu in the back of it. After two or
three minutes another car pulled over and I was put in the back
of that. The driver said to me: "I've been driving round the block
for the last half an hour waiting for you pair of dickheads to get
down. Did you not see me or do you think you're invisible?" One
of them rapped on my head with his knuckles: "Are you on LSD
son? That's what makes you fly isn't it?"

But when I was a boy such contempt for holy structures would
have been unthinkable because the Roman Catholic faith was
something that my family took very seriously indeed.

In the house of my paternal grandparents and maiden aunts,
everywhere you turned there were shrines to numerous obscure

saints and martyrs. In their back garden there was a grotto made from concrete and seashells, dedicated to the Holy Mother. Everyone wore rosary beads, carried a picture of the Holy Father in Rome upon them at all times and prayed to St Anthony when they couldn't find their house keys. At the foot of the stairs there was a holy water font on the wall, so you could bless yourself before climbing up to bed to prevent falling over and braining yourself on the steps ahead of you. For similar reasons there was a font at the top of the stairs to prevent you ever needing the services of a trip to Lourdes after falling down the flight and knocking yourself out.

Drawers were crammed full of prayer cards, benedictions, mass cards and religious trinkets. Everyone had their own roster of saints to pray to depending on their needs, which were often but not solely related to hypochondria or lost car keys. My favourites were the stigmatics and out of them I was most interested in Padre Pio. Stigmata were marks or wounds that would appear spontaneously on the wrists, feet and other areas of the body which corresponded with the injuries suffered by Christ when he was being crucified. Or rather they did if you were remarkably holy. Pio of Pietrelcina was a friar and mystic who suffered these gaping puncture holes in more recent times – he only died in 1968. As a child I had photos of him with his wrist wounds showing and three different bits of cloth that had been dipped in his blood. Fuck a splinter from the one true cross! Give me the blood of a stigmatic any day.

I would check my wrists and feet for the signs of stigmata every day when I was a child. And I would even spend hours trying to bring the bleeding on with my mind much in the same way I would spend hours trying to move objects with The Force, after watching *The Empire Strikes Back*. I'm not mocking; this was what attracted me to the Roman Catholic Church and what initially made me consider becoming a priest myself: the violence. The mysticism. The terror. The blood. The gaping wounds. The immense suffering.

Rainhill was split equally between working and middle class

inhabitants. In geographical terms it was handily bifurcated by Warrington Road, with mainly middle class folk living on one side – where the titular hill was – with the working class – my family included – living on the other side where the newer housing estates were and where the titular rain fell by the pail-full.

Father Mac executed his duties well and fairly as far as I can attest but the fact that he looked and talked like a bumpkin out of a JP Donleavy novel outweighed whatever spiritual, moral or practical attributes he might have had in the eyes of the more middle class parishioners. These folk who lived on the other side of the road longed to have shorter services enlivened by contemporary Christian folk rock music with participatory clapping in the aisles. And ideally they wanted a celebrant who looked a bit like Ian McShane. But more than anything they wished dearly not to be surrounded by martyred giants holding saws, knives and scimitars, with their angry wounds and bloodied robes and faces looming out of the dark. Father Mac did not want to leave but there was some kind of *putsch* and he was replaced by a more urbane Englishman called Bullen who had tanned skin and lacquered hair, a combination which made him look a bit like Bob Monkhouse. He also had his own car but how can you trust a man on matters of the gravest spiritual importance when he's got orange skin and drives an Austin Morris Princess with a vinyl roof?

Before long Bullen got the decorators in to modernise the church: the intricately patterned, lovingly detailed Victorian wall murals were covered by large blocks of magnolia, lemon and grey paint. He also had carpets fitted and installed an expensive lighting system. Luckily three of the martyrs and Christ in his firmament survived the decorators' officially sanctioned vandalism and they remain on the back walls of the church to this day, but transposed into this utterly tasteful, brightly lit space with its Habitat / show home vibes, the church immediately lost all of its power over me. I don't think I ever really believed in God – despite really wanting to – but now that I could see clearly into all the magnolia corners of St Bart's, I was no longer afraid of him either.

The changing balance of power between a new and an old world was also becoming apparent in my junior school, St Bart's. A collection of pre-fabricated buildings, it was connected to the church by a graveyard and a playing field. Half of my teachers were nuns from the convent. They were old with faces like chamois leather, and more likely to mete out punishment with a wooden or metal ruler than their lay counterparts, but they also appeared to be dying out as not one of their number seemed to be under retirement age. (More recently there has been an influx of new nuns from various countries in Africa into Loyola Hall according to my Mum but I'm not sure if they are employed to teach at the school any more.) The other half of my teachers were just regular folk, mainly middle class Rainhill people who were also involved in helping out with the church.

It being a Roman Catholic school with close ties to the local convent, church and religious community, there was a lot of faith-related teaching. But aside from the terrifying elderly nuns, after the old decor of the church had been covered in Dulux and Father Mac had been sent back to Ireland, none of it held much sway over me. None of it seemed to make any sense. I was a dutiful son and really wanted to have faith like my parents did but very little of it added up. Every time something bad happened we would just be palmed off from the altar with a platitudinal: "God moves in mysterious ways." I would have settled for the darkness of ritual alone but the modernisers insisted on removing it. The terror that religion can wield over the faithful was probably the most essential aspect of the Church; and deprived of that, what was the point? Churches – and by extension the Church – are supposed to put the fear of God into you. Making them inviting, homely and comfortable is missing the point by a country mile. By the time I was about 12, the Church to me was little more than a priest who looked like a stand-up comedian and a load of people clapping along to terrible music in a large, well-lit but badly decorated hall, usually at the behest of a guy called Steve or Dave or Pete with an acoustic guitar, a roll-neck sweater and brown leather sandals worn over black towelling socks.

As soon as I was old enough to question the justice of the random things that befell people in life, I also realised that the Church was unable to provide any decent or reasonable answers.

One morning at school when I was about eight or nine, we were having our first lesson of the day with Mrs Moss when there was a colossal bang from Warrington Road outside. It was the loudest thing I had ever heard. Mr Perry who was in the Saint John's Ambulance and did first aid, ran into the room and told her to get us all away from the windows and that we should all lie on the floor under our desks with our eyes closed. We knew it was serious because he addressed Mrs Moss by her Christian name.

We were kept like that for what felt like the longest time. We weren't allowed to walk home on our own. Mothers were summoned. Neighbours were summoned. Friends of mothers were summoned.

"There's been an accident," said a friend's Mum who had been tasked with fetching me as we walked on to Warrington Road. "The bus driver... accidentally drove into the bus stop... There were some people there... One of the ladies from the bus stop is in Heaven now."

The bus stop and the fence behind it were destroyed; bits of wood and concrete were all over the main road. The road was completely free from traffic – the only time bar Easter Sunday I had ever seen it so quiet. There were huge holes in the sandstone walls separating the main road from the convent. Large rust-coloured blocks lay scattered across the tarmac like a giant's Lego. Round the bend towards my best friend Stu's house two cars were on their sides and a bit further up there was another one on its roof. I wanted to run onto the road and run round the cars making squealing engine noises but my neighbour gripped me to her – even though there was no traffic about, just haunted looking adults with white knuckled grips on children, dragging them home. Then further still was the bus. It had been driven through the front of a house where a boy from my year lived. It was so bizarre, I thought. 'When they drive the bus away there will be no front on Alistair's

house. It will be like a doll's house. You'll be able to stand outside
and watch his family eating their tea from the street.'

"Alistair's house will be cold tonight!" I said.

"I don't think Alistair will be sleeping in his house tonight,"
said my neighbour's Mum in a strange high pitched voice.

As well as Mr Perry giving first aid, they went and fetched
Father Mac and he gave the young woman who was at the bus
stop the last rites. She wasn't Catholic though, so there wasn't any
call for me to do the service. By the next day the school was open
once more and although it was a long time until they fixed Alistair's
house, I was disappointed that the opaque, plastic sheeting and
scaffolding they fitted to the front meant you couldn't see inside
at any point.

Before hitting my teens I had plenty of interests. I was a keen
reader of books about manned and unmanned space travel; I was
a voracious consumer of science fiction novels and comics and
loved anything like *Dr Who*, *The Hitchhiker's Guide To The Galaxy*
and *Sapphire And Steel* on TV. I was also growing to like pop
music on the very infrequent occasions I heard it. My Dad didn't
really like popular music of any stripe at all. The advent of The
Beatles in the early 1960s had put him off for life. We listened
to the mainly talk orientated Radio Merseyside all day long on
Saturdays and Sundays when we were in the house and – if I was
lucky – in between all the interminable, jocular, sentimental chat
I would occasionally get to hear 'I Feel Love' by Donna Summer,
'Heart Of Glass' by Blondie, 'Telstar' by The Tornados, 'Popcorn'
by Hot Butter or some other song that would make me think of
outer space, or sometimes even make me feel like I was floating in
a vacuum – like Alexey Leonov, the Russian cosmonaut who was
the first person to perform an extravehicular spacewalk in 1965.

But I was also really into trains. And there were worse places
to grow up than Rainhill if you were a fan of the railways. Just
under two centuries ago, a one-mile stretch of track formed the
site of the 1829 Rainhill Trials. This highly publicised contest
was organised by the directors of the Liverpool and Manchester
Railway to judge which type of steam locomotive would be the

first to pull passenger trains on its newly completed line – the first modern example of its kind anywhere in the world. Five engines entered but only one completed the Trials – the Rocket, built by George and Robert Stephenson. This fantastic train, in striking yellow, black and white livery, was years ahead of the field and became known colloquially as the Rainhill Rocket... locally at least; I've heard it was known as Stephenson's Rocket in other, less enlightened places. When the actual railway line opened the following year in 1830, the inaugural journey of the locomotive was marred by the death of William Huskisson, an MP for Liverpool. The unfortunate politician ignored advice and got off the train when it stopped midway between Manchester and Liverpool to take on water and was hit by a locomotive travelling in the opposite direction. When leaving Rainhill by train today, if you know where to look for it, you can see a commemorative plaque on a sandstone wall near the point where he was hit. And as well as the world's first passenger steam locomotive and its first railway fatality, Rainhill could claim a third train-related number one: the world's first ever skew bridge – a road bearing structure that crosses a railway line at a pronounced angle.

But these kind of facts can only really remain significant in a young man's life for his first decade. There were two colossal presences lurking just out of view that would shunt innovative steam engines, oddly angled bridges and crushed parliamentarians into a siding for good – and they were alcohol and heavy music. These were the two things which would come to eclipse nearly every other consideration in my life for the following three decades. What chance did my collection of authentic British Rail issue brass buttons stand when confronted by the twin spectres of Special Brew and Iron Maiden?

In 1982, I started secondary school. St Edmund Campion Roman Catholic School was an all-boys comprehensive on a housing estate in St Helens that was knocked down the year I left to make room for more Barratt homes. One of my best friends at Eddie Camp was (and still is) Martin. His Mum and Dad were nurses at Rainhill Hospital, Europe's then largest insane asylum and their house stood on the massive grounds amid the imposing Victorian wards, the fields and thickets. Twice a week, when I would get off the bus with him after school to go round to his, other kids would yell at us: "MENK! MENK! RAINHILL MENKS!" Then they would belm over-exaggeratedly out of the rear window as the bus pulled away, slapping hands twisted into grotesque claws against temporarily spasticated wrists, faces warped into odd parodies of muscle malfunction, grimacing lip spasm and mental enfeeblement before resolving into laughter. And that was just our friends. No one seemed to realise that the people who lived in the wards of this majestic building were unfortunate souls suffering from lunacy, not those blighted with mental and physical impairment. Or maybe they did realise and just didn't care. Who knows what goes through the heads of schoolboys? A big thing at our school was that you could get beaten up if you had a big forehead. The tough kids, who were all Neanderthal looking, thick-browed cunts with tiny foreheads would go round and measure everyone from their hairline to their eyebrows. If anyone's "fodder" came in at over four inches, they would then kick the fuck out of them, screaming, "TEFAL head!" There was a TV advert for the French kitchenware company on television at the time featuring a bunch of scientists who had giant foreheads because of how clever they were, you see. And the relatively clever were feared and hated with a relative ferocity at St Edmund Campion RC.

Martin's elder sisters had gone away to join the Royal Navy and he had become slightly stir crazy due to lack of full-time companionship at home. He spent his time inventing games for us to play that didn't make any sense. One involved us sitting on the roof of his house, filling our mouths with Angel Delight powder and then blowing through cheap mouth organs until one or the other of us would faint and then slide down the roof and off the side. I remember him turning crimson, clouds of brown powder firing out of the end of his tiny instrument until he grunted, "Urgh, I'm going," as his eyes rolled into his skull, and his body slid limply off the side of the house.

Over years of visiting him there, I would come to regard the hospital as an amazing place, if cold and menacing. Occasionally a terrified inmate would make a bid for freedom, running howling down Rainhill Road in their pyjamas and we would be there to see it. There was no white van, no giant net, just harassed looking nurses who maybe spent a bit too much time in the hospital social club smoking John Player Specials or supping mild in local pub The Brown Edge to be sprinting after the powerfully insane. (These escapes didn't always end well. Martin came into school one morning ashen faced saying that while walking in the grounds the preceding evening, he had stumbled across the clean-up operation dealing with an escaped inmate who had been hit by a train. No plaque for that poor bastard.)

The hospital would occasionally attract some national glare because of the higher security Scott Clinic on adjacent ground and its temporary guests such as Ian Brady, who came in for psychological tests. (The bus driver who went mad at the wheel of the 10A driving it through people and cars before crashing headfirst into Alistair's house also ended up passing through their wards.) But Rainhill Hospital itself was a large, quiet place full of hidden nooks and crannies. We weren't supposed to wander round the grounds ourselves but the site was too sprawling and large for it to be effectively secured against curious teenagers and Martin knew the hospital layout – its fields, copses, roads, railway embankments and cuttings – like the back of his hand. The main buildings which housed the wards were impossible to gain access to however. Like St Bart's church, the imposing central structure had been built in the mid-19th Century from locally sourced sandstone. But they were mainly feature free, hulking and loved by few other than us. There would be no grade listing for the wards to save them from their fate in 1991, or, for that matter, to save the former inmates from theirs – care in the community.

And it was in Martin's house, in Rainhill, on the grounds of Europe's largest Victorian insane asylum that I had my first beer.

I think I'd just turned 13. I'd had plenty of small glasses of wine and sherry with my family before on special occasions at meal time, not mentioning whiskey when I was ill, but nothing touched me like this can of beer.

I remember with great clarity sitting in Martin's room with about four other lads. It was about 4pm and we were all in school uniform, talking about *Advanced Dungeons & Dragons* and Queen's superlative *News Of The World* album and sunlight was streaming through the sloping window in the loft conversion bedroom. Martin's Dad came in with some four packs of cheap lager. They'd been fetched straight from the freezer cabinet and they were covered in condensation. The can of Compass lager, a local supermarket own brand, had the map of some imaginary continent drawn on it, except it had been rendered with such little attention to what actual land masses look like that you could have been forgiven for not realising what these roughly sketched blobs were supposed to be, and presuming it was representative of the piebald pattern of a Friesian cow's hide, for example.

I removed the ring pull off the can – a surprisingly hard task to accomplish – and then let it dangle from my little finger.

Someone said that you could use the ring pull as a weapon to slice someone's throat open. The edges of the aperture – if that's what it's called – were sharp against my upper lip and the can started freezing my bottom lip numb. And the lager was as cold as glacier melt water.

The taste wasn't totally unexpected as my Dad let me drink shandy on some weekends, but bereft of the sugary lemonade, it tasted of unexplored adult vistas and untold levels of sophistication.

Everyone made over-exaggerated exclamations about how much they were enjoying their beer. How they always loved a beer. How this was a particularly fine beer.

There was something caustic, cleansing, scouring and metallic about the golden liquid as it burnt its way down my throat. During the first demonstrative swig, things in exterior life seemed to become time-stretched and then broke away from me in ragged chunks. The light from the window was ripping my throat open, letting the sun's rays slide into my mouth and then, gradually spilling warmth into my belly. I always knew that there was something missing inside of me. A hole the size of a grapefruit or a clenched fist in the middle of my chest where I felt my soul or something important like that should be. In church my priest, the one who looked like Bob Monkhouse, talked about how the Spirit Of Our Lord would fill our bodies – would we only open our hearts to his love. But I couldn't feel it. I couldn't sense his presence in the room and my heart was standing open and completely empty. I had ached for this sensation for so long with no joy and now Compass lager had given it to me.

I was on to my third can and as drunk as hell by the time everyone else was finishing their first. I got on my chair and started dancing and laughing and waving my arms around and I think Martin threw me out but I can't really remember.

It's weird; I don't really have any memories of prolonged good periods in my life before a few years ago. I don't really remember enjoying being a child that much or a teenager or even a young adult for that matter, and I don't really mind that much because I guess it's totally normal for a lot of people. But I have nothing but fond memories of being round Martin's house. I drank so much there one night that I ate three large Dundee cakes and then vomited currants so heavily that some got stuck to the ceiling. Later, when Martin's sainted mother cleaned up after me, my puke broke the vacuum cleaner.

I'm sure if Rainhill Hospital still existed and I went and sat in the grounds on the grass, a golden shaft of celestial light would pierce my life once more; if it wasn't all just Barratt Homes, shatterproof bus stops and nondescript newsagents now. They say that fishermen rescued from drowning at the last minute – tangled in the nets, dragged to the surface, the briny punched and poured from their lungs – can become obsessed with the area of ocean in which they nearly died; sometimes even returning physically later to try and find the exact spot on the sea's surface above where they were rescued. The act of water entering the lungs releases huge amounts of endorphins, apparently giving one a rapturous feeling of calmness and well-being. These melancholy fishermen return to where they nearly exited life and sit there in their boats, floating on the ocean waiting for the feeling to return to them, waiting to return to the state that was as close to God as they would ever get.

What's gone has gone, but I'd still go back to Rainhill Hospital if I could. And what would I give to have that can of Compass lager right now? And what would I give to have the roaring sun in my throat and in my belly once more?

Organised Noise (1987)

Fucking U2.

The stadium rock four-piece got me into more trouble with my parents than any other band when I was growing up. I dearly wish I could pretend it was Throbbing Gristle, Slayer or CRASS but no, it had to be U2.

I started buying records in 1982 when I was ten. (I had already inherited a scratched 7" copy of The Tornados' *Telstar* and a cheap but satisfying Johnny Cash greatest hits LP off my parents and in 1980 my best friend Stu gave me a cassette copy of the *Flash Gordon* soundtrack by Queen. But I broke my actual record buying cherry with a second hand vinyl copy of the *Kings Of The Wild Frontier* LP by Adam And The Ants and 'Love Of The Common People' by Paul Young on 7" from Woolworths a few months later.) Initially, for a very short period of time, when I bought records I did so with the full knowledge of my Mum and Dad but after a while it became clear that I didn't really understand the rules and this was actually violently unresolved territory.

Sometimes it seemed to be just fine for me to come home with a couple of 7"s and then at other times it caused a massive conniption that could last for days.

In 1984, there was a short-lived but excellent 'grey market' shop over the road from the HMV in Liverpool which sold foreign pressings of popular albums at drastically marked down prices. My first purchase from the store was a Greek edition of U2's *War*, which I bought because I liked the cover. When I got it home, I was so taken with playing it on repeat, I forgot to stop by the time my Dad got in from work. He discovered me listening to bombastic closing track '40' at full volume, and he was nothing, if not predictably angry about it.

"What good is this? It's a total waste of money!" he roared at me after turning the record down so it was barely audible. He then picked up the sleeve and waved it in my face. "You can't eat it. You can't wear it. It's useless!" In a rare moment of bravery I grabbed the gatefold off him, extended it out and put it on my head like a giant two dimensional, stove pipe hat and started marching up and down in front of him. "Who says you can't wear it?!" I shouted triumphantly. "Pathetic!" he shouted back and stamped out of the room slamming the door behind him with such violence that it removed all of the oxygen from the downstairs of the house and deposited it all upstairs.

He was more consistent when it came to TV and radio. For most of my childhood I wasn't allowed to watch *Top Of The Pops* at all or listen to Radio 1 outside of my bedroom. My sister Catherine and I were allowed to watch a little bit of telly every evening after engaging in lengthy negotiations with my Dad but nothing to do with rock and pop music or youth culture in general. I didn't realise at the time that this was more for his sake rather than ours.

Modern youth culture would light the touch paper on his easily ignited anger. When he was working overtime I would sneakily watch *Top Of The Pops*, though. The first time he caught me I was in the middle of watching 'Cars' by Gary Numan when I was eight. He made me promise never to watch it again and shouted about how disappointed he was in me. The second time a couple of years later I was watching the video to 'Stand And Deliver' by Adam And The Ants when he came in unexpectedly from work. I couldn't even come up with a convincing argument as to how this situation had occurred as my mind had been blown. ("It's a highwayman in pirate makeup on a chandelier! Bloody hell!")

"I'll give you a diddly qua qua", he said sternly, reaching for his belt. This is something he occasionally did. He reached for his belt. This was to indicate what he would do to me – what he would like to do to me – if he were a less reasonable person. And in this way he acted his violent and rageful impulses out in a healthy manner. He dealt with his depression and nihilism in a less healthy way though – taking to bed for days, or sometimes even weeks, at a time and staring at the wall in silence.

My parents had both grown up along Scotland Road – Liverpool's tough city within a city that was home mainly to immigrants – not just Irish, but Scottish, Welsh, Polish, Italian and German as well. After getting married in 1966, they moved to Rainhill but after a couple of years my Dad got made redundant from his factory job in Liverpool so he put his name down for a government plumbing course in St Helens and ended up on a waiting list. He then went to his union to ask about work nearer to where they lived and they put him in touch with a furniture factory in Widnes. He worked for the factory for some time on the clock (or as a temp, as we'd say now) and three months after I was born, in September 1971, he asked if he could take a week's holiday. His boss came to see him and said: "I believe you are going to have a holiday. We're thinking of making you up, putting you on staff. We want you to be in charge of different spraying departments at the factory." Then he slipped my Dad a fiver – the equivalent of half his weekly wage – and said: "Have a drink on me."

They went on holiday camping near Valle Crucis Abbey in Llangollen thinking things were looking up. When they got back he waited for months but the promotion wasn't mentioned again, so when he was offered a place on the government plumbing scheme the following year, my Dad took it and left the factory.

After the course ended he started work with a St Helens firm and things started looking up – the work was certainly more satisfying and varied than clocking on in a factory every day – but he was vulnerable on trainee wages with a young family to support and a mortgage to cover. His old boss from Widnes called round to our house one evening and promised my Dad he would be looked after if he went back to the furniture factory; that they were opening a new operation in Birmingham and would need someone to run it. So my Dad went back. Not long afterwards, in April 1974, my Mum gave birth to my sister, Catherine. But there was no promotion, no new factory, no new job. In fact the opposite was the case. He was stuck on the shop floor of a furniture factory, working with poisonous solvents and noisy compression machines that were making him ill and deafening him, earning peanuts for the rest of his life. But now thanks to a drop off in demand for what they were making, he would also have to work 'short time' (drastically reduced, part time hours) between November and Easter every year between 1978 and his retirement in 1999 on much lower wages. So from my seventh birthday onwards it was a struggle for him to put food on the table and clothes on our backs.

I didn't realise until he told me this year that these extended periods that he would spend in bed coincided exactly with him being on reduced hours. Overextended financially, unable to cope with the fact that he had been lied to and unable to do the one thing that he wanted to do – work – he retreated into his bedroom, demanding silence and to be left alone.

With unemployment as it was in Merseyside in the 1980s, him pushing 50, with a wife and two kids to support and literally no formal qualifications to speak of, there was no wriggle room on this, just years of inchoate rage and bitterness. He couldn't retrain or leave, it was just time to bed in. His mental health became more and more erratic. He held his boss, pop musicians and his family responsible for the position he found himself in. But he especially blamed U2.

Of course this was another example of capitalism's great cloaking mechanism in full effect. Blaming expensive hat wearing stadium rock divots for your lot in life is no less unreasonable than blaming immigrants, the police, the middle classes, those on the dole, claimants of sickness benefit, your neighbour who has a better car than you, those on your shop floor who have better shift patterns than you, the secretary you suspect to be fucking someone in middle management, the students who are only working in your office over the summer break, black people, Asian people, Europeans, people from Wigan, people from Manchester, people from London, people from Yorkshire, people from the other, better, side of Warrington Road... No less daft but probably a lot less morally objectionable. It's all a well-ingrained divide and conquer subroutine that stops anyone that works from putting their boss's head in a vice and turning the handle until they start weeping blood.

I should say at this point I love and respect my father – my son is named after him. He is a good man – good to a fault (both of my parents are) – and if I have any positive attributes as an adult, then most of them (patience; endurance; how to strip, repaint and re-hang a door etc) are down to him. He taught me the most important lesson of my life – you should never give a fuck what other people think about you – even if he didn't put it exactly like that. He certainly wasn't responsible for me smoking crack or spending so much time in Wetherspoons pubs for example. He would tell me every single day not to end up in the same position as him; that even if I was starving and homeless he wouldn't get me a job in his factory because of what a shower of bastards they were, that he would never forgive me if I didn't go to university and go far away. All I wanted to do was to sit in my room read sci fi and listen to Gary Numan – all I genuinely wanted was to be left alone. He made it impossible for this to happen. And for that, and many other things, he has my undying thanks.

But also he would tell me every day how fucked everything was. How you could not under any circumstances trust anyone. How the game was terminally loaded against people like me and him. And nihilism and anger blossomed in me like a teardrop of Indian ink efflorescing in a vial of clear water.

The last time I properly fell out with my Dad about U2 before I left home was, in retrospect, completely avoidable. With *War*, I'd been playing catch up but later in 1984 the band released *The Unforgettable Fire* – the first album by the group that I bought contemporaneously – and the one that I loved the most. And then the following year they aced it at Live AID. These two things bought my teenage loyalty and despite discovering Joy Division, The Fall, the Sisters Of Mercy, The Jesus And Mary Chain, Sonic Youth, Nick Cave And The Bad Seeds, The Cure and Siouxsie And The Banshees in the intervening years, this is why I found myself sagging off school to go to HMV in Liverpool to buy *The Joshua Tree* on the day of its release, March 9, 1987.

My school was due to be knocked down at the end of the academic year and everyone involved had given up trying. Most people had stopped wearing uniforms – me included – but such was my limited budget for clothes and taste for dark trousers and suit jackets from Oxfam that barely anyone noticed. The fighting which had already been quite lively got much worse – some students got expelled for battering a teacher senseless. At least two other teachers appeared to be having full-blown nervous breakdowns. It was really easy to get away with not going in – even for relatively bookish people like me. Even though I was just a few weeks away from my O Levels, it felt safer just to hang around in record shops, libraries and parks.

At the time I had a heavily dented and scratched steel water flask which I carried with me everywhere. It was designed to hold 75cl of liquid and had been bought for me to house a plentiful amount of blackcurrant squash which would ensure that I didn't need to waste money on pop from the local shop. However by this point it was usually half full of a mixture of whiskey stolen from my Dad and home brewed fortified wine and sherry stolen from my Aunties. Or when I had the money to buy alcohol, Thunderbird blue fortified wine and Gold Label barley wine; often mixed.

After buying *The Joshua Tree*, I could have taken the train straight back to Rainhill but the powerful blast of head and gut-warming alcohol persuaded me to spend the day in Liverpool, listening to Heaven 17 on my Walkman, taking trips across the Mersey on the ferry. I don't know what time it was when I left but it was getting dark by the time I got home.

When I walked into the house pissed, clutching a U2 album, my Dad was already home. He confiscated it off me. He kept it for so long I didn't even really want it when he gave it back. I think Martin taped it for me eventually – I must have been the last person in my year to hear it. I didn't think that much of it. It seemed really underwhelming to me, despite having a great guitar sound. Maybe my Dad had a point... what good *was* it?

What I find interesting about my recollection of these events is not what happened itself but the peculiarly clear details still imprinted in my memory. The clean but matte feel of the sleeve of the U2 album, which was ruined by a thumb print the second I took it off the cashier. Listening to 'Play To Win' by Heaven 17 on a bright red Walkman the size of half a house brick with orange foam headphones while carefully navigating the ankle deep well of urine sloshing about the floors of men's toilets on the Mersey ferry. How I always had to carry a pencil with me to help with the rewinding of cassettes. How the tape had become snarled and then eventually snapped and had to be carefully stuck back together using sellotape, resulting in a second's uncomfortable silence during the track 'Soul Warfare'. How I also had a cassette with me containing tracks taped from the John Peel show. One night I had heard 'Upside Down' by the Jesus And Mary Chain and despite the fact it gave me a headache I listened in again the following night in order to tape it. I didn't hear it but he did play 'Tempo House' by The Fall. I used to play this track over and over again, trying to work out what it was. I didn't understand why the singer's lyrics were so weird, or why he didn't sing properly or why all the instruments sounded out of tune. I would play this song to people and tell them it was my band and they would say, "Jesus. Your band is awful." And I had a third tape with me, recorded from two albums loaned from Thatto Heath Lending Library's vinyl collection. *Evol* by Sonic Youth on one side and *E.S.T. (Trip To The Moon)* by Alien Sex Fiend on the other.

A lot of my memory is ravaged. I kicked a hole in the side of it. Made myself an unreliable witness. But I can remember my history regarding all of these songs, records and cassettes with a certain degree of clarity – where I heard them, where I bought them, where I taped them. The context. The setting. The sounds. The people. But what about the rest of my memory?

I can't remember, for example, anything about sitting my O Levels or leaving school a few weeks later, or much about that summer holiday.

To be fair my long-term memory is great for someone of my age. You're not supposed to remember anything before the age of four but I can remember plenty from before my second birthday. Being burped by my mother over her shoulder and vomiting extra chunky marmalade down the back of her new purple cashmere sweater. Being in hospital for three different operations which apparently, all took place when I was one. A hernia, a circumcision and a sinus drain. I remember sitting in nappies on the black and white tiled floor of the children's ward in Whiston Hospital pulling at the scab on my ear until it came off and warm blood dripped out onto my chest. I was shouting and banging a bright yellow Tonka truck on the floor. I remember liking the hospital with its lurid pink and garish yellow desserts. I remember being in the bath with my mother. Being in the pram and looking up at the giant, ugly faces staring in at me. I distinctly remember being repulsed by the sight of men, with their hairy noses, staring right in at me like gargoyles. I remember my sister being brought back from the hospital after she was born and how I wasn't able to sit on my Mum's knee as she was still sore. I remember my Dad's factory with the roaring lathes and loud compressors which gave me nightmares for years to follow...

But if my long-term memory is better than average, my short and mid-term memory are now shot. Twenty three years of ecstasy, cannabis, amphetamine, cocaine, LSD, mushroom, plant food, ketamine, crack, grass, alcohol and MDMA misuse plus several severe beatings have seriously affected the way I remember very recent events. Sometimes it feels as if my cerebral cortex has been put through a laminating machine that won't allow me to form satisfactory new memories. I used to know why this deterioration happened. I have read a lot of pop science books in my time but I'm not sure to what use, as I can now barely recall any science whatsoever. If my life depended on it, I could no longer rank a gemstone using the Mohs Scale Of Hardness. My intimacy with the process of fractional distillation of crude oil has become a thing of the past. Even the stuff I have to try and remember for work is pretty hazy and I have to recap every so often. Is it true that musical memory is different to linguistic memory; that hearing various songs – or maybe even just being reminded of them – lights up different areas of the brain in different ways? It's time for another refresher perhaps.

The first of the proper hidings I took happened when I was 14 in Rainhill. I was walking down Warrington Road at about 9pm when I saw three older lads on the other side of the road. My instinct that they were going to beat me up was correct, my instinct to run up a side street and then down a back alley to avoid them was not. I slipped on some ice and had barely got to my feet when they caught up with me and got stuck in. These lads all had the right clothes on – flared Wrangler jeans, widened with triangles of different coloured denim, Fred Perry tops, Adidas Trimm Trab trainers, big Kappa jackets. I did not. I was wearing Dollar-Stretch spray on jeans, Puma tennis shoes and a grey towelling sweatshirt top that had the word 'STYLE' emblazoned in the Lonsdale typography on the front, purchased from a unit in St Helens Tontine Market. Luckily the top got covered in so much blood – thin strings of gore pulled from the inside of my mouth and wiped on it with shaking hands on the eventual walk home – that it never washed properly clean again and I was allowed to throw it out.

I was still to disabuse myself of the illusion that if I could just have the really expensive casual gear that all of the other herberts in Whiston, Rainhill and St Helens wore, I'd be like them – or at least pass among them unmolested. But of course, that wasn't how it worked.

After the beating the sight in my right eye got worse and worse but by the time my parents finally managed to find a specialist who didn't fob them off and I was diagnosed as having a detached retina, the horse had already bolted that particular stable.

I had surgery the following spring to prevent me from going completely blind in the eye – I would never be able to read through

it or even make out faces with it again but it was still good for depth perception in conjunction with the left one. One notable thing about the experience was that I did get to have an adult pre-med and morphine as a painkiller after surgery. I was shouting in my sleep after the operation so they put me in a room on my own where there was a telly, something I didn't have at home. No one came into the room to turn it off on the first night so after I said goodbye to my Mum and Dad I watched *Deliverance*. I'd always hoped there was more to life than *Last Of The Summer Wine*, being an altar boy and playing the euphonium in a marching brass band. Watching Ned Beatty get fucked savagely by hill men as neon skeletons leered out of the corners, laughing starfish danced on my bed and screaming ghosts walked through walls, I realised that there was.

This was the first time I experienced the reality-collapsing, personality-erasing potential of drugs. It was an experience I was very much impressed with.

I would come to spend a lot of time in hospitals and I would also grow to hate them by the time I became a teenager for very obvious, unremarkable reasons. It had just started looking like the depressingly inevitable, badly cleaned bookend at the other, less joyful extremity of your very linear life. Every trip there became a dry run for the real thing, whether for yourself or loved ones. It's easier to ignore the depressing narrative of hospitals if you don't end up in them all the time, something I didn't manage in my twenties and thirties.

My eye healed but the terrible fear I had developed of leaving the house got worse and worse. Synth pop became terrible. Science fiction started to seem ridiculous. The 1980s went sour. My life went sour. Reality went sour.

More recently I have tried to pinpoint the exact date everything went wrong midway through that decade and I have come up with a few potential suggestions as to when and why this happened.

September 23, 1984: I am sitting in my room and everything is right with the world. I am reading *The Hitchhiker's Guide to The Galaxy* by Douglas Adams and listening to *The Luxury Gap* by Heaven 17 on my Dansette. I love sci fi and I love music from

Sheffield – especially by ABC, The Human League, Heaven 17 and Cabaret Voltaire. My Dad shouts up from the bottom of the stairs: "Come down here. There's something on TV I think you should watch. It's called *Threads*." The next day I tearfully join CND. By the end of the week I am a vibrating nexus of anxiety and I constantly check the horizon for mushroom clouds.

February 15, 1985: I am sitting in my room, afraid of nuclear war but otherwise still essentially happy. I am listening to a group I discovered last year called Simple Minds. Not only are their recent albums *Sparkle In The Rain* and *New Gold Dream (81 82 83 84)* excellent to listen to on a massive Walkman while striding dramatically though snow and rainfall but you can also get their early, weird LPs from Woolworths for two pound each. My favourite is called *Sister Feelings Call*. Today, in St Helens, is the debut screening of a new John Hughes movie called *The Breakfast Club* which climaxes with the brand new song by Simple Minds. It concerns a disparate bunch of white American teens on weekend detention. One of them is a proto-criminal called John Bender played by preposterous tit mangle Judd Nelson. He wears fingerless leather gloves – the stylistic hallmark of a complete bellend. Apparently during filming Nelson insisted on staying in character between takes and mercilessly aggravated the angelic Molly Ringwald until she was in tears. It took an intervention by cast and crew to prevent a raging Hughes from sacking the actor, furious with his oafish behaviour.

If only Hughes had stuck to his guns then perhaps my life wouldn't have collapsed into ruin. But no, at the end of the film bad boy lummox Bender strides across a sports field as Simple Minds' transcendentally awful new song 'Don't You (Forget About Me)' comes on. He leaps up and punches the air – his fingerless leather glove becoming frozen centre screen. Jim Kerr roars like a hippopotamus that's fallen into a hay baler.

After that, I feel like the shadow of a giant concrete building without windows has fallen across my soul. I don't know it yet but this feeling is called depression. And unless I state otherwise from now on, just presume that I'm massively depressed and don't feel like getting out of bed. Or if I'm out of bed that I feel like drinking until it's best that I go back to bed.

July 13, 1985. I am round at Stu's house, in his bedroom. I am afraid of nuclear war and massively depressed but I still have faith in technology and the future. And today the future has arrived. We are both 14 year olds and we are just a couple of the two billion people who are watching Live AID as it happens on TV thanks to satellites. Satellites in outer fucking space. Phil Collins is in mid-air on Concorde heading towards America faster than the speed of sound. The screen I'm watching is only four inches across and part of an upright turntable and cassette recorder hi fi combo. The technology that is allowing today to occur is blowing my fucking mind. Stu's Mum comes into his room carrying a tray of roast chicken legs. Adam Ant walks on stage. "Yes!" says Stu. "Yes!" I say. He isn't dressed as a pirate or a highwayman wearing makeup but as some kind of rockabilly duffer but it doesn't matter because nothing can ruin this moment of righteousness and vindication. What is he going to play? 'Kings Of The Wild Frontier'? 'Prince Charming'? 'Mohok'? Two billion people are waiting. They play 'Vive Le Rock'. "What?" I say but by the time he does a scissor kick I know the 80s and my childhood are over. Humanity has peaked. The world has become a darker place. It's all downhill from this point onwards. I look at the chicken with tears welling up in my eyes. By the end of the day I am a militant vegetarian. By the end of the week I am an angry alcoholic who no longer speaks to his parents. And by September I have a Jesus And Mary Chain LP, back combed hair and winkle pickers.

And that's exactly how I remember it happening.

In reality there are people out there who suffer simply awful and calamitous experiences when they are young and this, if they are unlucky, can plague them for the rest of their lives. For the rest of us however – me definitely included – life just doesn't pan out like that. I had a moderately unusual upbringing but then, doesn't everyone? There wasn't anything in particular that made me an alcoholic or a drug addict or mentally ill. It just panned out that way. It was just my bad luck.

And anyway, there had been more important things
happening in the mid-80s than Adam Ant doing a scissor kick
or Simple Minds courting mainstream success in America, like
the damage done during Margaret Thatcher's second term in
office for starters. But I was just a boy and didn't really fully
understand what the Battle of Orgreave was. And I only really
started coming to terms with Thatcherism and how it affected
me and the community I came from during her third term in
office. However, on one level or another, all of these things were
actually connected.

In 1984 unemployment bottomed out at 3.3 million as a
year of miners' strikes took place. But what also happened that
year was that hope in a better future was dismantled. A lot of
cultural commentators take the 1960s to be a short decade in the
Eric Hobsbawm sense, claiming that the genuine Sixties – as in
the Swinging Sixties of liberalism and psychedelia – started in
1963 and ended in the murder at the Altamont racetrack during
a Rolling Stones concert or when Charles Manson's family
murdered Sharon Tate in the Hollywood Hills in 1969. But in
Britain, in the wider cultural sense, the values of 60s liberalism
and utopian counterculture were only ground into the dirt in the
UK during Margaret Thatcher's second and third terms in office,
between 1983 and 1989.

The 1960s were the most forward looking and inclusive time
in living memory, promising a new dawn in civil rights, an end
to racism, misogyny and homophobia as well as fair treatment
for the working classes for the first time ever. The biggest lie ever
told by the music press was that the punks were opposed to the
hippies. Bar a haircut they were the same people and the political
spirit of 1968 was passed down through smart punk bands such
as CRASS into the 1980s on to those brave few that carried the
flame such as Napalm Death and Extreme Noise Terror. Radical
political movements such as anarcho-syndicalism, class war and
socialism still promised (no matter how naively) that power
and money could be seized from the capitalist ruling class and

distributed fairly among people on the street.

And that was what Thatcher wanted to end... the 1960s dream. She wanted to destroy hope. As she said: "Go back, you flower people, back where you came from, wash your hair, get dressed properly, get to work on time and stop all this whingeing and moaning."

My favourite albums recorded in Britain during this period reflected the death of hope in the future. Skullflower's *Xaman*, Loop's *Heaven's End*, Spacemen Three's *Playing With Fire*, Godflesh's *Streetcleaner*, My Bloody Valentine's *Isn't Anything* and *Psychocandy* by The Jesus And Mary Chain. These records were the soundtrack to the death of liberalism and optimism. They sounded the retreat away from utopianism into nihilism and despair, which was not just to say that they were violent and inward looking but they even parodied the sun-dappled psychedelia of 1967. This was the brown acid really kicking in. And it felt like they had been written just for me.

I didn't know any of this at the age of 14 though. I knew five things. I knew that Judd Nelson was a colossal prick. I knew that you couldn't trust anyone. I knew that Gary Numan was some kind of genius. I knew that I hated hospitals. And I knew that I really wanted to take illegal drugs.

As I write this I'm sitting in a flat which is lined with shelf after shelf of vinyl in the form of albums, 12"s, box sets and crates of 7"s; not to mention a wall full of CD shelves, topped off precariously with hundreds of box sets and outsize CD packages; tote bags stuffed with CD-Rs; several computers, iPods, phones and tablets full of MP3s, M4As and WAVs and boxes of cassettes. The couch where I do my writing really needs replacing. It's coming apart where I sit, the cushions that I use are twisted out of shape and the arm where my laptop rests is dented. To the right of the sofa is my stereo resting on top of some vinyl shelving my Dad made for me, every spare space covered in piles of 7"s and cassettes. To my left is a large Expedit vinyl shelving unit I panic bought a year or so ago when I heard that IKEA were stopping making them.

14 of the 16, 13"x13" spaces it affords are already rammed full of records.

Now that I'm middle aged and twelve years into an accidental career as a music journalist I find myself asking the question that my Dad asked me in 1987 more and more – "What good is this?" What is the point of all these records? Most have been written about enough already and others are probably undervalued elsewhere with good reason. Some of them I used to love passionately but I know I'll probably never listen to again. Why do I own so many of these things?

What good is all music – not just U2? What is its function generally and what is its function specifically for people like me who listen to it obsessively and constantly as well as hoarding it in various physical and digital formats?

One of the advantages of being a music writer is I don't just have to come up with stupid theories on my own – I'm free to ask musicians and producers, who have spent lifetimes pondering the very same subjects, how they feel. Once when talking to Mark Fell, the visionary experimental sound engineer and abstract techno producer, I asked him about the role of music and he said: "The linguist Stephen Pinker described music as being like 'auditory cheesecake' but I think that it fulfils a much more fundamental role in people's lives.

"I think it was [Edgar] Varese who said that music was organised sound, but for me, that's a bit problematic. It's a bit like saying a car park is organised tarmac. It's not. So what is a car park? Take the white lines in a car park. Are they to do with organising the tarmac, or are they to do with organising all the movements of cars and people and social interactions that go on in the car park?

"So for me, music isn't organised sound. Music organises sound in order to deal with something else, and for me it seems that what it's organising is time. For me, music is organised time."

I'm just a layman compared to both Fell and Pinker but I agree with the former wholeheartedly. Music is more than mere decoration – it has to be more than mere decoration. It tracks both the passage and the measurement of time, on several different levels.

Just to the left of my head, three shelves up and two rows in on my Expedit unit, is a violent jumble of album spines – not filed by genre, country, age or alphabet. Metallica's *Kill 'Em All*. Ghostface's *The Pretty Toney Album*. Hawkwind's *Hall Of The Mountain Grill*. Ultravox's *Ha! Ha! Ha!* Aphex Twin's *Syro*. Arabrot's *REP.REP*. Pantha Du Prince's *Black Noise*. Horace Andy's *Sky Larking*. A near disintegrated copy of Judas Priest's *British Steel*. A mint copy of Bathory's first LP. *Vol 4* by Black Sabbath. A signed John Foxx 12". Patrick Cowley's *Megatron Man* on maxi 12" (the b-side 'Lift Off' is the killer track). A cheap reissue of Doris Duke's *I'm A Loser*. An eye-wateringly expensive double vinyl Velvet Underground live bootleg called *Sweet Sister Ray*. A glossy double vinyl reissue of *Funhouse* by the Stooges. A battered original copy of *'74 Jailbreak* by AC/DC. Dr Alimantado's *Best Dressed Chicken In Town*. Herbie Hancock's *Sextant*. The massively underrated *Judy Sucks A Lemon For Breakfast* by Cornershop. Motörhead's debut album. *I Am Kurious Oranj* by The Fall. A 12" of 'Eighties' by Killing Joke. *Nothing's Shocking* by Jane's Addiction. A 12" of 'Juice' by World Class Wrecking Cru. Afrika Bambaataa & Soulsonic Force's *Renegades Of Funk* EP. *No Agreement* by Fela Kuti. An unopened expanded vinyl reissue of Nirvana's *In Utero*. A one sided etched 10" of Zebra Katz and Njena Reddd Foxxx's 'Ima Read That Bitch'. A 7" of Fat White Family's 'Touch The Leather'. The Japanese issue 7" of 'Quiet Life' by Japan, *Realization* by Johnny Rivers... All of these records – to one degree or another – are markers that I throw down into the void behind me and shore up against the void in front of me. Most of them are living mnemonics, connecting me to people, times and places, via songs, tunes, lyrics, drum patterns and so on. And that's often via the secondary medium of the artwork, or simply a glimpse of the spine.

There's absolutely no sense to the way I store my records and it takes me ages to find specific titles when I need to. I have colleagues who have extremely well thought out filing systems who think I'm insane. Through overuse, the albums I play the most tend to end up on the middle shelves, at head or hand height, the less favoured ones tend to end up at floor level. But once in a while, when I'm on my hands and knees desperately searching for some misplaced disco 12" that I really want for a DJ set or a missing piece of my son's Lego, my eye will be drawn to the black and gold spine of U2's *The Joshua Tree* and instantly I think, 'Why do I still own this piece of garbage?'

And then I remember.

And When The Lamb Opened The Third Seal (1989)

In 1989 I left home to go and study English at Hull University. If anyone asked me where I was from I would say, "Liverpool".

This was a lie. I was from a small village nine miles outside it called Rainhill.

I felt shallow, inauthentic, provincial and afraid, so I wanted to hide my insecurity behind the giant mass of a city. But there were practical reasons for my subterfuge as well.

Despite it being home to the world's first official steam locomotive trials; close to the site of the world's first official steam locomotive-related fatality and the location of the world's first load bearing skew bridge under which steam locomotives would pass, I had no faith that anyone across the Pennines would have heard of Rainhill. I needed to pick somewhere big to identify myself with.

With most of my family being either Scousers or Irish I felt more comfortable claiming allegiance with Liverpool as opposed to Rainhill but it was a complete con. Rainhill lies on a fault line. It is a liminal zone between temperaments. No one wants you. You're a plastic Scouser to the St Helens lot and you're a woolly back to the Liverpudlians.

It would have been geographically more correct to tell other freshers that I came from St Helens, which was only three miles

up the road, rather than Liverpool which was nine miles away
to the west. St Helens is an industrial town which lies between
Liverpool and Manchester like a buffer; as do Wigan, Warrington,
Widnes, Leigh and Skelmersdale. But despite its proximity and
the fact that I went to school there, I didn't have much faith in
anyone other than the followers of rugby league and fans of Bernie
Clifton – a family entertainer famous in the 1970s for pretending
to ride an ostrich called Oswald – having heard of St Helens, let
alone Rainhill.

But I did not belong to Liverpool. There are no degrees of
separation when it comes to this city. You are either in or out
and I was out. Liverpool is a very insular place. As far as most
Liverpudlians are concerned, their city could break off from the
UK, float out into the Irish Sea, disengage itself from the Eurasian
Plate and then from gravity itself before drifting off into the
universe and people who lived there wouldn't mind so much.

My mate, the writer and punk musician John Robb has lived
in Manchester all of his adult life and he has written about the
city extensively. We often end up discussing how Liverpool and
Manchester, which are only 35 miles apart, can be so different.
It's my view that to people in Merseyside, Liverpool is more of an
abstract notion; that the city to them is really just the community
that lives there. Mancunians, I think, love the bricks and mortar
of their city, the architecture, the industry, the culture and the
geography, more. While immigrants from Ireland make up a large
percentage of the working class of both urban areas, elements of
the Celtic character have bled into the Scouse personality to a
definable degree – Manchester remains relatively more protestant
in its nature.

You can see this rift in many aspects of the respective cultures
of both cities but most clearly in the music they produce. Liverpool
is a crucible for warm hearted, psychedelic and romantic music – it
is the home of The Beatles, OMD, Echo And The Bunnymen and
the Mighty Wah!, while Manchester is a factory for groups that
are urgent, intellectual and dark-hearted such as The Smiths, The
Fall, A Certain Ratio and Joy Division. I love both cities but I do

admire Liverpool's lack of interest in what London and the rest of the world thinks of it. It must be the only modern metropolis where literally everyone 'knows' The Beatles went off the boil when they decamped to London. Although this is a sentiment that can ruffle feathers, I think that Manchester defines itself in opposition to London whereas Liverpool simply doesn't care about the capital. Manchester is determined to be the UK's 'Second City' (above Birmingham) and desperate to prove it has better home-grown music than any other major urban area, the capital included. The irony is that it easily beats London hands down in musical stakes and always has done – very few great groups are actually from London. They simply move there to get gigs and find fame.

This polarity is evident in how music intersects with drug culture as well. Merseyside is essentially an LSD and pot kind of place whereas Manchester is more speed and ecstasy orientated. I missed out on the first couple of years of acid house because I lived in Merseyside, where most people seemed to be only interested in acid-fried rock and prog. People would look at you like you were mad if you suggested going to a rave: why would you listen to electronic dance music when you could spark up a bifter and get *Space Ritual* by Hawkwind or *Ummagumma* by Pink Floyd on the stereo instead? Dancing? Have you gone soft in the head lad?

After 'Ace Of Spades' by Motörhead, my favourite all time rock song is 'The Four Horsemen' by Aphrodite's Child, a Greek prog trio that featured the late Demis Roussos and Vangelis. This track is the uncontested highlight of *666 (The Apocalypse Of John 13/18)*, a double concept album about the Book of Revelation, and ownership of it was a rite of passage for many true heads in the North West. (One of these true heads was a young Richard Ashcroft, who grew up in Wigan; if you have a copy of The Verve's ten million copy selling *Urban Hymns* LP to hand check out 'The Rolling People', and note the remarkable similarity to 'The Four Horsemen'. The similarity is no coincidence. "We are the people, the rolling people" go the lyrics to the Aphrodite's Child song 'Altamont', another track from *666*.) Among its many cosmic grooves, it features narration in both Greek and English as well

as the actress Irene Papas simulating an orgasm on the track '∞',
a twenty minute long cosmic jazz rock freak out called 'All The
Seats Were Occupied' and much sonic experimentation.

So depending on your point of view and geographical
location, this album was either an embarrassing folly or one of the
finest achievements of the 20th Century. Interestingly the LP also
features in an urban myth that gets repeated in both cities, exact
in every respect, with the only difference being an unspoken one
of interpretation.

The story goes that a young man comes in from a night out
to find that his flat has been turned over. Everything is gone, the
cupboards are bare, the furniture is missing, the fridge, the TV, the
cooker and even the bed have been nicked. In fact the only solitary
thing that remains in the completely empty flat is a copy of *666* by
Aphrodite's Child. The Mancunian who hears this laughs: "Not
even a desperate smackhead burglar wants a copy of *666*... what
a top diss!" The Scouser who hears this laughs, "You can rob a
guy's fridge and you can rob his bed but you can't take his copy
of *666* la!"

In reality the North West is fractured like crazy paving along
numerous other fault lines. It can be broken down into a myriad
of zones which are all slightly uncomfortable with one another
and these are mainly distinguishable by chip shop custom and
etiquette. (While I'm on the subject, if you ever find yourself
buying chips in Wigan or Parbold and the person behind the
counter asks if you if you want your takeaway "wi pea whet", for
the love of God say no. I wouldn't wish that culinary madness on
my worst enemy.)

So from when I left school at 16 until I was old enough to
leave the area I didn't have any particular stamping ground that
was my own and not feeling particularly comfortable or welcome
anywhere I split my time between Rainhill, St Helens, Liverpool,
Widnes, Manchester and Kirkby.

Rainhill was where I lived and worked.

I was a pot collector in the local Ex-Serviceman's Club – where
I once nearly got clouted on the head with a walking stick by an

irate retired RAF man because I was wearing a Dead Kennedys 'Holiday In Cambodia' T-shirt. To be fair to me, I think it was my whole appearance that got his goat, not just the punk sloganeering.

Being a big fan of David Bowie and The Cure, I would occasionally wear a lot of eye makeup and also had giant, back-combed, Robert Smith-style hair that extended my 6'4" height by an extra 12". And I was no stranger to the joys of diaphanous blouses, bangles and nail varnish. To be fair, not everyone wanted to beat me up because of the way I looked. By the time I turned 16 I was… well, not exactly beautiful, but certainly less visually dissonant than I ended up. I did have a clear and smooth, milk-white complexion and only weighed ten stone. (I was the same height and almost twice that weight when I hit middle age.) And I could turn a few heads back then, even if they nearly always seemed to belong to middle-aged men.

I used to do a bit of gardening for one of these men (among several other people on my parents' estate) for beer money. He liked his garden kept extra tidy and my services were required on a regular basis. Once after finishing the mowing I went into the kitchen where he was leaning over the sink with a bright red face looking out of the window: "You know John... it looks hot out there. Do you ever think you might be more comfortable doing the work wearing shorts and a vest?" I told him I was wearing shorts. He wiped a bead of sweat off the end of his nose and let out a strangulated reply: "No, I mean really short shorts and a tight string vest. I've got some upstairs you can borrow if you like." I turned down his offer but the following week it was very hot so I did his garden wearing just a pair of Daisy Duke cut-off denim shorts, some toe-capped boots and no shirt. He looked extra crimson when I picked up my wages that afternoon and gave me a one-pound tip.

But most of the time I hated being in Rainhill. My experiences with my eye had left me terrified of getting beaten up again. I had frequent panic attacks. I couldn't walk down alleyways at any time of night or day. I was always in a state of panic during the hours of darkness and during the hours of daylight too if there weren't people around or if I was stuck somewhere without a really obvious line of escape. I became the sort of person who just disappears from social functions without warning. Sometimes I couldn't be outside of my house comfortably, even to walk round to someone's house, without having a drink.

So Liverpool became one of the places where I went to drink in pubs, bars and clubs.

Even though it was statistically much less safe, I simply felt more at ease spending my beer money in Liverpool than the relatively uptight pubs of Rainhill but the way I looked meant I often drank in gay bars. This is not to say it was any less scary in Jody's than it was on the streets outside. This was a no-nonsense watering hole that had a proud 12" awning of rubber cocks standing to attention above the bar and two toilets, both marked 'Gentlemen' but with fairy lights round only one of the doors. One of the barmen was usually in some pretty bracing bondage gear/ biker leather combo and used to carry a riding crop with a feather attached to the end of it. If he was happy with you, he'd tickle you with the feather – if you weren't drinking quickly enough, he'd apply the crop with a biblical force.

I couldn't always afford to go to Liverpool though, so St Helens was another place where I drank regularly, especially mid-week given how close it was to Rainhill. St Helens was also where I learned to take drugs.

In 1987 I knew this punk in St Helens who would throw these top parties which were like the exact opposite of something out of *The Great Gatsby*. The punk lived with a complete lunatic. I don't mean that this housemate was angry, zany or unpredictable but as far as I could tell he was actually clinically insane. A friend of mine went round to their house once and told me that he had been sitting in the kitchen having a brew, only to see a cat walking out of the lunatic's room with an especially dour look on its face and its tail pointing bolt upright with the non-writing end of a bookie's pencil sticking out of its anus. To be fair, the lunatic directed his quivering madness at everyone, not just the cat. I had it on good authority that he had guests round for tea once and he cooked their shoes. And by that I mean he put two shoes in two frying pans, fried them to a crisp and then served them up on plates to their respective owners. He then sat staring intently at them while they figured out what to do – eat their own shoes or make a run for it barefoot.

This punk was part of the mid-80s UK indie scene and attendant toilet circuit. He often put touring bands up when they were playing venues like Planet X in Liverpool or The Citadel in St Helens, so it wasn't a surprise to see Paul Heaton of The Housemartins at the party. This was the night that Heaton met Jacqui Abbott, a girl who drank in my local pub, The Royal Alfred, more commonly known as The Alf. She must have impressed him, as some years later he phoned her up out of the blue while she was working at Wilkinson's home improvement shop selling shitty mop heads, paint rollers and plastic buckets, and asked her if she wanted to be the new singer in his group, The Beautiful South. She left the shop before the end of her shift and didn't look back.

It wasn't just a significant night for her, though.

I'd only ever had controlled drugs once before and that experience had been brilliant. When I was 15 I interviewed one of my favourite bands, a terrifying avant-garde industrial rock five-piece called GNARL, for a St Helens fanzine. They were kind of like a local version of The Spice Girls, in that you were supposed to identify with a different member of the group depending on what kind of St Helens man you were – you could pick from the angry drunk journalist, the angry psychiatric nurse, the angry drunk garage worker, the angry drunk and drugged dole claimant, etc. They sounded like Killing Joke crossed with King Crimson and the Cardiacs and used to punch each other in the face before they went on stage. Sometimes they had tape recordings of Hitler's speeches or choice snippets of dialogue by Darth Vader playing under their hellish grooves. (They were a genuinely fantastic band, but then St Helens had more than its fair share. I cut my teeth watching rock groups in St Helens in my mid-teens for a long time before I bothered to go and watch anyone famous. Ask anyone who saw Those Naughty Corinthians or The Volunteers play live. Those Naughty Corinthians achieved local notoriety by insisting on watching a football match on TV that they didn't want to miss while playing a gig. They performed their entire set at a 90-degree angle to the audience, facing a portable set on a barstool. This may not sound that surprising to you, but that kind of unorthodox behaviour was less common in those days and it was kind of like St Helens' Bowie and Ronson on *Top Of The Pops* moment. Only 15 people were at that gig but at least four of them went on to form bands themselves.)

I'd never taken illegal drugs up until the interview with GNARL but when I got to the singer's flat I didn't want to lose face when they kept on offering me joints. When I got home afterwards I sat on my bed watching lots of little red people climb out of the cover of a Sisters Of Mercy album sleeve and start doing suggestive dancing all over my duvet. "If this is what pot is like, I'm never taking acid," I thought to myself. I went to bed and had spectacular dreams about lying down in a pool of mud in my parents' back garden and looking up into the sky as hundreds of burning meteorites came crashing down all over Rainhill. (When I next saw the singer he said to me, "So, how did you like that opium?")

At the party the punk said: "I've got mushrooms in the kitchen. There are trays of them drying in the oven. You lads, don't have too many. Or if you do, fuck off somewhere else." I'd had four cans of Special Brew and half a bottle of Thunderbird so I didn't give a shit about anything. I ate hundreds of the tiny, foul tasting psilocybin mushrooms and drank about a pint of soup. Before too long it became apparent that me, and two other idiots, needed to be walked somewhere a bit quieter where we could attempt to calm down. The walk through the park was amazing. All my friends were talking in fluent Russian. I became utterly convinced I was Kevin Keegan. There were neon luminous insects crawling everywhere. Everything I touched retained bright green hand or fingerprints. That was the best bit of the night. It lasted for 20 minutes, which flew by. By the time I got to my friend's house I had become discombobulated. With no chance of return to normality, it seemed. They tried playing soothing music but album after album of Bob Dylan just made everything worse. Clocks going backwards. Demons from overspace. The smell of black holes. Spiders in my brain. The extra person in the room with chattering teeth. The whistling nuns at the window. The conviction that I was in a coma. The conviction that I was dead. The conviction that I was insane... well, I guess I was actually insane by this point. And 'Lay Lady Lay'. I still can't listen to that Mumbling cunt now without a shadow passing over my grave.

I remember one bit of it really clearly. I was standing in the bathroom trying to urinate looking at the bath. Then I was looking up at the moon. Then I was looking into the toilet bowl, which looked uncannily like a duck's gaping mouth. Then back up at the moon. Eventually I just fell to the floor, curled up in a ball under a tree and started gibbering. The carpet felt like grass.

My friend's parents were having a downstairs bathroom fitted and had left a bath, a shower unit and a toilet in the back garden. She had told me this several times, apparently, but I was incapable of understanding even the most simple of sentences.

There was one lucid interval. I remember laughing and saying: "I'm alright!" And then the waves of horror came slowly back over me. Another seven years of madness. Eventually they put me behind the couch and threw a blanket over me. When no one else was looking, one of my friends would bounce a tennis ball on my head and laugh to himself.

And then, at 8am the next morning, it stopped. Just like that.

And when I got home, I nearly cried with relief when I saw my parents' front door.

And when I got into bed I said to myself: "I will never take drugs again under any circumstances."

The Alf was the best place to watch local bands, despite it not having a stage or anything like that. Its status as such was probably aided by the fact it was one of the few places in St Helens where you could usually drink without bother no matter what you looked like and because of this it was always full of an uneasy amalgam of skinheads, goths, punks, metalheads, crusties and random odd bods. I did love that pub but I shouldn't romanticise it too much. There were some right violent lunatics who drank in there and I stumbled across people shooting up in the gents on more than one occasion.

Very early one morning, while attempting to walk away from the wreckage of an all-day drinking session at The Alf to a mate's flat several miles away, I ended up crashing on a bench near The Bird I'th Hand pub. When I woke up I was indoors on a fold-out couch in a bedsit. I was fully-clothed but with a crocheted blanket over me. Next to me in a chair by the bed was an old-ish looking guy, probably mid-60s. He had ill-fitting false teeth, his neck was in a brace and he was wearing thick bifocals. There was a cat sat in his lap.

"You were on a bench outside," he said, nodding at the door.

My head was swimming. I still didn't really know what was happening or even what city I was in.

"Do you like tea?" he said.

I nodded dumbly and he poured me a strong brew out of a teapot which had been sitting next to him.

"My name's George," he said. "Do you like cats?"

I nodded again and took the mug off him. I was having vague flashbacks to some nonsense. Walking down Prescot Road, falling over a lot, needing to sit down for a rest. A welcoming bench...

I looked at the clock on the wall. 6.05am. Either side of the clock there were big Athena posters of muscular and well-oiled sailors in suggestive poses, with massive bulges in their underwear. You could only really tell they were sailors due to their nautical hats.

"Do you like sailors?" said George.

"Where's your bathroom?" I snapped.

He nodded through the kitchen at another door. I pushed roughly past him, stumbled inside and pulled the lock shut.

Inside I pressed my head against the freezing cold of the cistern until my eyeballs ached. I wanted to sprint out of the toilet, past George, through his front door and out into the street. But standing was barely an option.

After some time I walked back out. "I suppose you'll be going," said George, clearly miffed.

"I'm sorry about that. I don't feel very well. I'd like to stay for a bit if that's alright," I Mumbled, sitting back down on the bed. "Would you mind making me another cup of tea?"

He nodded and poured me one.

"I can't stop drinking," I started saying to him, but I started crying and had to stop talking for a bit.

After a long time I started to feel a bit less gruesome. I nodded at the posters: "Do you know George, I'm starting to think they aren't real sailors."

He smiled slightly and said: "Y'know, that thought has crossed my mind as well."

Then we sat in silence looking at his posters until the buses started running again.

Despite the drink and drugs however, I was actually a conscientious student for a while after I left school.

Cronton Sixth Form College, just outside of Widnes, was great as far as I was concerned as it wasn't some collapsing concrete nightmare full of lads on steroids beating up teachers – or vice versa if it was time to play rugby. It was a collection of ramshackle, prefabricated classrooms surrounded by farmer's fields, one massive pub called The Black Horse and the picturesque Pex Hill Quarry. There was no dress code. There were girls there. I learned a lot about music. Most of the people I met were pretty cool and I had excellent teachers. For once in my life I managed to balance my drinking and my studying relatively well. I sat A Levels in English Literature, History and Geology, all subjects I enjoyed learning about and excelled at.

I would occasionally go out in Widnes to watch bands. I went to see very early gigs by the Stone Roses and the Happy Mondays there but for the life of me I can't remember anything about them because I was too drunk. My music tastes tended towards heavier fare than indie though and because of this I hankered after going out in Manchester where my favourites Joy Division and The Fall were from.

Every week both home grown and foreign groups like Loop, World Domination Enterprises, Faith No More, The Young Gods, The Butthole Surfers, Big Black and Pussy Galore were calling to me from Manchester venues listed in the live ad pages of the *NME, Sounds* and *Melody Maker.*

One of the first gigs I ever went to see in Manchester was the Pixies supporting Throwing Muses at The International on April 29, 1988, when I was 16. The first thing that really struck me about the four-piece support act was how weird they looked. Literally everyone in the crowd was either a goth or a punk or a psychobilly or a hippy or a metalhead or a crusty and then there were the Pixies who looked like office workers on dress down Friday, all plaid and denim and big grins. It was the 1980s and I'd never seen anything like it before. The gig was like a jet engine going off in my face and after they ended with a Beatles cover version, 'Wild Honey Pie', my teeth literally felt loose in my head. I realised immediately that I had witnessed something amazing but it would be a long time before I understood that it was the best gig I'd ever see.

A few weeks later my best mate Stu and I made the trip back over to The Rainy City on May 14 to see The Sugarcubes live at the University's student union. Björk was probably the most beautiful person I'd ever seen. She looked incongruous standing in front of what was, as I remember it, a very drunk and very ugly crowd. While the group played 'Water' someone was obviously spitting at Einar Örn Benediktsson, the group's other vocalist and trumpet player. He noticed that there was phlegm dripping off his black top and started tearing the sleeves off and dropping them on the floor as he said: "I don't think there are a lot of advanced people here. I've had to clean my T-shirt because somebody spat at me. I think that Manchester is… I think that Mancunians… Is what they call you? Mancunians?… aren't very advanced. I thought you were supposed to be advanced people."

As soon as I heard the stuff about Mancunians I knew we were fucked. I don't think I've ever felt as far away from home as I did at that very moment. I wanted to keep my head down but it's impossible when you're 7'4" including hairstyle and covered in makeup. Fights broke out everywhere. The bouncers waded into the crowd. People started kicking and punching each other while the band ploughed through 'Sick For Toys', 'Birthday' and 'Delicious Demon' and then disappeared off stage not to return. The full show barely lasted 25 minutes.

By the end of the gig Stu had both his T-shirt ripped off and his belt snapped in the fracas before being head butted on the bridge of the nose. When I found him afterwards he was just stood there in his black briefs with his trousers round his ankles and blood pouring down his chest. Another friend got kicked unconscious, had to be taken to hospital and ended up with bad concussion for a week. I still feel a slight twinge of guilt now in reporting that the night was amazing.

Toward the end of my time at sixth form college I became sick of being skint all the time so I looked for another job, and found one in Kirkby, a small overspill town on the outskirts of Liverpool.

In the run-up to my A levels I worked long weekends as a ride operator in the funfair and amusements section of Knowsley Safari Park during the first half of 1989 alongside my mates Stu and Steve. The words 'fun' and 'amusement' had been stretched way beyond breaking point by this dour fibreglass and concrete distraction zone. There was a long, red, bumpy slide, which was sun-bleached pale pink at the knuckles. It had a tendency, when freshly waxed, to eject the slidee in a violent arc over the safety mat and straight onto the gravel. And it was often freshly and vigorously waxed when I was working there. There were spinning teacups that you could sit in that went round in a lugubrious, extremely safe, circle. We had the world's smallest Ferris wheel and the world's smallest roller coaster. There was a bouncy castle which was, strictly speaking, actually a giant bouncy donkey. And there was also a 15-inch gauge miniature steam train that was very easy to derail. We were paid one pound per hour, in the knowledge that three shifts added up to £21, which was the most you could earn while receiving income support without incurring any kind of deduction. 'Most people who worked there were signing on; and after my A level exams finished in Easter, I was as well.

I wasn't really interested in animals and only went into the Safari park on one occasion and even that wasn't by choice. A well-spoken guy in a flatbed Land Rover who looked very official borrowed me as an odd body one day. He drove us up a long gravel road to a field that contained two rhinos. While they were certainly different to any other animals I'd seen before, they didn't really do anything of note. Which was just as well. The two cables that made up the electric fence were snapped and the beast nearest to us could have just wandered out if it wanted but it just stayed where it was sniffing at a tree trunk. I had to hand the man a series of tools with insulated grips while he repaired the wires. After finishing, he started up an interminable conversation on his walkie-talkie so I walked a bit further up the road. There was an elephant in the field. It wandered over to have a look at me. I do remember that its eyelashes were probably four inches long but other than that I felt short-changed at how unsurprising seeing an actual elephant was.

Nowadays I probably wouldn't set foot in anywhere that wasn't a rescue zoo but this said, the rhinos and the elephants at Knowsley seemed relatively happy as far as I could tell. That is to say, as much as a disinterested 17-year-old non-expert, Special Brew drinking Sisters Of Mercy fan can judge the happiness of a giant pachyderm standing in a field in Kirkby. They certainly seemed happier than the sunburned bellends who had paid to get in and would shout at us about their kids and how far they'd driven and how much their kids loved trains on the days that the locomotive was derailed, or the bellowing Dads going on about the windscreen wipers that the mischievous baboons had torn from their Volvos. Or shouting about how the slide was too slippy and had ejected their children straight onto the gravel.

I am certain that I worked at the Safari Park on April 15, 1989, but I can't remember anything about the shift. As soon as I got back home I phoned my mate Steve to see what time we were going to the pub. He was really odd and quiet and eventually told me that his mate had been crushed to death at a Liverpool game in Sheffield that afternoon. He'd been drinking with him the night before.

Your first experience of the death of someone close – when they aren't old – is always going to be abysmal; I didn't even want to think what it must have been like to watch it live on TV.

At college on Monday, my Geology teacher Tom said we didn't have to stay in class if we didn't want to, but if we did we could we read in silence as he was feeling out of sorts. It wasn't long before he started talking about being at the game though, telling us everything that he'd seen happen, his eyes full and watery but not brimming over. He kept on shaking his head and looking out of the window anxiously as he talked as if he was watching something awful unfold in the distance across a field full of golden rapeseed.

The rest of the summer was mainly great but I fell out with my Dad over some nonsense. He said some mean-spirited things to me and I said some mean-spirited things back. I left home under a bit of a cloud and didn't really talk to him for a while afterwards. But I did well in my exams, I saw a lot of good bands, I got drunk every day. One afternoon at the safari park the train was piloted full throttle – 13mph – at closed points and within the hour Stu and I had been told unceremoniously to fuck off and not come back. I didn't care. I knew I was leaving Rainhill and St Helens and the surrounding environs and didn't particularly feel the need to act graciously about the fact.

I moved to Hull with Steve in September and we got stuck into getting properly fucked up. About a week after we got there we had a great day exploring the pubs of the old town – the Steam Tavern, The Old Black Boy, The Bluebell, The William IV, The Green Bricks and a small bar that served 40 different types of schnapps. At the end of the session we were clattered and should have gone home, but we were passing a waterfront nightclub with some spurious fresher offers on combat lager and were dragged in as if by tractor beam. Inside it was a pine, chrome and mirror decorated disaster area, packed full of busy looking herberts freshly arrived in Hull, dressed up to the nines in ironed denim or pastel coloured shirts with button down collars and patent leather shoes custom built for the kind of fighting popular in new towns. After a miserable couple of hours of Stock, Aitken and Waterman and 'Love Cats' by The Cure, the DJ flung us without warning into the end of evening erection section. After 'Let's Get It On' we were treated to the charity version of 'Ferry Cross The Mersey' that had recently been at number one, and within seconds Steve was marauding across the dance floor to the DJ booth, steaming a path through abysmally drunk couples attempting to recreate *They Shoot Horses, Don't They?* He screamed: "Turn this off you fucking cunt. This isn't… entertainment." The DJ seemed genuinely confused as to what his point was, and to be honest, two and a half decades later it doesn't seem like the apocalyptic act of provocation that it did back then. But there was no turning back. He was red in the face and yelling blue murder while a bunch of lads slowly gathered round him mimicking him in over-exaggerated Scouse accents. I stepped in and immediately made the situation much worse.

A bunch of us were thrown out onto the cobbled street outside. Steve was in tears by this point, with a bunch of lads circling nearby yelling shit at him about the people who had died. All sorts of dark, rage-inducing, fight-igniting ideas were being given voice to. These were not their own ideas, though; these lads were merely cracked mirrors reflecting the astonishing moral abyss at the core of that human abscess, Kelvin MacKenzie. They were conduits for a hatred that they barely understood or registered. I was ready to fight and I had little or no appreciation of the mechanics that had brought me to that point.

There was so much violence when I was young. Literally everywhere I went. Healthy sexual energy corrupted into bloodshed between lads who were all utterly identical bar from which town they came from or which football team they supported or which band they followed or what haircut they had. You either learned to bang your head against a brick wall or to pummel your fists into your neighbour's face. Boys just being boys. Boys just beating boys. Imagine the power if they'd stood together.

The situation fizzled out into nothing. Luckily for us things were taken down a notch or two by a bunch of girls piling out into the street singing. Steve and I beat a hasty retreat back towards our flat and the lads rolled off in the other direction. The bouncer who had kicked us out watched us all slope off and spat after us: "Bunch of fucking animals."

If This Is Heaven I'm Bailing Out (1992)

So here's a question for you: is there anything that separates the alcoholic from the serious problem drinker? Really, is there any way at all to differentiate between the person who wakes up down the park in piss-wet clothes; who weeps inconsolably in the post office queue; who will sell every last thing they own just for some extra strong lager; who gets rushed to hospital fitting because they didn't have enough vodka to drink 24 hours previously; who will literally not stop drinking until they die in astonishing agony, sometimes decades before their time – and someone who's just having *a bit of robust English fun*?

Terrifyingly, I'm not 100% sure that there is.

The trouble with the word alcoholism is that not everyone agrees on what it means. Colloquially it can refer to any kind of serious drink problem – even though it is connected in most people's minds with the idea of ethanol addiction. However, the concept of being addicted to drink has numerous common interpretations – with some people believing that it is possible to recover from the illness despite there being not much in the way of evidence for this. There are even some people in the health service itself who believe that alcoholics are those who go through troublesome, extended periods of heavy drinking but can, eventually, with the right sort of detoxification and therapy, eventually go back to drinking sensibly. They look down on the perceived old-fashioned and quasi-religious nature of Alcoholics Anonymous.

Whatever other people think, all I can say is that the fellowship was a crucial aid to me stopping drinking. When I went to AA for the first time was when I stopped drinking despite having tried many many times before unsuccessfully on my own.

So, for the record, let me say that I am chronically addicted to ethanol and I believe I cannot control my drinking to the extent that my only options are to not drink or to die. And I believe this will always be the case. Even though I haven't had a drink for nearly seven years, if I were to have a pint of beer or a glass of wine now, it would probably have catastrophic consequences for me (and by turns for my family as well) within the week and that 'probably' is enough for me to treat the situation as a heavenly ordained certainty.

Even then, it's hard to define exactly where the boundaries of chronic alcoholism lie. But as blurred as they are on your way up, in my experience, you can be pretty sure you're on the team once you pass certain thresholds. It is straightforward enough to diagnose yourself once you are comfortably ensconced in end-stage drinking... should you have the stomach for it.

The easiest way to do this is to list all of the plans that you have hatched to reduce or control your intake of alcohol, while also noting how long you managed to maintain them. Here are just a few of the many schemes I planned for myself in order to curb my berserk thirst – all of which failed. Some within weeks. Most within days. Some within hours. Some within minutes.

I will never drink between Sunday at midnight and Thursday at 6pm. I will never drink between Monday at midnight and Wednesday at 6pm. I will not drink on Mondays. I will not drink on Mondays before 6pm. I will not drink on Mondays before midday. I will not drink anything stronger than lager. I will only drink real ale. I will only drink clear spirits with fresh fruit juice. I will only drink red wine with food. I will only drink white wine after food. I will only drink tonic wine. I will only drink down the pub. I will only drink outside of my own house. I will only drink with friends when it is a special occasion. I will only drink with friends. I will only drink with people I am on first name terms with in pubs. I will never drink on my own. I will always stop drinking by 10pm. I will never drink before midday. I will never drink before 10am. I will never drink between the hours of 4am and 8am. I will have a pint of water between each and every drink. I will not drink because it is January. I will not drink because it is the first week in January. I will not drink because it is before 6pm on January 1. Every fourth drink must be something lighter, like a pint of lager. I will not have a drink to get me back to sleep if I wake up in the middle of the night, no matter how bad I feel…

But I wasn't born like this. And even though I drank, I wasn't a chronic alcoholic at school, or in sixth form college. Not really. So when did I become one?

To be honest, I have no idea. All that I feel is that I am one now and that's me done for life. I kind of see it as being a bit like Schrödinger's experiment, except inside the box, when you finally dare look, there isn't a cat – there's either a normal person, with a normal life and a normal career or there's someone in a stained coat, sitting on a park bench with three litres of White Lightning looking at a cig packet containing five, slightly crushed Lambert And Butler Superkings, through rheumy red eyes.

It's close to impossible to tell if someone's an alcoholic when they're a teenager, simply because the cover is so good. Especially when they get to university. Listen to the senseless fresher chatter in any student union bar: "Yeah, I was a total alcoholic last term – I was down the bar by 7pm every day!" "She was a complete alcoholic last term but she's getting better now." "Let's get some drinks in – I've got some blood in my alcohol stream!"

And in my student union bar in 1989, I would laugh and rub the bottle of vodka or sherry in my coat pocket absent mindedly or say to the barman: "Four pints of lager and one pint of Guinness. And look mate, put two large vodkas in the Guinness…"

It's true that university probably can reveal an alcoholic's true nature to themselves eventually, if they're observant. Most students, even the boozy ones, get their act together in their second or third year and suddenly, without warning, there are only a small handful of piss artists left, grimly drinking on their own or with other like-minded souls or making friends with annoying freshers, while everyone else knuckles down to dissertations and final exams. Maybe this would have happened to me but I got kicked out of Hull University in the spring of 1991 for non-attendance after one year and one term.

I did go to Hull with normal ambitions and creative aspirations; it's just that they didn't last very long. They were vanquished by an all-out assault from Special Brew, Happy Shopper vodka and Cellar Five own brand pale cream sherry.

During freshers week I joined a creative writing group but only attended the first meeting. Someone was holding court about his short story based on TS Eliot's *Murder In The Cathedral.* I was angrily dressed down for calling the play boring ("You don't have the right!") and then when the irate Archbishop Thomas Becket fan in the group demanded to know what I wanted to write about all I could think of was: "Pylons and stuff." (Although, to be fair to my gauche, drunken, teenage self: Murder In The Cathedral is fucking dull and pylons are fucking boss.) I only saw one person from this creative writing group again – my friend Natasha. She was the first person I met at university and remains my friend to this day. Now that I think about it, she started encouraging me to write the first day I met her and hasn't let up since – over a quarter of a century later.

A month or so into our first term, she was already ensconced on the student newspaper and commissioned me to write an interview with fleetingly popular *NME* sanctioned, this week's saviours of rock & roll types, Birdland. I think I acquitted myself well enough but at the same time I'm glad to report that the article – like my other early attempts at music journalism from St Helens – seems to have vanished off the face of the Earth. All of the other things I was going to do with my time: write a book, pen short stories, host a radio show, start a successful band, learn how to DJ, become a filmmaker etc all got shelved in favour of drink and drugs.

I don't have many regrets. Not because I haven't wasted massive chunks of my life, made really terrible decisions and been a transcendental pain in the fucking arse but because people with regrets are generally still time wasting, bad choice making, pains in the fucking arse. I'm now trying to get shit done and better late than never. There genuinely is no point in crying over spilt milk as far as I can tell.

However, it has to be said, that I don't have very fond memories of my time at university, and this does bother me. It doesn't matter how you cut it: I could have spent my months in further educational facilities better. I may have been the first person in my family to go to university but I was the first person in my family to get thrown out of it as well.

Which begs the question: what did I actually learn at university during the four terms I was initially there?

Well, first and foremost I learned how to smoke cannabis resin through an empty coke can and then, later, an apple. I also learned how to say, "Fuck the Boer cunts" in Xhosa.

While it might seem obvious to you dear urbane reader, I learned the hard way that putting a traffic cone on your head is like fucking a sheep – you only need to do it once to get a reputation you'll never get rid of.

(On my way to a party down Beverley Road one night I came across a cone that was much bigger than any other I'd ever seen. I mean it was like five or six feet tall. It was the über traffic cone – the mother of all traffic cones, the Ur-cone. Looking back through the mists of time elapsed, the way I choose to remember the incident is this: it was such a massive traffic cone that I decided to put it on my head to take the piss out of students who put traffic cones on their heads, yeah? Because they're such wankers, right? I was being ironic, yeah? By the time my friend Conn helped me get the thing over my head I looked like some very early drawing board design for a dalek abandoned because there was nothing frightening about a giant orange triangle with a pair of army surplus boots sticking out of the bottom of it. He led me in to the party where I started jigging about and shouting: "Look at me! I'm an idiot with a cone on his head." Even though I could tell immediately even before I started knocking drinks over that I'd made a massive *faux pas*, there wasn't much I could do about it as I had a massive plastic cone jammed over my head that was stopping me from seeing anything, trapping my hands to my sides and preventing me from bending any joint in my body apart from my ankles. As I toppled over and waited for Conn and a couple of other people to pull me out by my feet I suddenly realised that my future was sealed as that guy who turned up at that massive party going, "Look at me! I've got the world's biggest traffic cone on my head!" before throwing himself off the Humber Bridge a few weeks later. It wasn't just the fact that my entire peer group was there, so any lingering hopes I had of a career in the Home Office or at Faber and Faber had evaporated before my eyes but literally, now that everyone knew I was a first class helmet, exactly what had been the point of reading all of that Franz Kafka and William Burroughs?)

I also learned how to spot when I was having a nervous breakdown.

(If you ever see the video to 'Why Are You Being So Reasonable Now?' by the Wedding Present on YTV's *Calendar* show and you start screaming because you're wearing exactly the same paisley shirt as David Gedge and you carry on screaming because you think that you're David Gedge trapped in the television and sending yourself messages from the future; you may well be having a nervous breakdown. If every time you pass a TV set you can faintly hear the theme music from *Raiders Of The Lost Ark* – whether it's switched on or not – again you may be having a nervous breakdown. As far as I can tell, all of this was part of the long tail of psychological problems that my severe beating, eye surgery and heavy mushroom trip had kick-started. Once I was watching the BBC News and John Suchet broke off half way through a report, leant out of the screen and snarled at me: "DORAN! What the fuck are you doing, you sloppy cunt?! Get your shit together!" You have to hand it to Suchet, he tells it like it is, whether you want to hear it or not.)

I don't think it's too much of a non sequitur to follow this up by saying that I did not learn how to be successful at meeting girls at university. My one and only attempt to chat someone up was not an honours performance. On the encouragement of Natasha to go over and "just say something natural to her – it'll be fine" I unleashed this Milk Tray Man classic: "Hey, would you like to hang out with me some time and listen to some reggae?" To be met with a fairly unequivocal: "Are you taking the fucking piss?" The phrase, "Hey, would you like to hang out with me some time *and listen to some reggae?*" would echo round my head for decades to come. I was delighted to find out in 2001 while watching the film *Ghost World* that this is actually still the international gold standard of douche-baggery when it comes to talking to women and I am right to feel mortified. To be fair, another completely natural thing I could have said to her was: "Would you like to come back to my flat, smoke cannabis resin through a half-eaten apple and look at my Revolting Cocks picture discs, while I hum the *Raiders Of The Lost Ark* theme quietly to myself?" so things could have been worse.

Natasha used to call me jolly lad. And then she would say, "Well, perhaps, more lad than jolly!" and start laughing to herself. I'd laugh along with her but think to myself, 'What the fuck is she talking about?' To this day she looks exactly the same as when I met her in 1989. She claims not to have a portrait in her attic, or an attic full stop, so instead I attribute her youthfulness to good genes and Oil of Olay.

Most of my friends around this time were local to Hull but my best friend at university was a student called Albert. I met him via Natasha at 3am at some terrible house party in 1989. He was standing in a room full of people who had taken the knock and were lying down. He was listening to Hot Chocolate and doing something odd with his hands, roaring: "HA! HA! HA! I'M DOING THE HITCH HIKING DANCE!" He said I should come round to his flat the next day and he would cook tea for me. I visited with a litre bottle of sherry and he made us Birds Eye Potato Waffle sandwiches. "It is the ground black pepper that makes this dish," he told me. He made me lie down on his bed after that with my eyes shut. I was worried he was going to do something mad to me but he just wanted to play me the soundtrack to *The Good, The Bad And The Ugly* at full volume. "It sounds better after a good meal with your eyes shut," he told me.

We drank together every night and the majority of days for about four years and then whenever we met up after that. Bleached out memories of us waking up outdoors with blood on our hands; howling as we kicked my own front door in; a friend's ribs being broken in a car park 'game'; being dragged in headlocks out of pubs and clubs and so on suggest to me we weren't always particularly nice to be around. Albert lived above an off-licence and this is where we sourced most of our cut-price alcohol from. It served cheap red wine that retailed for one pound per bottle. The brand was Monsieur Bertier and the label featured a crudely drawn cartoon of a French man replete with beret, striped T-shirt and string of onions. The label on the back proclaimed it to be perfect for those who knew "little or nothing about wine" and also declared it ideal for those who liked drinking outdoors. By the time you'd put away enough of the bottle to see the large red crystals it contained, you'd already be well on the way to not caring.

I miss the intensity of the times. We didn't have a physical relationship in the gay sense but we were peculiarly close nonetheless. I guess when you're less than ten years into alcoholism it still engenders a sufficient amount of romance to stop you from realising what a bellend you're being, but the self-recognition is there from the start. I knew he was like me and we enabled each other in a guilt-free manner.

After getting hoofed off my course, I ended up in a quasi-derelict squat which backed onto the train tracks just outside Paragon Square Station in town, living with a local couple called Rob and Caroline. There was gas and electricity but there was also a big hole in the wall that let the elements in and no boiler to provide hot water or to warm the radiators. On some winter nights, literally the only way to keep warm was to put as many layers of clothes on as possible (Rob was best at this and once managed to fit 12 outfits on at once) and stand, with chattering teeth, next to the cooker with the oven on and the door open, the grill on and all four gas rings ablaze.

Rob was a muscular but cherubic dosser and guitarist in a band called LIMB, who sounded like Big Black covering *Metal Machine Music*. He painted the band's name onto a railway bridge one night. A copper clocked him when he was about 80 percent of the way through his act of vandalism, causing him to run off. To this day if you are walking up to De Gray Street from Princes Ave you can still see the word LIMP in massive letters above the road.

My Auntie Kath, who lived in Childwall in Liverpool, would come over once a month and leave me a sack full of leftover food she got off a dinner lady friend. She did this because she thought (correctly) that I spent all of my dole money on sherry and cigarettes.

Once I arrived back from Cellar Five with a litre of own brand pale cream to find that Rob had made an entire 1kg cylinder of dried Marvel milk up into liquid form.

Every receptacle in the house was full of lukewarm synthetic milk. The saucepans were full of milk, the mugs, the saucers, the bowls, the casserole dish, the pressure cooker, the washing up bowl were all full of milk. The fucking bin had been emptied and half-filled with milk.

"Look at all the milk," said Rob with a big smile on his face.

"Why . . . why would you . . ." I started saying but I could tell I was going to start crying so I went upstairs and drank enough sherry to put me to sleep.

The following summer we did get our shit together to throw one of the best parties ever. His friends brewed us several litres of screened pure ethanol. We lined a bin, poured it in and topped it up with fruit juice. It didn't taste too bad but you were reduced to a state of frantic imbecility by less than a mug full. Two people brought acid, someone brought pills, everyone brought speed, weed and beer.

All my furniture got put on the bonfire, as did all my spoons and all my toiletries. There were people dancing on the roof and general carousing everywhere.

The next thing I knew I woke up in the back garden next to Rob. I only had my boxer shorts on and I'd pulled a bike up to my chin like a duvet. Rob had no shoes on and someone had drawn all over his face in red Biro.

The garden was on fire and there were firemen with breathing equipment everywhere.

"Are you inebriated sir?" asked one of them sternly.

"Take a fucking guess," said Rob.

I always wonder if it was delayed shame over this incident that made him become a fireman. After I left Hull he ended up stationed on the lip of an industrial estate in Immingham. Rob would complain that there were very few fires, so there was nothing to do, but when there were they tended to be terrifying. A lot of stuff seemed to happen to him. Like once he saved a parrot by giving it the kiss of life and air from his oxygen mask, resuscitating it and landing himself on page three of the *Immingham Post*.

His girlfriend Caroline was a tough, heavy drinking lass from Hessle but very funny and generous hearted with it. In retrospect her presence probably stopped me and Rob from getting too out of control given the decrepit nature of the property we lived in. Despite how horrible it was, she forced us to clean the place like it was a regular flat but I have no doubt that the grim lodgings played on her mind as well as on ours.

I used to have a small carbuncle on my face until I got it removed at the age of 40. It wasn't so bad when I was a kid but it seemed (to me at least) to get bigger and bigger each year through my teens, finally driving me to distraction by the time I lived with Rob and Caroline. I tried to remove it in 1991 using a Stanley knife. It was fucking horrible and it hurt a lot even though I was really drunk. There was a lot of blood in the bath and all for no good reason, as after the wound on my face healed properly and I took the plaster off, the thing had grown back exactly the same as before. I had no idea how moles and minor facial disfigurements worked. I wasn't a surgeon. (I was a drunk living in a squat in Hull.)

There was blood in the bath quite a lot in 1991. I came in one night, drunk as hell and Caroline was missing. There was a matted clump of hair, treacly, clotting blood, a smashed mirror and a pair of scissors decorating the chipped enamel of the tub that only ever got used for the hand washing of clothes. The window was broken as well, and there were bloody palm prints on the frame. I looked up and down the train tracks at the back of the flat, scoured the surrounding streets, rang the hospital and rang her friends but couldn't find her. She came back a week later, seemingly right as rain and it wasn't mentioned. Well, she asked me a few days later to put a bit more effort into cleaning the bathroom but I think that was an entirely separate issue. Then her friend the nurse had to come and stay with us after her boyfriend – a fucking giant, heroin-depraved, site labourer – had kicked her head in trying to get her wages off her. She couldn't open her eyes when she arrived and took some cleaning up. She looked a million dollars when she left a few weeks later. We asked her not to go back to him but we were pretty sure that was where she'd end up. "She's like Florence Nightingale," said Caroline, "But with a smackhead for a boyfriend."

At some point after the Gulf War started, we started watching a lot of it on low-grade acid. Terrestrial television was just taking its first faltering steps towards rolling news. My black and white portable was taking its final faltering steps towards a skip however. It had been in my family ever since I could remember (the mid-1970s) and I had a feeling it was even older than me. The casing around the screen was partially built out of wood. I had to stop people from leaving lit cigarettes resting on it after it caught on fire once. I remember sitting there one night with my comrades Rich and Stimmy listening to the match pre-amble from George Bush while we were coming up, when the horizontal and vertical hold went dramatically and his head started stretching and stretching until he looked like Jabba The Hutt saying: "This is the new world order."

Rich groaned in terror: "Why is George Bush talking about New Order?"

Stimmy started laughing demonically. He was holding a smoking apple in one hand and jets of smoke were billowing out of his nose and joining a halo round his head as fractals and sparks shot out of his ears: "HA HA HA! It's the war! On drugs!"

I signed on after being kicked out of university but didn't even last a year on the dole. There simply wasn't enough money to get drunk every single day for a fortnight on a giro. I worked in a series of pubs and warehouses all over Hull and signed off when I couldn't get away with it any more. After Albert graduated in 1992, we both ended up working in the same aerosol factory called Macbrides, based out on East Hull Industrial Estate.

On the first day, Albert was put on a production line making *Beverley Hills 90210* Body Spray ("You've watched the show, now try the all-over fragrance") and I was put in a giant storage warehouse to clean the floors. After about three hours I heard a siren going off and thought that it must be lunchtime. I went to put my broom in a cupboard and retrieve my sandwiches from a locker. I didn't get as far as the pokey dining area. I looked out of a window and saw that across the car park there were men and women bottlenecked by the small pedestrian gate in the huge chain link fence.

I realised that the siren was still sounding. People were shouting and several had panicked and started scaling the fence. There was a sound like popcorn cracking and occasionally a small blackbird would fall out of the sky. On the other side of the fence some people would duck with their hands over their heads when this happened. "Why are there birds falling out of the sky? Is the world ending?" I thought. I wanted to run and join the other people but I had legs like Bambi on ice and had to sit down on the cold warehouse floor for a few seconds and wait for the crippling adrenaline rush to pass so I could stand up again.

Outside I started jogging toward the gate, which was now

clear, but stopped to look backwards for a moment. There was a massive fire in the building next to the one I had been in. I could see the top of the giant sump, a kind of gasometer for storing enough liquid accelerant for tens of millions of cans of aerosol. I stood and watched how the fire and the gas tower were in roughly the same spot. Every so often another bird would come blazing out of the sky and hit the ground with a dull clatter. They weren't birds, they were exploded aerosol cans. Giant cans of bug spray intended for the United Arab Emirates. Litre cans of extra spiky hair spray. Mr Muscle oven cleaner. Cheap, generic floor polish. Burst, blackened, empty.

I started running down the street and saw Albert sitting on a wall smoking a roll-up and grinning. "It looks like we've got the rest of the day off," he said. I'd been at the safety briefing the day before that he had skipped, so I told him about the sump's three-mile blast radius. We stood in the road and frantically flagged down a flatbed truck. We gibbered happily in the back of the speeding vehicle, looking backwards at the rising plume of smoke as we headed to town. Sadly, neither of us were able to beg money from girlfriends or mates that night, so we sat in our separate rooms swearing and sweating with not a drop to drink. To add insult to injury, the factory reopened the next day despite one entire storage building being rendered unusable and the sump having a giant scorch mark up one side. After a week I got switched to working nights, ten while ten, on the production lines, which is where I stayed for the next year and a half.

It was around this point that my drinking really stepped up a notch or two. I was now working so I could drink constantly during my down time, and because of the hours, I had plenty enough money for what I wanted. University was over so I had nothing in the way of plans for myself. Mid-week this drinking was mainly being done on my own between 10am and when I went to bed, usually around 5pm. At the weekend I tried to maintain a sense of normalcy but the disjunct between my working week and how I wanted to go out pubbing and clubbing on Fridays and Saturdays started running me ragged at the edges.

After a difference of opinion with some young soldiers home on leave outside of the Spiders nightclub in Hull in 1993, I had to visit A&E at Hull Royal on a Saturday night, which was mainly remarkable for two reasons. I don't know if it has changed since but entering Hull Royal's A&E ward at 2am on a Sunday morning two decades ago was like being transported into a particularly bloody painting by Pieter Bruegel The Elder but where everyone was wearing Global Hypercolour T-shirts and really expensive, blood-spattered trainers. And on top of this I ended up on a documentary about street violence in Humberside. If you ever go for a job in Hull Prison or De La Pole psychiatric hospital you will get shown this hour-long YTV film as part of your induction. I'm the one leaning against the reception desk with blood pouring out of my face – wearing some kind of 'ethnic' pull over hooded top as was the style among crusty raving idiots in those days. Unfortunately it was crimson coloured so the incident did not lead to me throwing the top in the bin. The best bit of my debut TV appearance is when the lady at reception asks me if it is a head wound and I say, "Take a guess" as blood drips through my fingers onto the counter. The funny thing is – I don't look too shocking in the film considering but by the following tea time both eyes had swollen tightly shut to the extent that I couldn't press a roll up cigarette between the hard, distended, purple dunes of flesh that had closed up in front of my eyelids; and my nose was the colour and shape of the kind of banana you might find in a skip at the back of ALDI on a Sunday evening.

I had a week off work and it was during this week of sitting on my own, unable to see – the temporary blindness, bar the merest slits of light, exacerbating the already terrifying effects of severe concussion – that it occurred to me that I might have the kind of drink problem that wasn't necessarily going to go away. It was bad enough during the day: unable to concentrate, constantly forgetting what I was doing and what was going on. Sometimes even forgetting my own name, bringing on panic attack after panic attack. I would be convinced there was someone in the flat with me, the smell of food rotting on the hob getting worse and worse, the buzzing flies, the dull drone of the transistor radio tuned in to a local station, all but drowned out by the ringing in my ears. But it was worse at night time. I really wanted to try and go over the evidence. Suss it out. Was I an alkie? Surely not…

I remember sitting in my boxer shorts shaking with fear, opening my last can of super strength lager from Iceland and lighting an Embassy Filter. I couldn't assemble my thoughts; they fell down around me as fast as I could try and piece them back together again.

"Focus!" I shouted. But there was no focus and there was no answer. Only confusion, ugly noise, fear and near darkness.

I pressed the lit tip of the cigarette into the smooth skin on the inside of my upper left thigh until it went out. The pain was excruciating. It did not help me to focus.

A year later, when having all the various indignities my nose had suffered over the preceding decade straightened out, I had to go back to Hull Royal and stay overnight. I had become very, very nervous about hospital visits and almost didn't go. The last thing I remembered was being pushed on a trolley into surgery by a very pretty female nurse. I asked if they put the good looking nurses on jobs like this to keep pre-op men sedate and did women going under the knife get good looking male nurses to accompany them into theatre and what if the patients were lesbian or what if they were gay? Despite me begging for one, there was no pre-med.

Something went wrong on the table and I died. I ended up standing on a cloud faced by a bar that stretched from one horizon's vanishing point on the left all the way to the vanishing point on the right. Behind the bar was an angel who started pouring me a pint of Guinness. It was white all the way up to the top with a little black head. I had a sip and I knew I was in Heaven. "This is beautiful," I told the angel. "Fucking beautiful man. FUCKING BEAUTIFUL!"

I was shaken roughly awake by a nurse who looked like Dennis Hopper in Myra Hindley's wig. She shouted at me: "Mr Doran! Stop swearing! You're upsetting some of the older patients on the ward." I was shown the door a couple of hours later. It was too soon and on the way home an old lady had to help me across the main road by my flat.

It was around this time that I started drinking into blackout quite frequently. One night I went over to Manchester to watch the industrial metal band Ministry. I went to a party afterwards, got a lift in a van back to Hull the next day and got to the pub at opening time to meet Albert and a few others. About 12 hours later we decamped back to Albert's and I offered to go out and get everyone pizzas. Only somehow I got lost on the way back and ended up 'trapped' in the grounds of old people's secure accommodation. (I'd somehow wandered in there but couldn't find my way back out, like it was the large scale version of a humane mousetrap or lobster pot.)

Or at least, this is what I was reliably informed happened afterwards – I have literally no recollection of anything after Ministry coming on stage late. So when I woke up, frozen to the marrow, a row of 15-inch pizzas along my body like a particularly useless dough and cheese blanket, in a weird, high walled garden, it didn't even occur to me that I was anywhere other than Manchester.

According to my watch it was 6.15am. I climbed over a wall with one of the pizzas under my arm like a big, tasty bread discus. The road was almost entirely empty but the door of a 7-11 style newsagents was open. I walked inside to see a man sweeping the floor.

"How do I get to Piccadilly?"

He looked up: "What are you talking about?"

"Piccadilly train station. How do I get there?"

He snapped at me: "Don't you mean Paragon Square?"

"Errr. No, Manchester Piccadilly train station!"

He lifted the broom and swung it at me. It connected with my temple. He shouted at me as I stumbled away from him back on to the street – it was obviously Beverley Road! Why hadn't I noticed?!

He followed me out on to the street shouting: "Are you on

drugs lad? This isn't Manchester – this is Hull! YOU'RE IN HULL, LAD! YOU'RE IN HULL!"

So I went back round to Albert's and we laughed about it. And we waited for the pubs to open.

I don't see Albert as often as I'd like to, but when I do, it's a real pleasure. I lost touch with him after the 90s – both of us falling into our separate black holes. But he got back in contact six years ago, a changed man. He'd been sober for a good few years, thanks in part to AA, when we first met up again, whereas I was just shy of 12 months dry and still slightly shell shocked. He was as thin as a whippet and handsome as ever, despite suffering some catastrophic coastal erosion of the hairline. He'd also become quite a snappy dresser in the intervening years – a benefit of sobriety that I've yet to experience. He had started dating an old friend of ours from university and was living what seemed to be a rewardingly quiet but bohemian lifestyle of books, studying, writing and long walks.

It's not my job to speak for Albert and I won't but I think it's fair to say that both of us owe AA a great deal, despite the fact that both of us would be critical of some aspects of the fellowship.

Is it possible for people like me and him to drink sensibly if we are taught how? I guess in theory… on paper it must be. Say for example there was a person assigned to stay with me every hour of every day, who was ordered to shoot me dead if I drank any less than one and a half beers a day but also to kill me if I drank more than four, then I guess there is a chance that it might eventually become normal for me to drink sensibly. However, even under such abnormal circumstances, I cannot imagine for a second, the gnawing, all encompassing, monomaniacal desire for ever yet more alcohol abating, even if this situation lasted for a decade or two. I remain sceptical towards the idea of retraining – despite how logical it can seem when explained to me by certain people – because I have to.

Let's say, for the sake of argument, it is possible to train a true alcoholic into sensible new habits – how many attempts would it take? Each time I fell off the bike, picked myself up and got back on for another attempt, what effect would this have on me and those around me?

I've heard it said that you only have to eat something 17 times to get used to the taste of it, no matter how vile it seems at first. Could I endure coming crashing off the wagon up to 16 times first before I got the hang of it?

I had another thirsty friend that I met via AA when I first quit in 2008. He left the fellowship not long afterwards to try a more modern approach to controlled drinking. The last time I spoke to him he informed me gleefully: "The people who run this centre I'm going to think you lot are idiots. Living in the dark ages. All that talk of God and higher powers. You need a scientific programme like the one I'm trying that trains you how to drink sensibly, that gives you tools to use to cope with your urges and proper cognitive behavioural therapy… not this fucking dark ages, Moonie cult thing you're into."

I'd love to be able to tell you he's doing well these days but he's not with us anymore.

It's Midnight! I'm On The Soul Train! (1995)

When you're asleep, you have a circle round you. You're in a chain of hours. A chain of years. A chain of planetary positions. And when you wake up, there is a fraction of a second when you have to place yourself on that chain. Where on the planet are you? What time of day is it? What year is it? And during the night, the deeper you have flung yourself into the void before sleep, the more difficult it is to place yourself on that chain. But then a lifeline is thrown into the blackness to pull you out. You're so far away that you could never do it on your own. An alarm clock goes off. A lover elbows you in the ribs. Curtains are thrown open. A light switch is flicked on. A policeman shines a torch in your face. And there is a rush of civilisations screaming before you. And all of your days and hours and places rush before you but where have you woken up? And when? And what time is it?

And after I became a dad on April 27, 2011 and would be woken with a start in the middle of the night by noise from the baby monitor, I would feel like getting out of bed, sinking to my knees and crying tears of thankfulness because I was in the here and now and no longer trapped in the there and then.

By the time my job ended at Macbrides I was at a low ebb both physically and mentally so decided to move somewhere else for a fresh start. I arrived in Manchester just in time to witness the North's utopian house / techno / acid revolution get shut down by violent hoodlums. There was to be no ecstatic release for me. I would drink heavily from dawn 'til dusk in back street pubs and dark rooms that stank of piss before waking up in rented flats screaming in fear.

I didn't know it at the time but I used to live on the same street as The Chemical Brothers, back when they were The Dust Brothers. The Dickenson Road / Birch Grove area of Longsight, Manchester was a pretty realistic neighbourhood back in 1994 / 1995. They told me once (later, during an interview) that they went out raving one weekend and when they got back, people had broken into their flat and stolen the floor. All the basement flats in the area had heavy stone flagged floors. (As did ours.) They said it didn't stop them from having some pretty righteous but muddy house parties later that year.

I had my first epileptic fit in Manchester. I do not suffer from epilepsy *per se*, it's just that some of the symptoms of alcohol dependence and withdrawal can identically mirror other illnesses temporarily – the symptoms of epilepsy and schizophrenia being two that would plague me on and off during my career as a drinker.

Alcohol withdrawal seizures are one of the commonest forms of tonic clonic – or grand mal – fits in adults, except they usually tend to happen to people in their 50s and 60s. I was 23. Massive, constant doses of alcohol suppress the nervous system, eventually causing tolerance and dependence. When the source of alcohol is removed too quickly, this can cause what is known as 'synaptic misfiring' sometimes leading to tremors, hallucinations and tonic clonic seizures. Commonly, among drinkers, this is just referred to as the DTs or withdrawal.

The dark irony about alcohol dependence is that you often can't do good for doing bad. Kicking booze can kill you. Carrying on drinking can kill you. The only sensible course of action, once you're sodden with the stuff, is a slow decrease in intake of alcohol over a period of time. And if you do stop too quickly, well… your body lets you know that it is displeased with your course of action.

Heavy drinkers will know the vice-like tension that starts building up in the base of the skull, slowly increasing into spasms throughout the body when a heavy session is terminated too quickly. These are the tremens which start visiting hand-in-hand with the delirium. This is one of the reasons why seasoned alcoholics should not kick without professional help. If a slow reduction in the amount of alcohol taken over time isn't an option, then they need anti-spasmodic medication like temazepam or clonazepam to stop a potentially fatal seizure or heart attack.

As was fast becoming the pattern, I moved to Manchester with fairly high hopes. I got a job as a teacher of English as a second language to first generation immigrants. My classroom was below a needle exchange programme in a community centre in Cheetham Hill and at first things, both personally and professionally, went relatively well. However the education programme got shut down and without a job I devolved almost immediately.

After a fairly miserable fortnight-long session celebrating my last pay packet as an adult education teacher, where I'd drunk myself into unconsciousness every single night, I stopped drinking far too quickly. I woke up one morning and found that I'd written in really big letters along my bedroom wall in crayon: "Stop drinking, you cunt." Downstairs in the front room, the house was filled in a shin-deep carpet of empty and half-empty cans of "Inca Brew – The Beer of the Aztec Kings". They formed a sickening meniscus between the floor and the walls. They were all over a year out of date.

I couldn't stop shaking and crying and my skin had turned bright yellow. I was, indeed, a cunt and needed to stop drinking.

Over the course of the day I tried to pour away beer and spirits and expunge the evidence of the previous 14 days. The following night, I started feeling the sick spasmodic sensation at the top of my spine, which over the last two years had come to be a precursor of the waking nightmare which could only be staved off by more ale. But obeying my note to myself I decided not to drink anything.

By the time *The Sky At Night* came on I was starting to slip in and out of hellish hallucinations. Patrick Moore announced that astronomers had discovered a gigantic lake of alcohol in outer space and then said that it rained diamonds on Neptune. As I started to nod off, I became aware of horrific figures standing in the corners of the room. They started telling me things I didn't want to hear. They told me I had died with my family in a car crash four years earlier.

Lying in bed later, I was tormented by disembodied voices and what sounded like crazed techno music. When I closed my eyes I could still see the room as if my eyelids were translucent. With my eyes shut the room was the same, except there was a man sat in my chair. I opened my eyes and he was gone. I close my eyes and he's there again. "He's in the room. He's in the fucking room…"

At one point in the night it all seemed to stop, and I heard a soft popping sound. When I looked up, there was an angel in front of me. It was holding a mug of tea and had a big, shiny bullet instead of a head. The shakes had become distinguishable spasms that were becoming more and more violent. I felt like the inmate of a psychiatric ward undergoing EST. I was flapping up and down on my bed like a dying fish. This was eventually interrupted by a feeling of warmth. Everything went orange and I zoned out.

I came to on the other side of the room. I'd knocked my writing desk over and my arms were hurting – I'd obviously come crashing out of bed, over my desk and into the corner.

Whatever had happened had opened the dams in me. I started sweating profusely. The feeling of toxins pissing out of me made me feel tolerably better and I eventually fell asleep.

When I woke up my bed sheets were sodden and ice cold, and Neil Armstrong was stood at the end of my bed. He was wearing a space suit and holding an American flag. The flag was flapping as if in a breeze but in his visor I could see Buzz Aldrin holding a camera, standing on the lunar surface.

I felt very ill for about eight days and stopped drinking for ten in total. Bar two dry Januarys and one severe illness, this would be the last significant pause in my drinking in the next 14 years.

During this time I both kept bad company and was bad company. I made terrible choices and compounded them gleefully. I had little in the way of self-respect. I blamed everything and everyone but myself for how miserable I was but it wasn't just the drink and drugs, it was the flat I lived in itself. I simply shouldn't have moved into the place down Dickenson Road but it had been born out of necessity and opportunity. The massive old house where I'd previously lived had carbon monoxide leaking from the gas fires and was getting turned over on a monthly basis by crackheads. This other flat was standing empty. It had been vacated in a rush by our drug dealer Peter Dailor, who'd had some sort of nervous breakdown.

"Would you jump in his grave as fast?" asked someone about the unseemly haste with which me and my mate Steve, who had come over from Hull with me, moved into Dailor's freshly vacated flat but we didn't really like him that much, so didn't worry about it. He wasn't even a good drug dealer. All he ever had was shit cannabis resin. He had no work ethic but he did have a large menagerie of exotic insects. Occasionally he would turn up at our house brandishing a cassette. He recorded his insects eating and would then ask if he could play the cassette on our stereo because it had an LED graphic equalizer on it. He could sit there for ages listening to this monotonous clicking sound, staring at the shifting fields of red and green rectangles of light.

Being quite mentally effervescent, he attracted rumour and urban myth like a bad story magnet but we managed to boil them down to some actual facts. He'd moved to Manchester to study zoology at the MET in 1991 but got kicked off his course for doing unnecessary homework – basically he got busted for taking four zebra legs home with him (one of the things left in the house when we moved in was a very heavy work bench and a bunch of G clamps and saws). He had a live-in girlfriend who sort of kept him on the straight and narrow but then she got pregnant. She asked Dailor to stop spending all of his spare time sitting in the dark smoking pot listening to his giant millipede having its lunch and to start getting the flat ready for the new arrival. When he refused to get with the programme she left and he deteriorated quite quickly.

It was good fun moving into the loon's flat at first. He had a first-rate collection of oil paintings of communist leaders all over the place and a box full of vinyl-laminated business cards in the form of drinks coasters with a crude cartoon of a clown holding a saw with his address and phone number (now our address and phone number) printed on them. They also bore the inscription: "Pete Dailor – inventor and children's entertainer".

The only insects left in the flat were decidedly unexotic, however. Every day on waking, there would be cockroaches everywhere. You couldn't do anything before removing all of them, which was a depressingly and distressingly Sisyphean task. We got on at the council about them but they just told us to forget it. "Every house in your entire area has them… once they're in a block forget it… It sounds like there are more in your flat than average but there's still nothing we can do."

After a while, it didn't matter that the landlord never bothered us for the rent and there was a large portrait of Chairman Mao in the hallway. The idea of the entire street being infested with multitudes of insects was starting to play on my mind. I started having nightmares about Dailor's girlfriend and what she was pregnant with. I couldn't be in the flat without a drink in my hand. I'd crack a bottle of sherry the second I got up. I guess it was bothering my flatmate Steve as well as he was on the bong at all times.

One night after the pub, toward the end of my stay there, there was a bunch of us messing about, jousting in the kitchen. This basically consisted of us getting on each other's shoulders and engaging another pair of combatants with saucepans. When we accidentally knocked the first polystyrene tile out of the false ceiling I didn't notice the couple of roaches that fell onto the linoleum floor. We started howling and smashing at the roof tiles until someone started screaming because they'd realised they had cockroaches in their hair.

Steve was the first to see the large suitcase. We dragged it down and spent ages looking at it. We were totally wasted and buzzing off what it could be... body parts... money... drugs... please let it be drugs!

When we opened it though it was over half-full of cockroaches. They were mainly dead but with quite a few still moving. I always thought that cockroaches were the least human insects I ever saw, that there was no way you could ever anthropomorphise them without losing sense of what they actually were, until I saw one as a sidekick in the children's CGI film Wall-E. But back in 1995 I was left staring at a suitcase of sluggish, senseless, alien creatures, trapped inside a box, listlessly climbing over piles of thousands of corpses, slowly starving to death, with no chance of rescue or reprieve.

I lasted another week in the flat. I packed as much stuff as I could carry in a large suitcase and moved down south for good. I left at 8.13am on a Tuesday morning. Steve was taking a break from filling his own suitcase for work when I left. He had another day of selling tat round the alehouses of central Manchester ahead of him. Novelty lighters adorned with ganja leaves and gonks for the Granby. King-sized rolling papers with cartoons on them and hash pipes for the Ducie. Packs of pornographic playing cards for the Piccadilly Gardens. He didn't even look up from his bong when I said goodbye and walked out of the door.

I moved in with my girlfriend Helen in Welwyn Garden City, Hertfordshire and this undoubtedly saved my life. She undoubtedly saved my life. I'd known her since I was a teenager and she was the first of the two serious, long-term relationships I would have as an adult. We lived in a tiny granny flat with a single bed, a portable TV, piles and piles of books and piles and piles of cassettes and bottles and bottles of wine. Times were often very good and for a few years it didn't even matter that it wasn't enough to temper my raging thirst which was just getting more and more entrenched. But I need to be clear about this – it's great to be young and in love and drinking all the time. What an adventure it is. What a romantic life to lead. It's just – what happens to your youth and what happens to the love because of the constant drinking? If I was a philosopher I would have used dialectical means to study my situation which was happy but also harmful and untenable. But I wasn't a philosopher. I was a drunk working in a factory.

By this stage I now had to plan everything around my drinking and when I didn't there was often trouble. And it was difficult because I was working peculiar shift patterns in a local warehouse. And when I woke with a shout or a scream in bed in Welwyn Garden City, in 1995 at 5.25am with the piercing screech of the alarm clock, I couldn't imagine feeling worse. With only four hours sleep and several mugs worth of unprocessed cheap whiskey still sloshing round my belly, too sick for breakfast, too late to shower, every step between my bed and punching in at the warehouse at 5.58am was sheer fucking agony.

If you fly over Ebenezer Howard's 1920s utopian new town, heading South away from the Satanic mills of the North, it looks like an inverted crucifix. Perhaps this is a Northern perspective because most of the inhabitants of this godforsaken place fled up from London, approaching from the South. It was the first small town in England to develop a bad heroin problem... but was that because of or in spite of its Quakerite lack of pubs in the cross-shaped, manicured centre? The relative scarcity of pubs in WGC didn't make them any friendlier however. In the few ale houses there were dotted round the perimeter you could often look forward to seeing a fight, even if other types of entertainment were thin on the ground. Well, maybe not in The Pear Tree where they had the same incidental music that is played in the psychiatric wards featured in *One Flew Over The Cuckoo's Nest* on a constant loop in the background during licensing hours.

A few months after arriving in town, when a large international logistics firm and a large supermarket chain opened the huge central food store, refrigeration centre and bonded warehouse on Black Fan Road near Panshanger, I got a job as a shop floor goods-in clerk working the early shift one week and late the next. There were literally hundreds of these jobs going and pretty much anyone who went to a temp agency that month to enquire about work got one. When I went for a celebratory drink on finding out I now had work, luckily I chose the Pear Tree, because on revealing my good news I was quickly surrounded by high blood pressure, shaven-headed bruisers in canary yellow shirts chanting things like, "Southern jobs for Southern lads not Northern cunts" at me while I supped up quickly and left. The pacifying effect of the syrupy faux classical music piped in through the idiot calming ducts just about prevented them from erupting into actual violence. This peace was not something that would pervade the actual job however.

On the whole, working early shifts is worse than working lates or night shifts. Or at least they are if you go to the pub at 2.30pm straight after work, promising yourself you'll be home by 9pm at the latest but then never are. I don't want to tar everyone with the same brush or indulge in stereotyping but at the same time I'm pretty sure there are a few postmen out there who know what I'm talking about. Sweating cheap whiskey through cheap clerical clothes in an air hangar covered cityscape constructed of tower blocks of crates of cheap whiskey, writing down numbers referring to cases of whiskey on sheets of paper, trying not to vomit when bottles of whiskey smashed on the floor near me, counting down the hours 'til I could have my first whiskey of the day, was all I did, professionally speaking, for the first year.

They're odd places, bonded warehouses. They're officially Customs property and, as I understand it, police cannot enter the premises. Despite rigorous searches at the only gate in and out and CCTV cameras absolutely everywhere, a lot of people (not including me, I didn't have the nerve or the initiative) were trying to smuggle cases of alcohol out of the place. When caught, most people would hold their hands up, despite the fact that getting nabbed with a trunk full of Bells just before Christmas could land you in jail. There were however a sizeable number of stupid people working there as well who seemed unable to comprehend that just because there were never any police on the actual site, that this didn't make it a frontier town like Deadwood or Mos Eisley Space Port. Big Customs and Excise security guys with glittering eyes would properly row with these men who were deranged by constant night work and hangovers and not in the possession of clear-sighted long term planning. These guys with their hangdog looks who were pathetically trying to steal bottles of cheap liquor they probably didn't even like that much, to sell on in pubs – they didn't stand a chance. Blood would sometimes be spilled on concrete flags at unusual hours of the day as policemen stood outside the chain link fence, leaning on cars, smoking cigarettes, waiting to be handed their new charges.

The razor wire topped perimeter fence was far too high to be worth throwing bottles over but once at Christmas I saw some frozen turkeys achieve the kind of escape velocity and flight paths that would have proved impossible for them while they were alive.

I was good friends with four of the guys who worked in the warehouse. Two of them had girlfriends who were prostitutes. And one of the other two guys who were single was sleeping with one of the prostitutes but in a not on the books, not on the meter and not with knowledge of her boyfriend kind of way. I was, let's say, conflicted by all of this. While I prided myself on coming from a working class family and kidded myself that I was pretty street smart, I also acknowledged that it felt like I'd taken a wrong turn somewhere, that I was somewhat out of my comfort zone.

No disrespect to anyone who was born in WGC and works in a factory there – after all I'm from St Helens and my Dad worked his entire life in a factory in nearby Warrington – but I later realised that the wrong turn I'd taken was at Junction Four of the M1 for Hatfield. I should have stayed on the motorway until it penetrated the heart of London, stopping only to pick Helen up on the way. I was disconsolate about the high percentage of prostitutes I knew – and they weren't even nice prostitutes like they would have been in a Ken Loach or Richard Curtis film. I was kind of stunned that no one else seemed to think it was weird. Every time the fourth guy went out on a date with a woman I would become irrationally afraid that she would end up on the game as well.

It's one of those things I'm really embarrassed about now but everyone else there pretty much hated me and most of them didn't really feel any reason to hold back from telling me. The worst part of it is, I totally get it. Not only was I a bit of an annoying bolshie prick but after growing up in a culture where it's totally normal to fight men from the town down the road from you, of course you're going to hate some kid with scruffy long hair and a nose ring from 230 miles away with a completely different accent. Some giant bald ex-army prick with a chin that looked like a snow plough who worked on the pallet trucks used to call me Fenian scum on account of my surname. Used to talk at length about all the hidings he'd dished out to "my sort". He would go on at length about the several tours of Northern Ireland he'd completed – the men he'd put in hospital, the women he'd fucked – like this was somehow relevant to me. I was sick of the way he curried favour with the other drivers at my expense, they already disliked me enough as it was without him sticking his jaw in. I decided an act of largesse on my part was necessary to improve relations.

One late shift the unthinkable happened and we actually got finished by about 10.30pm. The vegetables, beer, spirits and wine for the nation's entire chain of Safeway supermarkets for the following day were packed neatly onto pallets, which were all in the right trucks and ready to be driven to their destinations. It was nothing short of a minor miracle. People were in a giddy frame of mind. We were going to get off shift well over two hours early. I had a brain wave. I said I'd run over the road to the Attimore Hall pub and get a couple of pints in for everyone and they could settle up with me when they came over after putting the battery trucks on to charge for the night.

I jogged over to the pub, hitting the bar at 10.45. I ordered 27 pints of Stella, nine bottles of Bud, four whiskeys and five Jack and cokes.

"Is that all?" asked the barman.

"No. I'll have a bag of Frazzles as well please", I said.

"Would you like a tray?" he added.

He was OK the barman, he even gave me a hand carrying the giant round to a long table at the back of the pub but as soon as he left me he went to fetch the landlord. I looked at all the gallons of ale in front of me and felt a massive amount of tension lift from my shoulders. I could imagine Lance Corporal Bollock Face taking them all to the Ludwick Arms instead just to drop me in it but I didn't care.

The landlord was a touch passive aggressive when he turned up. "There's not going to be any trouble, is there", he said, pitched halfway between a statement and a question. I downed a pint in one and looked at him. I imagined the headline on the front of the following day's *Welwyn And Hatfield Times*: "Northern Idiot Dies In Ill Advised Last Orders Stunt".

"As soon as it turns twenty past I'm calling the police", he added.

But the rest of the shift barrelled through the door at ten past eleven and got stuck into their drinks. Aggravatingly, I'd already finished mine and I had to sit round watching everyone else sipping away at theirs.

Little by little the knives were being slid back into my flesh. When I first sat at the table surrounded by 36 drinks I initially felt free but now I just felt trapped again watching these clowns drink them all... far too slowly. I only had to wait for another twenty minutes before getting thrown out though and then I went home and had a real drink. In my flat I poured myself the first of many well deserved whiskies and didn't stop until I slipped into the deepest of voids. Helen was already asleep and I would drink quietly in the dark, smoking cigarettes, listening to *Young Americans* and *Station To Station* by David Bowie on my Walkman, feeling my brain unclench. Feeling my teeth unclench. Drinking until I stopped sweating. Drinking until I stopped hurting.

Even though I was a bad piss artist, I still had standards and goals. I knew that just slugging down whiskey out of a Teletubbies mug in the dark was bad form, so I started aiming a little bit higher. I was a late starter with cocktails – up until moving South I didn't even know what cocktails were. And when I say cocktails, I include such drinks as vodka and orange. Or to be more specific I had no idea of the potential a vodka and orange could offer when made outside of St Helens. In my teenage local The Alf, you could get a potato distilled spirit with a shot of congealing, glow in the dark, syrupy, sunset orange cordial if you wanted but it wasn't what I now recognise as a vodka and orange. This noxious combination always managed to somehow separate completely in your mouth so you had double the displeasure of drinking both constituents individually, as if you'd just necked a glass of turned milk and cod liver oil or Castrol GTX and rancid bull semen. So to a young man desperate for alcohol it was very bittersweet to experience it, much like sex in prison on Christmas morning. (Lags actually brew their own hooch by leaving orange cordial on the radiators to ferment and I'm reliably told it tastes remarkably like a vintage V 'n' O served in The Alf.)

An effete, blouse wearing ponce like myself couldn't really take the St Helens vodka and orange experience, I'd just tip a large shot of Smirnoff into my Guinness, sometimes eliciting a screeched, "Ooh, look at him... *Oscar Wilde*", from a perpetually angry barwoman called Betty. It was better to leave the foul Dr Jekyll-esque concoction to the only people who could handle it: old women on pension day. They were the sort of folk who looked vacuum-packed from the inside and acted like they were cast from bronze, despite having skin like dried chamois leather and only being four feet tall. Every Thursday they would barge up to the bar, sticking their Ray Harryhausen-designed bony elbows into your ribs to get pole position for ordering a drink. They would always go for bottles of Special Brew, Gold Label barley wine or Thunderbird blue label that stood on sticky wooden shelves at room temperature, to be followed by a V 'n' O chaser. Then they would leave like a flock of angry, de-cloaked Jawas in crimplene for the scoop and weigh and Wilkinsons, their spiritual load seemingly unleavened by the massive lunchtime injection of brutal alcohol and crudely refined sugars they'd just main-lined.

I remember some poor sod (presumably returning from university, France or a Communist run homosexual indoctrination camp) asking for vodka and fresh orange once. The reply from Betty was simply: "*Fresh...* orange?" But executed in such a withering manner that people were still talking about the incident early the following week.

But when I left St Helens in 1989, it was clear that change was in the air in more enlightened locales – that drinking culture had to change. I don't want to get all 'Four Yorkshiremen' about it but there were more than a few pubs when I first started drinking who literally wouldn't serve women pints of beer and frowned upon them ordering their own drinks if they were below retirement age. And there were plenty of others who wouldn't treat a woman on her own as anything other than a prostitute with her meter ticking or a cock ravenous Mata Hari. Some men I know get slightly misty eyed at the perceived authenticity of this time, of 'proper' Northern drinking culture, before craft beer, quinoa salads and internet connected touch sensitive juke boxes featuring Bon Iver, but most of it was shit if you ask me. I'm deadly serious about it when I say I only went into ten pubs prior to 1990 that weren't fucking horrendous places to be. All up and down Beverley Road, Hull, in 1989, many, many hostelries were announcing another kind of change. They had posters in their windows declaring that all-day drinking was coming; apart from The Rose – a spectacularly pre-lapsarian, madness-infused pugilism shack – which had a poster announcing: 'Coming soon: "MILD"!!!'

It wasn't until 1995 that I experienced an honest to goodness cocktail, made and served with ingenuity and craftsmanship. During the summer I had read an article on how to mix the perfect dry martini in the *Guardian*. I'd never really known what the difference between the actual cocktail and the hyper-powered cheap Italian vermouth was. The former was favoured by international spies and high powered American business people while the latter was preferred by those who had relinquished their quest for leading a happy life and by those who lasted until after 5am at house parties. I chewed this feature over in my mind while working a late shift in the bonded warehouse in WGC. I determined to go to Claridge's in Mayfair on the weekend with Helen so we could drink a proper martini. Otherwise, literally what was the fucking point of getting out of bed in the morning?

Wearing smart clothes, her in a cocktail dress and me in a suit, we propped up the West End hotel bar and watched as the cocktail waiter fetched a frost encrusted eight ball glass out of a freezer cabinet and placed it on a paper doily. He produced an expensive looking solid steel perfume atomizer and held it a foot above the glass before giving the bulb a gentle squeeze, releasing a mist of Noily Prat vermouth into the air. Some of this eventually descended slowly onto the inner surface of the glass. It seemed like a homeopathic recipe for making the drink. Only the world's most sensitive atomic scales would have registered the increase in weight the glass had undergone. Then he reached into a small freezer unit and brought out an expensive bottle of imported Russian vodka that had almost, but not quite, gone waxy with the chill, and topped the glass up the brim. He used a razor blade to carve a thin translucent rectangular slice of lemon peel and rolled it up, squeezing the resultant citrus oil into a slick onto the surface of the drink. Then he speared the roll of rind with a cocktail stick, used a miniature flame thrower to singe it and placed it into the drink.

We had several each then walked all the way back to Kings Cross. My pounding heart was made from the finest patent leather and pumped onyx squid ink round my crystal veins, my eyes had become pearls and shone under street lamps – each of which flickered into warm sodium life as we passed underneath in the twilight. I ran a hand through my hair which was finer than splinters of glass and the strands chimed together. My teeth met in harmony as mutually embracing rows of stalactites and stalagmites. I purred like a tiger and my long coat swung with each step, just so. With each echoing crack our shoes made on the Portland stone flagged pavements of West London, shop front windows bulged outwards and car alarms sprang into discordant song. The GPO buckled, swayed, and then regained its composure as we strode past. The primary neon of Soho singed a message onto my retinas – all of this and more is yours. The after effect of the experience lasted all the way back to the bedsit in Welwyn Garden City and I can still feel a faint echo of it now.

That Christmas I couldn't get enough time off work to go up north to see my Mum and Dad so I stayed in Hertfordshire and my best mate Stu came to visit. When we woke up on the morning of the 25th I suggested we have cocktails. I sloshed vermouth round two mugs and then filled them up to the brim with Smirnoff.

"Jesus Christ", said Stu after his first mug full. "How does James Bond get anything done?"

We had another and Stu cooked breakfast, which was made out of 40 cloves of garlic, two tins of butter beans, three packets of super noodles and a tin of Campbell's cream of mushroom soup. I made a third martini but on sitting down I realised that I'd forgotten the vermouth. Looking at the clock, which read 10am, and then at the cracked Dr Who mug full of vodka, my eyes started to brim with tears.

"I think I've made a terrible mistake", I said querulously.

I don't remember much about the rest of the day and what I do is pretty grim. Some people apparently received phone calls from me after 11am tearfully saying that Stu was lying motionless behind the sofa and that he might be dead.

When we woke up the next day, we swore we'd be more careful in future, and determined to get it right, we started the day off with breakfast first *and then* made a mug of martini each.

Around this time there were many good times. And these times were far from unremarkable for me, just maybe unremarkable to other people reading, so I'd like to draw a veil round them; to keep them for myself. The opening line of Tolstoy's *Anna Karenina* usually posits the intriguing proposition: "All happy families are alike; each unhappy family is unhappy in its own way." However there is a French translation which widens this idea right out by changing the opening gambit to: "All happinesses are alike but every unhappiness has its own features." Which I think is a fair assessment of how things in life tend to be.

A Sound Like A Tiger Thrashing In The Water (1997)

When I moved from Welwyn Garden City to London with Helen in April 1997, I started drinking into blackout. And after a while it was like big chunks of my life weren't even there anymore.

It's difficult to drink yourself into a state of complete en bloc retrograde amnesia. This is total blackout where not even the tiniest shred of memory remains like a tatter of meat on a well gnawed bone. Entering this state means you won't remember anything that happened over a relatively substantial amount of time. And it happens to the extent that even after days or weeks have elapsed, the period remains mysterious to you like an obsidian ball in your consciousness. It remains forbidding, sealed off, senseless, kept in permanent quarantine.

But once you break the seal, it happens again and again. Blackouts punch holes into your permanent record. They cluster. They spot like black mould in a petri dish. These areas of totality with their impermeable event horizons are like puncture marks in your existence. Short, unrecoverable gaps of nothingness. They gather in lines like perforations on a sheet of stamps. And these are the lines along which your life is ripped apart.

By 1997, I had been working in pubs, clubs and factories for well over a decade and it occurred to me that this might be my lot for the rest of my professional life. I was starting to become desperate to get away from it and tended to spend weekends in London, clubbing, drinking and watching gigs in a desperate utopian blur, slouching back to the warehouse in Welwyn Garden City for another five nights of grind the second they ended.

The few friends I had left from university had already embarked on careers – an idea I had all but given up on for myself. Helen, who was a teacher, was my only point of contact with a professional life outside of shift work in factories.

But toward the end of my time in Hertfordshire, early in 1997, Aunty Kath, one of my Dad's elder sisters, gave me a few thousand pounds, not wanting to pay death duties on her intended bequest and in doing so, threw me a life line. My Aunty Kath and her elder sister Aunty Mel, really looked out for me when I was younger. Perhaps even more so than with my parents, I was crippled with guilt about the idea of this pair of elderly sisters who lived together finding out about the amount that I drank and my trouble with narcotics. I tried to think of something useful to do with the cash – quickly – and all I could come up with was night school or college.

I hadn't previously held any kind of desire to be a news journalist but the more I thought about it, the more it seemed to make sense, especially with the job's boozy reputation. When I found out there was an intensive, five month NCTJ (National Council For The Training Of Journalists) course being offered less than 40 miles away in Harlow, Essex, I couldn't think of any good reason not to do it.

Around the same time Helen accepted a teaching job in a large comprehensive secondary in Tottenham meaning we could both move to London together at the same time. If the future had previously looked like a void, it was as if someone had suddenly thrown a handful of glitter into it, directly in front of my eyes.

Toward the end of my course, we moved into a flat in Leyton, East London, with a small back garden and plenty of space for books and CDs. I wasted no time in finding a large, convivial Irish pub called the Northcote Arms to drink in. It appeared to hold selective lock-ins until all hours of the morning, so I immediately set about decoding the selection process; something that took me less than six weeks to accomplish.

I believe the pub has changed a lot now and Bernie and John – the couple who ran it, who I had a lot of affection for – have moved back to Ireland. Twenty years ago it was a boisterous and mainly friendly place that acted as a focal point for the local London Irish community. It also functioned as a second home to a crew of very thirsty people from all kinds of backgrounds, who mainly worked in the building trade.

After completing my course I got the first job I applied for, as a trainee reporter at a press agency called National News. This independent outfit based at the eastern lip of the City essentially employed a team of reporters, photographers and editors to cover current stories right across the soft to hard spectrum in both a news and features capacity, either specifically commissioned by a publication or to send out generally on the wires electronically to all titles. Their main clients were all of the national newspapers, the London locals and plenty of regional titles, not to mention a wide range of magazines. Within a month, I had a court story in the *Sunday Mirror* ("Air Rage Maniac Asks Pilot To Step Outside For A Fight At 37,000 Feet!") and a short news piece, or nib, on the front cover of the *Evening Standard*.

Our office was situated in a lovely building called Zetland House on Leonard Street, just off the Old Street Roundabout. If you turned right out of the front door you'd soon end up in the City, which was initially a visual treat for someone who wasn't used to seeing anything taller than the stinking Shredded Wheat factory in Welwyn Garden City and if you turned left you'd end up in Shoreditch, a locale I already knew quite well from my regular trips down to town to go out clubbing.

About two years earlier, I went on my first ever night out dancing in London. I selected an event at the Blue Note Club on Hoxton Square, because the show had been hyped to the rafters by the dance press. The night featured sets by a pre-success James Lavelle and a pre-fame DJ Shadow. I met up with some friends from Hull, got there before the doors opened but the queue was already round the block and we barely got in.

I must admit, I was dismayed by the music at first. There was a lot of smooth hip hop, jazzy breaks and fusion-y noodling going on and I almost left at one point, but then I ran into my mate Lee from back home in St Helens, and he gave me and my mate Frank a couple of pills. I don't even remember taking them. We went into the main room to watch DJ Shadow and again, the signs weren't good. There was a flock of deck hanging geeks in expensive trainers crowded round the DJ booth, clutching notepads. "This is the lamest thing ever", I said disconsolately.

Shadow was clearly as annoyed as we were however. He placed a 7" of 'Back In Black' by AC/DC on the turntable and literally dropped the needle on the plastic haphazardly, pressing play without queuing it up. All the trainspotters looked uncomfortably at one another. At the end of the track he picked the vinyl off the deck and smashed it, throwing the shards at them. Then he repeated the process with 'We Will Rock You' by Queen.

This was so exciting that it sparked an adrenaline surge in me but instead of dying off immediately, it kept on building and building until it became almost unbearable. I got momentarily embarrassed, as it felt like I was going to ejaculate – except, not in the conventional way but internally, across my entire lymphatic system. It felt like glands I'd never previously been aware of were bursting their caches of delicious electrolytes. There were tiny land mines going off in my pelvis, behind my knees, in my neck, deep inside my shoulders, in my ankles and wrists, all the way up my spine, flooding me with pure, tactile pleasure.

"Holy shit" said Frank, clamping his hand onto my arm. My skin felt electric where he touched me. It was analogous to something darkly erotic and erogenous, but completely asexual at the same time. His hand left a Kirlian outline of coronal discharge on my arm. There was a pleasantly acidic glow to everything, but none of the cephalic carnage I associated with LSD or magic mushrooms. We started grinning wildly at each other. I had a complete realisation – no matter how vacuous – that everything had been leading up to this point. No matter what had happened before, and no matter what happened afterwards, this would make up for it one hundred fold.

My friends over in Manchester and some other mates in Leeds and Hull had been on one for years. Despite loving acid house, hardcore, techno and jungle, I always resisted taking ecstasy. It was too expensive – "You can get three and a half litres of vodka from Aldi for that!" – and more to the point, it just didn't sit well with my bleak aesthetic. I genuinely believed that having that much fun was somehow like letting the side down. Acid, speed and mushrooms slotted into my ragged, melancholy lifestyle much better. I was instantaneously happy to admit that I'd been completely wrong. Very, very happy to admit it.

Shadow dropped 'Soul Power 74' by Maceo And The Macks, and all bets were off. Weird details were rising out of the music. Aeroplane noises, baby glossolalia, giant engines revving, ecstatic moans and groans. I became immediately aware of how much reverb and echo were being applied to Maceo Parker's burnished saxophone. The three-dimensionality of the recording was really apparent. Normally a good club PA gives you the illusion of being inside the music, but this was a literal immersion, a communion. I started dancing, immediately locked into a groove that wouldn't release me. I knew this record was twenty years old, but it sounded like the most modern thing ever recorded.

A tape recording of a man's voice – "The senator's been shot… been shot… he's died!" – rang out, suggesting a dark significance that I couldn't quite put my finger on. But if I was aware that there was both darkness and light, the light was winning. Another voice intoned: "Well, I don't know what will happen now. We've got some difficult days ahead. But it really doesn't matter with me now, because I've been to the mountaintop!"

To the mountaintop. This was where we were going. Up to the peak where the air was purest and the sun brightest. At the summit, the light would scorch our retinas.

The chant of The Macks intoning: "Open up the door… I'll get it myself" locked itself into my brain, looping in my head for the rest of the summer like a mantra. I realised that everything on ecstasy was about loops and imagistic flashes. Perfect moments captured in amber, time-stretched 'til they broke apart into honey-coloured fragments. A twanging bass note played with much vibrato became a ridiculous wave, travelling along a guitar string like the ripple of an earthquake along a giant suspension bridge. The parabolas of vibrating lines formed a pulsing network; from my nervous system, to soundwaves in the air, to vibrating speaker cones, to electronic pulses, to a vibrating stylus, to the hand of a DJ, to the past, to the future.

I don't remember everything, or even that much, about the night. I felt at one point like there were giant church bells tolling in the ceiling. After the club, we went to an illegal rave in a disused NCP Car Park and danced to techno til 8am. The next day a big group of us went to Brockwell Lido, drinking red wine from the bottle in the sunshine, watching the multi-coloured flags flutter against a light blue sky over Brixton. The afterglow was strong. The entire weekend was perfect, really. I genuinely believed that every single night out I had in London would be that good, but in reality it would be a long time before anything remotely comparable happened.

A big aspect of my job as reporter was knocking on doors, a practice called door-stepping. If a big story broke I'd ring someone's bell hoping for a comment and then hang around and wait for them to turn up if they weren't home. This was very boring and almost intolerable during deep winter; although it did lead to my cryptic crossword skills improving. Seasoned hacks and snappers would trade war stories on freezing cold assignments about hapless former colleagues. If you listened to them, it seemed inevitable that you would get caught out if you sloped off home early and then phoned the office from a phone box at the end of your road, asking to be sent home, when you'd already been there for hours.

One of these cautionary tales concerned a smudge, aka a photographer, who was staying in a seafront hotel in Brighton. His picture desk phoned him up and asked him to describe the scene he could see out of his window. When he failed to mention Eugenius Birch's much mistreated West Pier in flames, blazing a vandalous shade of orange against the night sky, he was fired on the spot. (He hadn't seen the fire of course because he was at home in Catford watching *Only Fools And Horses*, and not ensconced in the hotel room where he was paid to be awaiting a job early the next morning.)

Someone I knew thought it would be a waste of time door-stepping Colin Stagg, the one-time suspect in the Rachel Nickell murder in Wimbledon, and decided to vigorously explore the pubs of Raynes Park instead. Little did he know that an hour after he was due to be *in situ*, a man would turn up outside Stagg's next door neighbour's house on a motorbike and start firing a shotgun through the living room window as part of some on-going disagreement over the provenance of a batch of narcotics. It was always particularly painful to get read the riot act over this kind of thing the next day, as the very fact that you'd slunk off the job almost certainly meant you had incurred a terrible hangover as well.

With some reporters however, you simply had to be thankful that they hadn't become surgeons, hostage negotiators, diplomats or airline pilots. One cub reporter in my extended circle of peers was eager to make a name for himself, and decided to impress potential employers at the tabloids by gaining access to Bill Clinton while he was on a state visit to see Tony Blair. Fearing that the official channels would not prove that fruitful to someone whose CV only included a London agency and the *Barking and Dagenham Post*, he rented a room in the same hotel and abseiled down four storeys until he was outside the President's window clutching a Dictaphone and a sheaf of questions. After a few seconds some very angry American soldiers stationed outside the hotel at ground level trained a light on him and informed him that he should stop moving as he was in the sights of several snipers holding high-powered rifles and there were helicopters on the way. He didn't impress any potential bosses and he didn't get to ask Bill any questions. He was, by all accounts, at the receiving end of a lengthy interview himself later that night, however.

My own errors were slightly more prosaic. I wasn't a brilliant news journalist and that wasn't just because of my tastes in fuel. There was (and doubtlessly still is) a hardcore of hacks who mainly specialised in court reporting, whose appetites made me look like a choirboy. Yet despite this, they still managed to turn in sparkling copy every single day. One of them, it was rumoured, was completely homeless and yet still getting complex court copy published in *The Times*. It is hard to work out how some of these journalists make it past the age of 30. On an average day, the dungeon-like press room situated right in the guts of the Old Bailey, looked uncannily like a really distressing scene from *The Walking Dead*. For me though, I eventually had to admit to myself that my heart wasn't really in it enough to get with the steep learning curve expected of me. After a couple of years, I could barely pretend to be interested in the celebrity stories, the political tidbits and the court cases. This, combined with the drink, led me to become careless. The mistranslation of one small line of shorthand during an employment tribunal in 1998 necessitated an apology and clarification be run in every national newspaper in the UK bar *The Daily Express*, on my account. The agency – who always treated me well – could have sacked me but moved me onto feature writing instead.

When it looks like legal action will be taken against a big publication because of something you have written – and the fault clearly lies with you – I can't describe how dismaying the feeling is. I'm very aware of libel action these days – perhaps a lot more than I need to be given that I run a music website. In the world of online journalism, getting sued is less of a threat because of the ability to remove offending articles quickly without too much hassle. However it remains something that will make all print journalists blanch with fear. And rightly so.

My friend Phil, the former editor of the very fine and sorely missed music paper *The Stool Pigeon*, got sent a lawyer's letter a few years ago, when I used to share office space with him. On the face of it the legal document made it look like his entire operation was about to be shut down.

He and his editorial partner at the paper, Mickey, had run a fake advert before the last general election suggesting (as a satirical joke) that Heinz – the baked bean manufacturers – had gotten together with the British National Party and produced a limited edition run of canned pasta swastikas in tomato sauce. Mickey, a lovely man who looks and dresses like Theodore Kaczynski, The Unabomber, had even stayed up all night, cutting out swastika shapes into actual pasta, so he could photograph them.

It was only a few days after the paper hit the streets that a Heinz lawyer got in touch. When Phil opened the letter all the air got sucked out of the room as if a nuclear bomb had gone off in the atmosphere half a mile above the office. He blanched visibly; the bloodless ivory pallor of his face throwing his burnished coppery ginger locks into an even sharper relief than usual but after regaining his composure, he dealt with the whole affair in a commendably stoic manner.

It turned out that the Heinz Company has been plagued by (completely unfounded) rumours that they actually used to produce 'pastikas' during the Second World War, to the extent that it has become an urban myth. Not only was founder HJ Heinz a kindly and progressive businessman but his company helped the Allies during the war effort by making CG4-A glider parts crucial to the Normandy landings in their factories. And then, when the conflict ended, they also aided war-torn Europe with food supplies, helping stem the spread of starvation. It also turned out that *The Stool Pigeon* was not the first publication to come up with or fall for this preposterous story and that another well-known magazine had found it necessary to apologise and make amends to them.

Phil spoke to a friendly music lawyer who, when he had stopped laughing, had one word of advice for him: "Grovel." The food manufacturers graciously (and effectively) allowed the paper to continue printing after the necessary abasement took place.

For me, nearly getting every national newspaper in the UK sued for lots of money wasn't the wake up call I needed. It was only after I left the agency at the end of 2001 and tried my hand briefly

as a Fleet Street hack that I fully realised it wasn't for me. My heart wasn't in it and I wasn't cut out for it. Operation Enduring Freedom – the start of the bombing in Afghanistan – proved to be the final straw. I discovered where my line in the sand was even as a drunk. I simply wasn't able to square what I was being asked to write – especially when it came down to politics. My career as a tabloid journalist barely lasted 12 weeks.

In 2002 I tried to launch myself as a freelance writer with a questionable degree of success, getting features published here and there in magazines like *Loaded* and *Marie Claire*. But now that I didn't have the framework of regular shifts to get me out of bed in the morning, I became practically nocturnal and my mental health sank to new lows. My relationship with Helen began to crack under the weight that I alone was placing on it. And this was despite her best efforts to snap me out of my ill-advised routines. My local pub had started exerting a vice-like grip on me. I couldn't walk past it without going in for a drink and as it was on the corner of the estate where I lived and I could get someone to let me in during all but four hours of the day, this was a big problem.

I was starting to see non-existent spiders everywhere. And whether this was down to drink alone or because I'd recently started throwing a lot of cocaine into the mix as well, is a moot point.

By the way, if you're presuming that my introduction to the habitual use of cocaine was through Fleet Street, then I must disabuse you of that notion as understandable as it is. I was doing chisel on my home turf at my local because so many other people were – builders, electricians, bar people, plumbers, supermarket workers, clerks, chefs, taxi drivers... A snowstorm rolled through London in the late 90s and from my vantage point it seemed to swallow up nearly every other person I met. But I wasn't doing loads of coke with people in the media. Credit me with some civility.

I have mixed feelings about ecstasy. It has, no doubt, damaged my mental health to one degree or another, potentially for good even, but on the other hand, it changed my perspective on life in numerous positive ways. Even with LSD and magic mushrooms, I cannot ignore the mind-opening potential they unleashed in me, despite clearly being damaging for my psyche. On the other hand there are few positive things that I can say about cocaine. Aside from the fact that I've seen it destroy the lives of many people, and the fact it temporarily reduced my existence to being on a treadmill that was near impossible to jump off – the sad truth is I'm not even sure that I enjoyed taking it. However, it was a tool that had a very specific use for me. It allowed me to rapidly cut down on the amount of time I needed to spend doing things like eating and sleeping, thus allowing me to drink much more.

After one all-night session in the Northcote which ended about 5am, I found myself standing just yards from the pub's front door at 9.14am, waiting for a bus to take me to a temp job – subbing on a women's magazine in Central London.

On this morning waiting at the bus stop I felt very bad, which was odd because I'd felt great on leaving the pub over the road just four hours earlier. I couldn't breathe through my nose, someone had obviously used an air compressor to fire asbestos fibres and wire wool through my ear into my skull and I felt like an X-ray of a photocopy of a Polaroid of a ghost. The fact that I was going to make it into work was something. The fact I was going to be on time was something else again. That said, I was only 20 minutes out of the bath but could already feel a poisonous sweat prickling beneath my skin. In each pore was a chitinous arachnid sac containing flat, body-temperature Stella Artois and spider-hair thin splinters of glass dipped in syphilis and tequila sourced from a bottle with a plastic red sombrero for a cap.

There were very deep wells of this noxious liquid within me at most times. It pooled in my kidneys. It pooled in my liver. My lungs were sodden with it. My brain was a sponge dripping with it. It used to pool in my pancreas as well, until, that is, my poor, overworked endocrinal gland burst after an all too standard night sat in the flat in Welwyn Garden City drinking mug after mug of whiskey. It left in its place a raging thirst and an area of bright, burning pain the size of a tube of Parma Violets deep in my innards, like someone had impaled me with a soldering iron.

Liquid was spotting on the back of my shirt. I could only wear black or white shirts to work due to the mugs of liquid that poured out of my back on a daily basis. My kidneys weren't really working at optimum power at that point, so the shirt was bound to end up soaking in what was essentially a mixture of urine, alcohol, acetaldehyde and sweat. This would rapidly cool to a temperature which felt like the coldest thing that man could experience: zero degrees kelvin. And eventually, with some assistance from the hot air blower in the toilets at work, my top would become dry once again but would now have strange contour lines weaving across the back of it, sketched out in thick ridges of salty mineral deposit. I should have scraped this stuff off, jarred and sold it. Those crystals of despair would have made a bitter condiment for sado-masochists down on their luck or those who liked to get a mildly distressing psychedelic buzz while eating chips.

I told myself that I might as well get the first cigarette of the day out of the way. It became near impossible if I left it until mid-evening. With the first drag my head became a concentration camp, an inverse wunderkammer, a writhing well of debasement and horror. I could imagine my hands doing appalling things so – mentally – I slid them into an industrial press, crippling my digits good. I took a second drag of the cigarette with shaking hands. A deformed dwarf was at the bus stop pointing at me with its mouth open like Donald Sutherland at the end of the 1978 version of *Invasion Of The Body Snatchers*. Its face a contorted mask of orange, black and yellow scar tissue.

"Is it time? Have you come to take me?" I tried to say but it came out as a strangulated cry, which developed into a terrified scream.

I only realised it was a child wearing face paint to make her look like a tiger when her angry looking Dad came and scooped her up and walked off with her, crying, under one arm.

"Dear God. If you could just make this stop, I would do anything. Anything..."

Later that evening, after a few pints in the very same pub, I angrily demanded to know of no one in particular: "Who paints their child's face like a tiger at 9am on a Tuesday morning anyway?"

At this point I'd like to give a big shout out to myself for the few things I have managed to not get addicted to. There are two in the context of this book that are worth mentioning. The first was heroin. I smoked it once in 1993 in Hull and vomited copiously. I hate being sick; in my 20s and 30s I was only sick about ten times because of drinking, despite being blind drunk every single day. However, I'm sure I would have got the hang of chasing the dragon sooner rather than later if I'd stuck at it. People always say, "I'm afraid of needles, otherwise..." But my guess is they'd get over this fear pretty quickly if they smoked smack regularly and started feeling like they needed a more efficacious drug hit.

There are no degrees of separation with heroin. You either want to take it or you don't – and I had no interest in becoming a smackhead.

The second however was crack cocaine and I certainly smoked enough of it in 2002 to pick up a habit but that was a bullet that I didn't even need to dodge. It just never happened and if I'm ever tempted to think of myself as being unlucky, I just think about this situation for a bit and remind myself that things could have been much worse.

The House where it happened was in Maryland, fifteen minutes' walk away from Stratford bus station. Everyone who lived there or was a regular visitor sounded like the Second Class Fare To Dottingham man from the Tunes advert in the 80s. And I did too because it was where I picked up my chisel from.

The House, to be fair, looked like the kind of place where you'd end up smoking crack sooner or later. It was falling apart and full of pornography: I never remember being round there at any time of day when there wasn't a hardcore grumble DVD playing. For some reason, everything in The House looked sepia no matter what time of day it was. There were always people playing chess there to a frighteningly skilful level as well. I made the mistake of playing once or twice and my "clown's chess" was mopped up in minutes each time. By their own admission, most of them had learned in prison – chess and cryptic crosswords are honourable pursuits inside when you want to keep your head down and just do your time. There was one room downstairs in The House where no one, not even the live-in landlord, would ever enter. They'd just sling white goods and furniture in there when they'd stopped being useful. I was round there on the day that a stud wall collapsed and a landslide of newspapers, pornography, mangled chairs and broken toasters slid into the kitchen, blocking access to the back garden for several days.

The House was a constant magnet to men who had just split up with their wives. It was also a constant magnet to men who were just about to split up with their wives (whether they realised it yet or not). And it became a magnet for me. The last birthday present Helen would ever give me was a really nice push bike which I cycled round there one day to score. Sometime later after I moved out of the place we'd bought together and into rented accommodation I went back round to The House to pick up the beautiful bike. I'd only used it once but the thing was rusted solid in the back garden. It was fucked beyond repair.

I think I said earlier in this book that I don't have any regrets. This isn't true. I was being glib. I have many regrets which cause me deep amounts of shame and sorrow. And the fact that I refused to value my relationship with my girlfriend above my relationship with alcohol and cocaine is primary among them.

There's no uplifting, triumphant way to do coke when you do it all the time every day. Fumbling through your pockets for a note that isn't rolled up, thinking, "Please dear God let there be some notes left... if there are no notes left I am fucked. Please let there be a blood stained £20 note in a tight tube that I've missed..." Searching in a wallet past photographs of family and loved ones for wraps, thinking, "Please dear God let there be a wrap left... if there are no wraps left..." Digging out otherwise useless bank, credit or gym membership cards to chop out lines... none of it is a recipe for triumphalism or self-respect.

The trouble with cocaine is it gets you ready for the party but doesn't take you there. What happens when a house full of people do a lot of cocaine every single day is very simple – everyone sits round anxiously waiting for something to happen.

And in The House, eventually something did happen.

Any idiot can make crack cocaine – and that is a pertinent point to remember. Unlike making the much purer and more effective freebase cocaine – which takes a little bit of practical science knowhow, an ability to find 10% ammonia solution and ethyl ether, a steady hand and a clear desire and aptitude to not set yourself on fire – literally any idiot can make crack cocaine. You can do it right now if you like. Put the contents of your wrap in a metal ladle or big soup spoon and add about a quarter the amount again of baking soda before adding some water and stirring it in with a matchstick. Heat the underside of the spoon with a cigarette lighter until it bubbles and then use a butter knife or something similar to pick out the oily lumps of yellow precipitate that form in the liquid. What hardens and eventually dries on the blade of the knife is a rough and ready form of crack cocaine.

In The House, the opening gambit on the first evening I tried it was direct and only a half lie: "The coke got wet. So we dried it out in the microwave. No point in throwing it away though; might as well smoke it."

It was such a ridiculous thing to say that everyone started laughing their heads off. And three minutes later I was smoking a rock.

To be fair, crack has a pretty punchy hit the first few times you do it but then the first few times you do pretty much any drug properly is always mind blowing. Here's a more interesting way of looking at it: smoking crack was fucking hectic but nothing compared to the first time I smoked a cigarette, the first time I smoked dope and inhaled properly or the first time I drank half a bottle of whiskey in my mid-teens if I'm really truthful about it. I didn't slide onto the floor with my brains seeping out of my ears and forming liquid patterns on the carpet and I didn't run round The House with a cricket bat smashing stuff to pieces while listening to the Ramones on full volume. And when it comes down to it the real measure of a drug is what it's like when the dust settles. What it's like when you settle into your steady pace with it. And smoking rocks is a bit joyless to be honest. A bit of a bloody chore if you want to know the truth.

The standard of chess playing plummeted. Several games were forfeited dramatically. Levels of unintelligibility rose. There were some world class outbreaks of gibbering. The smoker's anthem of choice became 'Moaner' by Underworld played at window rattling, ear disrespecting volume but on the whole not much of anything other than scoring, smoking and clown's chess happened.

I stopped because I changed jobs and left the area not long afterwards and never thought about doing it again. But as far as I know everyone else did as well. For me, when it was sinking its claws in, it was only just a little bit more gnarly than plant food and not as heavy as speed. Which essentially means that I found it very hard to stop during a heavy session and it was obviously open to habit formation but I'd say it certainly wasn't as addictive as smoking cigarettes for example. One hit was brutally immediate but then you would drop down to way below your starting point very quickly in terms of mood and nerves; so you would essentially get the equivalent of a hangover maybe a quarter of an hour after smoking. And there was a very easy way to deal with this… especially if you had fifty quid in your pocket. Just pray that you weren't supposed to be doing anything the next day.

I'm not working for the Crack Marketing Council though. I don't really care that much if crack has a slightly worse rep than the one it deserves. My take on it is this: on the balance of things I'd give it a miss. It's not that nice. Having a meal with your girlfriend is nice. Going to the pictures with your girlfriend is nice. Smoking crack isn't.

Bad Liver (2003)

Here's another question for you: where is the line that separates the mentally ill from the merely eccentric? How do you determine where to draw the boundary between the psychopath, the sociopath, the fractured personality, the schizophrenic, the bipolar, the suicidal – and someone who's just *a bit of a character*?

I wouldn't claim to know the exact location – to have a map with an X marked on it – but since becoming a music journalist I've had a lot of opportunities not only to observe roughly where the transition zone exists but also how it shifts depending on a number of other factors such as fame, money, class, country of origin, gender and job title.

I became a music journalist more by accident than design at the start of 2003. I went for a job on a film magazine and even though I didn't get it, I ended up in the pub with some people from the publishing company afterwards. I don't remember the evening with that much clarity because I got rabidly drunk but I do remember going into some kind of extended angry rant about how I would like to execute all of Coldplay in a car park after making them watch as I tortured their pets first. On the strength of my performance, some maverick soul offered me the news editor's job on a new monthly music title called *Bang*. So professionally it was a great year – I was suddenly rubbing shoulders with a bunch of great music writers and larger than life characters that I had looked up to for years – some of them since I was in my early teens. I got to commission Swells, Carol Clerk, Taylor Parkes and Andrew Mueller; work on a team with Simon Price and Tommy Udo and socially I would meet people like Chris Roberts, Sylvia Patterson, Dele Fadele, David Stubbs, Holly Hernandez and Brother John Robb. (Some of the rock stars I got to meet weren't that bad either.) But best of all, I met Maria, who would, some time after the magazine closed, become my girlfriend, the love of my life and the mother of my son. And sure enough, it didn't take long for the magazine to close because it wasn't that good – but most of the relationships I forged then remain very strong today; as does my impetus to write about music.

After the magazine crawled to standstill I struggled at first. In fact I struggled a lot. In professional terms I felt like I'd been wandering aimlessly in the dark for decades before catching a glimpse of light in the distance; only for it to be snuffed out the second I started heading towards it. Writing about music for the print press felt like a closed shop. (It wasn't really, there were just more knowledgeable, time served hacks than there was paying work to go round and the publishing industry was only just facing up to the severe goring it had taken at the hands of the internet. So of course it was hard for an angry drunk dilettante to find his feet.)

It is fair to say I probably wouldn't have stayed the course if it wasn't for *Metal Hammer* magazine. This redoubtable monthly became a constant in my life and has remained a beacon to me ever since, providing me with gainful freelance employment, interesting travel and brutally extreme metal CDs and downloads to enjoy. They signify what is by far and away the longest stretch of unbroken employment I've ever had. And, to be completely candid, this is despite them having several very strong excuses to drop me along the way. One Monday evening, after spending all weekend at Download drinking heavily with Dimebag and Vinnie Paul from Pantera and all of Machinehead, topped off back in London with a Monday all-day session in the Stamford Arms with legendary mature lensman and incomprehensible cockney rhymer Tom Sheehan, I went to *Hammer*'s annual 'heavy metal Oscars' – The Golden Gods Awards ceremony held in a big nightclub in Hackney. I have no idea what I did there but apparently it warranted me being given an option the following day: forfeit an entire month's pay or never work for the entire publishing group again. Whatever it was, I was worse behaved than Slayer (Kerry King turned up at the venue with a giant brass crucifix that he "broke off a church") and Damageplan (Dimebag narrowly avoided hospitalising several people when he ran through the venue swinging a Les Paul round his head). That said, the following year I wrote something which caused much mirthfulness in the office and they doubled my wages for the month, so who knows what kind of experimental mind control tricks they were playing on me?

Back in 2005 one of my regular jobs was writing the demos column and I had a relatively touchy feely approach of being encouraging to anyone who wasn't a session musician playing new age Celtic rock, a 50-year-old teacher living out his NWOBHM-based nervous breakdown in public or a pro-active evangelical fascist. It was nice being positive for a change as I was seen as a bit of a hatchet guy in the normal reviews section. One day a CD-R bearing the name Marie Antoinette written in spiky Slayer-style, felt tip lettering, was given to me by the magazine. The music was unbelievably basic; what sounded like two-channel demos of quarter written songs played with little or no practice, ability or vision. It was so raw – featuring a guitar plugged straight into a cheap stereo and vocals sung through a condenser mic – that it was almost fetish-worthy. But not quite. On one track I heard the lyrics: "You're a fucking disgrace to your fucking race" and some other throwback boot boy stuff that sounded like it was about murdering "fags" and dashed off a bracing zero out of ten review, thanking them for the fiver that they'd included in the package.

A few months later, another parcel arrived at the *Hammer* offices for me. Marie Antoinette had self-released two singles, one called 'Why Don't You Stick This CD Up Your Arse John Doran, You Sarcastic Little Creep' and another with the more prosaic title 'We Hate You John Doran'. They were accompanied by an ominous looking C90. The tape was part biography, part death threat and, most uncomfortably, part session in the psychiatrist's chair. Marie Antoinette were a Great Yarmouth-based punk metal band with one member, Sauron Five, who sang and played guitar. His other mates would sometimes join in on songs (seemingly after the pub had shut) and occasionally there would be beats from a Casio keyboard. Sauron Five was also, he explained, "Great Yarmouth's fastest rapper" and was "heavily influenced by Ice-T". I remember when I first listened to it, there was one bit where it seemed to go really slow as if the tape player's batteries were running down. His voice was thick East Anglian: "You know, I've been really depressed since your review. I haven't been this depressed since the last time I was in prison for assault. I'm going to find you and break your fucking head open. I'm going to kill you."

The tape wasn't going slow, though. I was just having a panic attack. Not so funny now Mr Fancy Pants London Media Wanker, laughing at the authentic punk rock, gangsta rap, black metal music of the provinces, was the subtext I was getting from it. It's time for you to deal; your number's up.

I can't remember why I decided to review the next batch of Marie Antoinette singles in my column and give them zero out of ten but whatever my reasoning was, it was completely faulty and I genuinely wish I hadn't. The snide trolling had the depressingly obvious effect that I knew it would and another batch of CD singles with a cassette-recorded death threat arrived at *Hammer* a few weeks after publication. I wanted to review these but luckily my editor Jamie called time on the idiocy, and I was banned from mentioning them in the magazine again.

Hammer were less fortunate, though. Sauron Five got it into his head that I worked – or possibly even lived – at their offices and he started bombarding them with threatening calls; which, after a few months, always came at 9pm when sometimes he would even use up the entire message storage capacity of the magazine telling them how much he hated me, how brilliant his band were and what he was going to do to me; sometimes in the form of improvised gangsta rap. Ignoring their usual policy of not answering the phone after office hours, Jamie picked up the receiver to him in sheer exasperation once when he was part way through leaving one of his epic rants. The next day he told me that he'd had a very long talk with S5 and had come to the conclusion: "He is totally mental. I don't mean he is a bit of a nutter. He is clinically fucking mental."

The death threats stopped for a while but when they recommenced the magazine called the police and I had to visit Marylebone CID to talk to a couple of detectives. One of them asked for a summary of what happened and for my opinion. I started: "Whatever happens, as far as I'm concerned, I don't want this guy to go to prison on my account. Whatever is wrong with him, prison hasn't worked for him in the past and I dare say it won't do now. But mainly I just don't want it on my conscience. The guy's obviously got problems."

The detective stopped me: "Oh no. It won't come to that. He's not fit to plead. He'll never get as far as trial." I must have looked confused so he explained that some time after I had started reviewing Marie Antoinette demos in *Hammer*, S5 had gone round to his neighbour's house and attacked him with an ornamental samurai sword, breaking his arm in several places. It wasn't the first time he'd been sectioned and he was now detained indefinitely in a secure psychiatric hospital.

"Well, in that case, what I'd really like is for him to have his phone privileges removed," I said to the detective, who agreed that under the circumstances it probably was the wisest course of action.

Lunacy wasn't just restricted to the powerfully shit, unknown and provincial though. It seemed to stalk every level of the music business. Back in 2004, I interviewed the relatively talented, urbane and famous Sid Wilson, the DJ from Slipknot, while his band were touring Europe with Slayer and Mastodon. Being a rock star automatically gets you a free downgrade from "slightly mad" to "very eccentric" should you want it, but Sid was suffering from the kind of rigid delusions that couldn't really be compared to Patrick Wolf's dress sense or Robert Smith's haircut. Before our interview began he measured out five teaspoons of sugar and used a small wooden stirrer to level off the surface of each one before lowering the spoon slowly into his cup of coffee. Then he stirred each measurement of sugar five times clockwise and five times anti-clockwise counting out loud as he did it. Even though we were indoors and it was hot he was wearing a bandana wrapped around his head and two hats on top of that. He said it helped control the flow of information pouring into his head from "back home".

In the way he carried himself he didn't come across as mad in any traditional sense, in fact, going by the many interviews I've carried out with nu-metal musicians in the past, I'd say he was unusually intelligent and polite for his peer group. But then he also claimed that he was an alien sent from the constellation of Orion to help save mankind and to prepare the good people of Earth for intergalactic warfare, like he was an extra-terrestrial Second Coming. "I believe I am from Orion," he said, "but I am proud to be here on Earth completing this mission."

He talked to me for three hours about his belief system, which was a mixture of the rapture, *2001: A Space Odyssey*, *Blade Runner*, *Battlefield Earth* and St John's Book of Revelation. In fact he talked to me for so long that someone had to come and get him because the band were due on stage and were waiting for him in the wings. It came as very little surprise to hear that once, while a high school drug dealer, Sid had eaten a blotter sheet of 75 tabs of LSD during one evening. He phoned me the next day apologising for not showing me the tattoo which had revealed his purpose to him. It was of the World Trade Center on fire. A tattoo he says he got done in August 2001.

But if the music industry provided good cover for rock stars who were falling apart mentally at the seams, it initially also gave me the framework within which I was able to deteriorate even further myself. Because suddenly, if I really wanted it, I could be surrounded by people doing drugs, drinking heavily and behaving outlandishly all the time, and no one would think anything of me joining in as long as I had the money, the staying power and filed good copy on time.

At the end of 2006 I was offered my first potential cover feature for *Hammer* on young pretenders to the metal throne, Trivium. I conducted an extensive phone interview with them, which was fine but a bit stilted. Musically gifted frontman Matt Heafy was still a teenager and not long out of school. His monastic dedication to guitar practice and making his band famous hadn't exactly left him with a well-rounded personality and an abundance of anecdotes to tell journalists like me. He had one bad habit, he told me: buying a bottle of French wine older than he was at the end of a tour. Or should I say, asking his dad to buy it for him, given he wasn't old enough to drink legally back home in the States.

Luckily for me, a few days later on December 22, the band were rolling through town as support for Iron Maiden, who were playing their war themed album *A Matter Of Life And Death* in full at Earl's Court. I could arrange a follow up interview with Trivium for after the show. They would be heading back to the US for the winter break the following day, so it would be a great time to catch them – with no show to prepare for they were sure to be letting their hair down. Maria and I were going away for Christmas ourselves the following day; we had a cab booked for 8am to pick us up from her flat but I reassured her that it would be fine, that I'd be back in plenty of time to get a good night's sleep before us getting out of London for a few days.

I got to the cavernous venue at 7pm when the doors opened and was in time to see Trivium play a very early set to a mainly empty room. There was a lengthy delay as Maiden's road crew set up the stage to look like a front line trench, complete with a giant tank perched at the top of it. This, and an unexpected power cut to the venue, allowed me time to go backstage and get to grips with Maiden's fearsomely welcoming hospitality. They had cleared a space the size of a large school gymnasium and erected a temporary pub with a free bar inside it. I ordered five long island iced teas for myself and marvelled at Maiden's generosity. They were so very well mixed that I ordered another five and then repeated the process with some more of my favourite types of cocktail, starting with five long glasses of dark and stormy.

All pretences to holding it together went out of the window. Fucking Christmas was the one time of year when everything was guaranteed to start unravelling for me. People would go from not wanting me to drink to expecting me to and by the last two weeks in December I barely knew what was happening any more. Throw a free bar into the mix and it was game over. I was fucking destroyed by 10pm, wandering through a sea of faces concerned, disdainful, horrified. Although the actual show – what I can remember of it – was brilliant.

I was barely able to walk by 1am, the time that I got to the K-West – an upmarket rock & roll hotel in Shepherd's Bush – where Trivium were staying. And after we had some more drinks, I was barely able to talk as well. I didn't get very far into the interview before I got thrown out of the hotel for drunkenness by security. The exact details of what happened remain something of a mystery to me to this very day but I use the word thrown advisedly. I was certainly so clattered that I was unable to express verbally to the security guards that my coat, containing my mobile phone, travel card and wallet were still inside. While standing in the alleyway directly outside, roaring angrily, trying to work out what was going on, I was approached by a gang who showed me a knife and then asked for my money. Being hyper-emboldened I grabbed the knife – by the blade – and the guy holding it pulled back quickly, leaving me with a deep cut to my palm. One of the muggers looked visibly disgusted at me and pushed me into a pile of bin bags, before they ran away empty handed.

I struggled to sit upright and sat dozily with my head in my hands for quite a while, only vaguely aware that blood from the cut was pouring onto my face. After a while, still not fully realising that I was without money, phone, cash card and means of travel I staggered up to the main drag in Shepherd's Bush, thinking dimly about getting home. A police car on the other side of the A3220 flashed its lights and sirens once at me as its window rolled down.

The sight of the car gave me enough of a burst of adrenaline to momentarily clear my head.

I suddenly realised what was going on. It was probably about 2am, I had no ID, I was so pissed I could barely stand, my face was probably covered in blood if not dripping in it, my shirt was certainly heavily stained red: if these coppers got hold of me, I would be spending the night in the cells for sure. I had to get out of there quickly and back to Maria's flat in South London. I ducked back down the side streets until I was sure the police car would have driven off before trying to find my way to my girlfriend's on foot.

By the time I arrived at 7am Maria was terrified and had been phoning round friends and hospitals. She poured me a hot bath and asked me what had happened but I couldn't answer because my teeth were chattering so hard.

I used to fantasise about being an alcoholic writer when I was 18. "Just imagine how amazing it would be", I used to think to myself. "Just think of the lifestyle."

And now finally – at long last – I was where I wanted to be. Living the fucking dream.

But the truth of the matter was I felt like I could handle this kind of punishment in the same way I could handle the hangovers. As much as it upset Maria – it was just another war story as far as I was concerned. I was disappointed when my palm healed without a scar. What was really becoming untenable, as far as I was concerned, was how my sanity was coming apart in pieces like a daddy long legs in a car wash.

Withdrawing from alcohol is abysmal. It is, at the core of it, temporarily indistinguishable from schizophrenia when it really kicks in. I wouldn't wish it on my worst enemy. And the trouble is, once you get to the stage of having proper delirium tremens, it gets worse every single time it happens. Due to a process called kindling, each withdrawal session gets progressively more appalling than the last. The hallucinations get worse. The levels of fear and anxiety get ever higher. There is no bottom to how deep you plunge into dementia. The regularity and severity of seizures increases. And all the time as your head cracks open wider and wider, nightmares seep out of the other place and into your daily life; into your field of vision. I knew there was only one last stage for me below where I was now: alcoholic psychosis. To drive myself into permanent and profound madness. I wasn't afraid of dying as long as I had a drink in my hand but I was afraid of going mad and then being locked somewhere where I couldn't drink.

If I wanted to avoid psychosis I only had two options open to me as far as I could see – to stop drinking for good or to stop drying out.

Just as water finds its own level, I sought out troubled and hardened drinkers to spend time with. It was all the normalisation I needed to persuade me to take the stop drying out option. I had a network of pubs and bars all over London where I knew I could always get a late drink, where these jovial 2am wraiths would congregate. Where everyone knew my name and they were always what passed for glad that I came.

But I sought out this normalisation everywhere. Home included. At that time I lived with my landlord Simon who charged me a very reasonable sum of rent on a box room big enough for a mattress, a stereo and a pile of vinyl. Any discount could genuinely have been chalked up as danger money as far as I'm concerned however. Once I returned from a weekend away but could smell natural gas pouring out of the flat and through the front door, from the pavement outside. Walking up the stairs, I fully expected to find Simon dead in the kitchen, but it was empty. One of the hob rings had evidently been on but unlit for a few days. I turned the gas off, opened all the windows and went out to look for him. I found him in the beer garden of the nearest pub and confronted him angrily.

He said, "Oh I wondered what that smell was. It got so bad I was having to lean out of the window to smoke."

Simon's brackets had been loosened drastically by a decade sat in front of a giant radar dish, decoding Soviet weather reports when he was an RAF spook. This had left him with a terrible thirst, debilitating night terrors, a functional pension and a high-level security clearance. He was too unbalanced to put the latter to any worthwhile use, though, so he drifted into security work. As I heard it, he didn't even last one shift when he was contracted to work for the Tate Modern. His job simply involved walking through all the giant exhibition rooms on one floor once an hour, using a scanner to swipe sensors in each area to prove that he'd done his rounds. One of the shows on his patch featured work by a renowned Brazilian artist. She had spent months weaving and hand-knotting a gold lamé fishing net which hung in splendour from the gallery ceiling. Halfway through the room, Simon's torch failed, he tripped and fell headlong into the artwork and lay in it, thrashing and screaming in the dark – much as he did in his room every night I lived with him – until there was a giant, idiot-shaped hole in the beautiful and massively expensive exhibit. He was frogmarched directly out of the building and deposited into the freezing cold night.

Despite how much I enjoyed it, initially I treated music journalism like any other job – something that was secondary in importance to the ingestion of drink and drugs. It's true that research wasn't exactly top of my list of priorities. I still feel like punching myself in the face when I remember asking junglist motormouth MC Dynamite if he was related to Miss Dynamite. I realised that my core knowledge was somewhat lacking on the day I requested an interview with a rock star just to be told, "That's a nice idea except that he died 15 years ago." (I thought he'd been going through a fallow period.)

Just as you've probably always suspected, most music magazines have run live reviews where the journalist hasn't actually attended the gig. In 12 years of live reviewing I have missed two gigs that I needed to write about – both through sheer absent-mindedness rather than laziness or incapacitation, I hasten to add. One was kind of OK because I got to see the band at a different venue the following night and could at least write something truthful about them. The other one was trickier. I didn't know anyone at the gig and I had a sizeable 800-word report to file. So I did the only thing I could do... take some diazepam and phone someone in the band. "Er, hi. You don't know me but I've got a bit of a favour to ask you. Would you mind describing your gig last night to me?" And then some time later: "So would you describe the trousers you were wearing as bruised crimson or arterial burgundy?" And later still: "When you threw the guitar in the air did it trace a parabola, an arc or a semi-circle through the air?"

But little by little this attitude began to change.

I was thrown a lifeline – in more ways than one – by my brother Manish. I say brother, we're not actually related, he watches too much Buffy for us to be actual blood kin and no one should own more than one Harry Nilsson album, but you know what I'm saying. It was a great time when we lived together. We'd get up late and then listen to six Killing Joke albums back-to-back or watch every single David Bowie video in consecutive order while eating cheese on toast.

Being a music journalist when you're an adult is like a public admission that you have low-level mental health problems on its own. It doesn't matter how you cut it, there's something odd, bordering on wrong, about it; and this profession attracts more than its fair share of fragile characters – myself included. Really the key for me has become doing the job while maintaining the maximum amount of dignity possible; which is certainly not the way I entered the profession.

While Manish would be the first to admit he was probably suffering from slight OCD problems when I lived with him (his album filing system was like something out of *Driller Killer*) he was on the side of those doing music writing for the right reasons. After a while he started rubbing off on me and I started dealing with my cynicism, laziness and opportunism. I started taking my job seriously for the first time ever. I started taking *a* job seriously for the first time ever.

Shamefully we would both take cruel advantage of each other's mental infirmities, though. When I was on a catastrophic comedown he would wage sonic warfare on me. One Monday morning, after three nights out clubbing with very little sleep, he insisted on playing me all of *The Drift* by Scott Walker at full volume. When it ended he said, "That was amazing. Let's listen to it again."

Every November 5 we threw a party because it was his birthday. He'd always work himself up into a state beforehand. On one of these days he was doing my head in, flapping about food and people coming round. He was pacing up and down getting stressed out about what crisps to buy. I knew I had to get him out of the flat for a bit so I said, "You know how people are about crisps. Get some of all of the varieties you can think of. Then you can't go wrong." He disappeared for ages, only coming back to the flat when he was laden down with bin bags full of snacks, as I knew he would. There were a lot more than I had envisaged though, and when I saw all the crisps I started having a panic attack.

"Ahhh dear God, look at all the crisps," I said, scrabbling for my asthma inhaler. "What shall we do with them?" said Manish pacing up and down, getting even more frantic. We opted for piling them all in the corner of the kitchen with bags of crisps forming the middle of the slope and then using multi-bag packs and grab bags as sloped shoring walls to build a kind of big, omni-directional, crisp bag pyramid front leading up the sides to the plateau which was flush with the worktop. On the plus side we had Worcester Sauce French Fries, something of a rare treat these days I'm sure you'll agree.

At first it ended up being a good party. The flat was rammed and we were listening to *Vol. 4* by Black Sabbath, but then after a while there was a commotion. This roaring oaf of a ukulele salesman was trying to kick the bathroom door down. He claimed he had to get his coat and wouldn't wait for the girl inside to finish up. After some fine negotiation work he was calmed down and then Manish suggested he should leave. I returned to my pint of red wine and Quaver, Chipstix and Monster Munch sandwich in the kitchen, but the oaf came blazing into the room behind me, upset at being chucked out, swinging his fists wildly and shouting at Manish. Luckily my man Danny was there – a tough, ursine guy who drinks cider and listens to stone cold funk rock, seriously, you wouldn't fucking mess – but between both of us we could barely hold onto him. He slipped my grip, and before I had chance to grab him again he landed a punch square on Manish's jaw.

In my mind's eye, I can see my flatmate flying through the air backwards in slow motion, arms outstretched like Rio De Janeiro's Christ The Redeemer but wearing a SunnO))) hooded top. He landed square in the middle of all the crisps, his impact being absorbed by hundreds of bursting bags and thousands of critically impacting Space Raiders and Nice 'n' Spicy Nik Naks. Out of the corner of my eye, I could see him lying amidst all the crisp carnage laughing as we bundled the guy out of the flat. Apparently the angry guest been drinking on medication, but given that as soon as he was outside he punched his girlfriend hard in the face, it's safe to say his factory setting was Objectionable Arsehole, regardless. It took something like another hour to sort the whole mess out but we still managed to get another hour or two out of the party until someone set my amplifier on fire and then it really was time to call it a night.

Of course, you don't need to be a music journalist to come face to face with madness and degradation. If you live somewhere like London and you want to see sociopathy, you merely have to step outside your front door.

Once, after a day spent writing, I went to meet Maria, her sister and some of their friends in a Sam Smith's pub near Victoria Train Station for a post-work drink. Despite the well-meaning, righteous and reasonably priced chain doing their utmost to repel one and all with their transcendentally undrinkable beer and wine, the place was heaving. (Have you ever tried their merlot? It speaks of that old school, can-do British grit and determination: "Well, I've got some grapes, a spare dust bin and two feet – just how bally hard can this wine making caper be?") Because of this we ended up sharing a table with a couple wearing matching light blue and grey shell suits. There was a pile of camera and laptop bags between us all and the couple were making me nervous by staring at them intently. The man could have been any age between 35 and 55, his hair was slicked back with Brylcreem and his skin was dry and leathery while his eyes sparkled. He had a mesmeric smile of yellowing, sharp teeth.

He leant in close to me then whispered in a wheezing rattle the wrong side of 50 B&H a day: "You want to watch yourself in here mate... someone – a bit like you – he had his fucking throat cut in the gents last week."

He stared at me and nodded slowly in the direction of the toilets. I replied: "That's nice." I held his gaze for a while but eventually had to look away. As soon as I did he leant in smiling again: "Cut him from ear to ear." I wanted to tell him to fuck off, my heart was racing. But it was much worse than your usual pub fight pre-amble because the guy wasn't drunk or shouting. I had no point of reference. I couldn't work out what his game was.

People on the table next to us got up en masse to leave. I hurriedly barked at everyone to grab the other table. They didn't know what was going on so I picked up all the bags, laptop cases and coats and walked over forcing them to join me. Maria came over to ask what I was doing, I told her quickly that I was worried about the couple and went back over to pick up our glasses of wine. They didn't even look up when I did. I started to wonder if I'd overplayed the whole thing in my head.

Soon afterward we finished the drink and it was time to head back to Lewisham for the evening. We weren't in the pub for more than an hour and during that time I had my first two drinks of the day, a couple of regular glasses of house red but I can only just remember leaving. By the time we arrived at Victoria Station I had my arm round Bob from The Dentists' shoulders to help support me as I could barely walk. There was much laughing and we parted ways. I then had one of the biggest blackouts I've ever suffered. It wasn't a complete en bloc, I have two fragments from the following 16 hours that I can drop into the void – but it was a very, very long period of near complete darkness.

During one fragment I was on a bus, sitting downstairs with Maria. I think we were on the two seats very close to the driver because I was afraid. They were the sort of seats you have to give up if you see pregnant ladies or the disabled or the elderly. I wouldn't have been able to get up to offer a seat to anyone however. Maria's head was on my shoulder but it was in a savage parody of loving affection. Her head was rolling about and her eyes were tipping back into her skull. It was dark outside the bus windows, so it must have been at least a few hours later. I got my mobile phone out of my pocket to ring someone and after several botched attempts I managed to phone my best friend Stu in Cornwall. What I wanted to say to him was: "I'm afraid. There's something wrong with Maria. I can barely move. I need help. I don't know what's going on." But the noise that came out of my mouth was just a grunt, a slur, a nonsense of ugly glossolalia because my tongue had dissolved into hot viscous treacle and my brain was a sponge that had been wrung of all useful information.

And then later, more of the same. But this time on a train.

The next day I woke very late in the afternoon and only stayed awake for minutes at a time before falling asleep again. The only time I got out of bed was to crawl to the bathroom to be sick – which was odd because drinking never made me vomit. Maria had to have two days off work. I contracted a lung infection which I had for five weeks.

A full 30 hours passed before we realised we'd been spiked with a large dose of Rohypnol or something similar. I pieced together our movements from cash withdrawals and transport tickets. It was insane, we'd been halfway round London in the weirdest route possible... The trip from Victoria to Lewisham took over four hours and it was via Clapton. Stu said I sounded really upset but he just couldn't get any sense out of me to ascertain what was going on. He thought I was drunk. But who can blame him? When I felt so bad and couldn't remember anything the next day, I just presumed that I'd been drunk as well.

During the first few days of recovery, I couldn't keep any food or drink down. I'd already slept through my alcohol grace period, so the onset and the viciousness of the withdrawal from it was brutal and fast. I was so ill there was nothing I could do, just lie weakly in Maria's bed in Lewisham, sweating, spasming, swearing; staring bug-eyed at the non-existent insects all over the bed and the walls.

It had gotten to the stage when sweating it out that I would lose contact with the external world entirely unless someone was directly in front of me and talking to me. Millions upon millions of randomly misfiring synapses cast me into an internal space that might as well have been 600 miles cubed with me at the centre. It was an all-enveloping alien terrain with no sight of external life. A three-dimensional ultra-pointilist, ultra-pixelated nightmare of rapidly fluctuating noises, colours, sensations, thoughts and recall; all of them lasting for the merest fragment of a second – all flashing by too rapidly for me to grab onto any one of them. It was like the end point of all avant garde endeavour combined into one impossible to comprehend, impossible to describe and near impossible to endure experience of pure open-channel sensory chaos and mental confusion.

After a day or two I was still too ill to move. I was too ill to read. Too ill to want to listen to music even. Unable to distract myself I couldn't stop myself from thinking about what had been going on over the last few years. About how I had messed things up with Helen and how it would almost certainly happen with Maria as well if something didn't change. And then inevitably I couldn't hold it at bay: "Maybe I should stop drinking before it's too late."

And then: "What will it actually be like to never drink again?"

And when I considered it seriously it was as if a huge object the size of a mountain rushed by overhead, blocking out the light and warmth of the sun.

Dead Flowers New Romney (2006)

When I arrived in Rye Harbour at midday Jonny Mugwump was asleep on the grass outside of his ancient VW camper van. It was the hottest day of the year so far and he had roasted the colour of a sexually active mandrill's arse with pillar box red highlights along the crest of his nose.

"Jonny! Wake up!" I shouted. "You've fallen asleep in the sun."

He opened his lizard eye, with its stripe-like pupil, and croaked: "Not again."

He was taking an esoteric holiday on the coast and had kindly asked me to tag along. I needed some time out of London. My doctor had finally convinced me that my lifestyle as a music journalist had caught up with me. She wanted me to consider the idea that I was an alcoholic with a drug problem and I needed some time to weigh things up. And the idea of going away in a van with a load of booze and drugs in order to consider giving up booze and drugs didn't seem that incongruous at the time.

As we rattled along in the vintage van – it was of the age where it had a fitted carpet cut to accommodate the gear shift – Jonny played me some music by The Caretaker. It was a CD-R only project by Leyland James Kirby who sampled old big band records and processed them through a lot of echo, reverb and other effects creating a haunting, misty sound. It made for a weirdly appropriate soundtrack to driving through the Romney Marshes.

As we approached Dungeness we trundled past miles of chain link fence separating the road from a barely extant airstrip, gutted and levelled pre-fab buildings and partially abandoned army land. There was little to break the uniformity of the flat land bar advancing columns of thousands of pylons carrying electricity from the nuclear power station on the horizon.

Up ahead we spotted a static caravan park with about 20 trailers in it; in the middle of them stood a huge pylon. Someone had placed plant pots round the base of one of its giant legs in an attempt to prettify it; to give the place a more homely vibe. Nearby, there was a white plastic recliner but with no one sitting on it. We slowed down to a crawl to look at the park.

On the gate next to the park entrance there were bundles of long since dead flowers attached to the fence. Jonny grimaced and put his foot down.

When we got to Dungeness we parked up by a shack which had obviously been made entirely from material scavenged from the beach including planks of wood, plastic sheeting, twine and netting. On the roof of the shack was a bucket seat from a sports car but it wasn't facing out to sea. It was pointed at the power station.

We stopped and took each other's photograph outside Prospect Cottage.

A man dressed in a grubby Santa Claus costume chugged past on a 50cc scooter decked out in tinsel. He had a ghetto blaster strapped to his ride and was playing the Bing and Bowie version of 'Little Drummer Boy'. We waved at him and he waved glumly back. We stopped and watched as he disappeared off toward New Romney in the blazing May sunshine.

We walked along the slowly curving road until we hit the beach and when we got there, it was something like perfection. I felt, temporarily, like a brand new person. The dull ache in my liver, brain and kidneys and the sharp pain in my pancreas subsided for a while.

There was nowhere else quite like this cuspate foreland of red, ochre and liver-coloured pebbles; a perfect vision of flint shingle, pure bar from scratches of aged driftwood and scraps of fish netting. It was a little nipple of virgin cherty beach on a newly terra-formed planet, awaiting its first ever visitors. A spirit-level flat stony stretch whose uniformity was only broken by nuclear power stations, lighthouses, acoustic mirrors, monochromatic fog horn stacks, weather beaten fishing vessels, expensive looking brushed metal airstream caravans, rusting tin shacks and extremely well-designed wood framed huts built by slumming architects.

We walked down a pathway of slatted, sun-parched decking and, where it terminated, stood on a pebble dune by a rusted wincher, looking out to sea at distant cargo ships.

"What will I do if I give up drinking?" I thought to myself. And the first answer that came into my head was, "Start a secular pilgrimage."

Later on in the day, the wind started picking up and giant black clouds huddled on the horizon like muggers so we drove back to Hastings and parked on the promenade next to the sea wall.

Inside the van we made short work of the several bottles of red wine I'd brought with me. And then we started on Jonny's box of Blue Nun and his low grade ecstasy. He eventually retired by tipping the driver's seat as far back as it would go and pulling his coat over his head. He fell asleep almost immediately leaving me to sit on the inside wheel arch of a van which was now rocking in gale force winds, formulating my plan.

Every time I tried to give up drink and drugs I got consumed by one of these slightly eschatological plans. Last time it was militant beekeeping in Hackney.

It always felt easier to arrive at significant life-changing choices when the weather was up. I felt like the van was rocking me into action. How would I start the UK's first secular pilgrimage? When should I start it? Why not right now? What would happen if I just said, 'Fuck it', got up, left the van and started walking along the coast? Literally climbed down onto the pitch black beach, turned left and started walking.

I wondered how far I could cover in two or three weeks before running out of money. Would the people I loved come and find me and ask me what I was doing? Would they meet me a few days up the coast and bring me packed lunches and a change of clothes when I refused to come home? What would happen by the time I got up to Yorkshire, when I crossed the Humber Bridge? Would a local newspaper reporter come and meet me and ask me what I was doing? If she did, I would explain that I was inventing a new concept in leisure activity. I would explain that I believed that people should stop booking foreign city breaks and instead try walking up the coast for as far as they could go. To maybe do the entire circuit.

Would old mates and people I didn't know read about me in the *Hull Daily Mail* and come and join me on the walk? As we approached Scotland, would we be met at the border by a team of pipers and a kindly lady with shortbread biscuits? As the crow flies, it is about 2,500 miles round the coast of Britain. But I am not a crow and I do not fly. Even if I covered 50 miles a day, it would take a very long time to get all the way round Scotland's coast and back into England. By the time we got down to Merseyside and a Granada TV crew came to meet us, there would be more of a story to tell.

Why was this small group of people walking round the coast of Britain, picking up new converts on a daily basis? By now opinion writers for national newspapers would be penning columns about it. Some in favour. Some against. What does the walk around the coast of Great Britain say about us in 2006?

By the banks of the Mersey my Mum and Dad would come and meet us. My Mum would give me a £20 note folded up as small as possible pressed into my palm: "It's for food, not drink John." And my Dad would say that I was wearing the wrong kind of footwear for the trip: "You should have worn a pair of light fell walking boots with ankle support. It would have been easier that way. And where's your high vis jacket? And have you got any spare batteries for your torch? Wait a second – where is your torch? Take these spare batteries for your torch. And take this torch. And here, take some sachets of Rise And Shine dehydrated orange juice. Just add water for an orange juice-like drink."

It would start to become clear to everyone what we were doing as we approached Dungeness from the other direction, maybe about three months later. They would start to understand my big idea as they saw thousands of us approaching in a long string formation spread out over several miles. And then as I approached the nuclear power station people would cheer and clap. And then they would stop and stare open-mouthed as I *kept on walking*. Yes! That's right! I would keep on going for another lap! And this time I would start writing a guidebook on where to stay, what sights to look out for, where to bivvy down for the night. The path would become world famous. Students would spend their gap years walking it. Enterprising hoteliers would open up bunkhouses along the routes. The long-suffering UK seaside tourist trade would experience a rejuvenation in fortune not seen since the 1950s.

I needed to empty my bladder, so I opened the door of the van which snapped out of my hand with a bang. Jonny whimpered under his coat. I walked gingerly along the side of the vehicle and grabbed hold of the promenade railing with one hand and reached for my fly and unzipped myself with the other but the immensity of nature caused me performance anxiety. In front of me the onyx black night and onyx black shore met in a central void and the wind felt strong enough to carry me off into the nothingness.

The second time around would be magical. Triumphant. The black shale beaches of Ravenscar littered with golden trilobites and ammonites infilled with iron pyrites. The garish pennants of Eilean Donan fluttering in the breeze. Pipers at the gates of Lindisfarne Priory playing us a fanfare faintly across Foulwork Burn. The mournful ghosts of cockle pickers would be my companions and guides across Morecambe Bay. The lone and level sands of Rhyll, which on a good day stretch all the way to America and back.

I felt it with every fibre of my being: "I could just leave now.

Just turn left and start walking. I could take control of my life. This time next year everything will be alright." But a massive gust of wind like a freewheeling Range Rover hoofed me over the railings and upside down onto the pebbles below. The shock opened my bladder with a vengeance. It was a good ten seconds before I managed to stop pissing all over myself. I ran around shouting and screaming, punching the wall and booting pebbles up into the air, piss in my hair and all up my duffle coat. When I got back to the camper van, Jonny woke up, looked at me and said: "Have you just…" But I told him to stop talking and to pass me a mug of Blue Nun.

For the time being at least, I did not have what it took to set off on my seaside walk and it would be another three years before I gave up drinking.

The Prize (2008)

So, let me tell you how I stopped drinking.

In 2008 I moved into a shared house near Finsbury Park with Maria, my sister Catherine and her husband Paul. It came close to being the last move I ever made.

I've always gotten on well with my sister, even though in many ways she's the polar opposite of me – good looking, skinny, athletic, gregarious and a lover of travel. Perhaps it's apt that she and Paul eventually moved to Tasmania to build a house and start a family together on the other side of the world. Things were fine for the most part during the first few months we lived under the same roof. But my drinking soon put an unprecedented strain on our relationship as I started to devolve rapidly from high functioning alcoholic to barely holding it together mess within a space of weeks. After twenty odd years, the descent was vertiginous. I'd taken to just going to sleep in the street half way home after punishing sessions, on benches, in bus shelters or in doorways. It was like I was having trial runs at being homeless. Sometimes I made it home as far as the front door but then couldn't get my act together enough to get through it. I'd gone up to 20 stone and I was in a large amount of abdominal pain at all times. My liver was giving me so much grief, that most mornings when I woke up, I'd have to roll out of bed and onto the floor. I couldn't bend over to any great degree until I got moving. I stopped being able to tie my shoelaces and I was starting to waddle a little, like Vito, the gay mobster from *The Sopranos* who looks like John Prescott.

After a long weekend of really pushing it at an experimental rock festival in Birmingham that July, doing a lot of ecstasy, cocaine, ketamine, wine, tequila, rum and grass, I collapsed coming back to London and had to be carried off the train at Coventry. It was lunchtime. People looked disgusted. The proximity of death seemed unremarkable. Mundane. Par for the course.

On returning my doctor forced me to have blood tests and told me in no uncertain terms that I would not see the end of the year if I did not stop drinking and taking drugs. I nodded mutely but I still didn't really intend to quit; instead I made plans to make my transition as easy as possible if it turned out I had cirrhosis or something else final: I had stockpiled about 40 diazepam tablets in case of a very rainy day.

When my results came back it turned out I had fatty liver disease and that over 95% of my organ was affected. I was standing on the threshold of cirrhosis. I didn't know what else to do so I went out and got leathered. When I came back in, feeling my way back along the walls to the kitchen, wheezing with every step, sweat dripping off the end of my nose, my sister and Maria were already in there. Voices were raised and Catherine was waving the doctor's letter around: "Can't you see? He's going to die soon. He's going to fucking die."

I poured myself a pint of wine. They were talking about me like I wasn't there. And despite being 20 stone, 6'4" and having the lengthy beard and hair of a Hell's Angel or death metal musician, they were right. I was barely there at all.

I tried to ignore what was going on but this strategy only lasted for another week.

I went out to do a bit of DJing in the West End but my bullied innards had clearly had enough. My tolerance had plummeted rapidly over the course of the previous seven days but my thirst raged on and this discrepancy left me a bewildered, aggressive, close to psychotic mess. After I finished DJing I hit a couple of metal bars, the Intrepid Fox and The Cro Bar, but even in these spectacularly non-judgemental places, my behaviour and countenance were clearly not meeting minimum entry requirements. On the street outside I had some kind of epiphany and gave my laptop away to a rough sleeper.

Maria split up with me the next day.

I decided to give up drinking that morning but I think I recognised that I was so brutally sodden with alcohol that stopping dead was far more likely to finish me off than any liver complaint. My good friend John Tatlock had just arrived in town from Manchester and I really needed to get out of the house so I suggested the pub. "After all", I said with a hollow laugh, "it's not going to kill me."

(I should point out that this was far from the first time I had woken up, decided to give up drinking and then set about implementing this by going out for a drink; but to date, it remains the last time.)

My 'one for the road' was, against all odds, a really great night. I felt really bad that Maria had split up with me and that it seemed likely I was going to die soon but at the same time I was happy to be going back out for a drink and really perversely excited about the idea of attempting to give up drinking for good this time – even if all the available evidence made it seem highly unlikely that I would stay the course. It just felt that fate had forced my hand; that whatever was going to happen, was going to happen very soon.

I went to my local in Kings Cross. We got there about seven or eight, drank til last orders and then had a little bit of a lock in, during which we had a few more pints and a couple of lines and that was it. I haven't had a drink since. Of course, it's not the giving up that's hard, it's the staying sober after you've made the decision to give up that's next to impossible.

The next day after John left I went to talk to Maria, hoping against hope that she hadn't split up with me and it was just some misunderstanding but unfortunately not. Luckily she didn't throw me out of the house however, so I moved into the tiny spare room with a pile of books, a mattress, a duvet and a reading lamp.

I have an idea that I stopped drinking on August 1, 2008 but am not entirely sure – it's just the date I ended up choosing, roughly a year later, to acknowledge my first year of sobriety.

I had a real evangelical zeal for it at first. It was a pretty good attitude to have as it took the outer edge off withdrawal for the first day or so. Withdrawal is such a grim business that whatever you can do to be lowered into it as gently as possible is a good thing. But in the end you just have to get on with it. And it definitely gets much worse before it gets better. This time the really savage bit only loosened up a little after about a month or so. I was so fucked up I had a hangover that lasted for two and a half weeks then after about six weeks I could I feel myself getting marginally better physically each day. My liver sorted itself out in just over half a year, which is apparently very speedy.

I only told a handful of trustworthy people about what I was doing. I didn't talk about it on Facebook or Twitter or to casual acquaintances or business contacts or anything like that. I didn't instigate any kind of big ritual, like crossing off the days on a calendar with an X like I was in prison. I lost track of how many days it had been within the month because I wanted it to become normal for me to be sober as quickly as possible. So I tried not to treat it like some Herculean task. If you look at sobriety like it's something you can do, it starts looking more like a task that you might even possibly get away with.

In the spare room, the first two weeks were pretty bad. I'd gone cold a few times since moving down south but hadn't dried out properly and thoroughly all the way for nearly a decade. The hallucinations were baroque... real *Event Horizon*, HR Giger, insects coming out of the walls, angels hovering in the corner shit. Even going on past experience, the music I was hearing was crazy, kind of like Anaal Nathrakh and Gnaw Their Tongues mixed with Whitehouse and Perc. I have to say I did enjoy this music – it's just a shame it had to come hand in hand with the rest of it.

Withdrawing from alcohol in a full-on way does have an extreme metal/ industrial/ noise aesthetic about it. I'm certainly not saying I enjoyed it but perhaps there was about 5-10%

masochistic awe, at just how vicious and weirdly psychedelic the experience was. It would be facile to say to someone in a similar position, "Try and enjoy withdrawal." No one, not even the insane, enjoys being plagued by imaginary insects crawling right through them. As unpleasant as it was – kind of like taking bad acid that lasted, on and off, for a fortnight, it was a genuine psychedelic experience; and genuine psychedelic experiences can be used as tools of self-improvement, if you chose to view the situation in that light. And I did.

The experience was so psychically violent that it thrust me into a state of deterritorialisation that lasted for literally weeks before I became reterritorialised again. The clarity of thought I achieved on some fundamental questions about myself was terrifying. It was, in some ways, the best of all times to ask myself the sort of shit that I would otherwise find too pompous or ridiculous: who was I, what was my purpose, what was I doing and where was I going? I was presented with a picture of myself in such simplistic clarity while I myself was in such a state of relative plasticity that it became strangely easy to contemplate genuine personal change. But it should be said that the picture I was presented with was not particularly nice.

This is not to say that all revelations during the period of deterritorialisation were to be trusted fully. During this time I experienced what I felt to be a blinding clarity about drinking – feeling I'd uncovered some objective truth about alcohol culture. (This was a bit like the scene in *They Live* where Roddy Piper and Keith David have a massive fist fight, before the former finally persuades the latter to put on the sunglasses). Christ almighty – I couldn't believe it. I was slap bang in the middle of some living Hogarth illustration. The alcohol advertising was everywhere demanding that I drink! (I thought it had been banned years previously…) Where I lived I was surrounded by places that were either off licences or premises that served drink. There were drunks in doorways, on buses, on trains, on the pavements, in church porches.

I did not know that drink had undone so many. But here they were. Mortal. Legion. Leathered.

The empty spirits bottles, beer cans and wine bottles piled up in bins, in skips, along pavements. The privet hedges throbbed with empties. Every front door I passed seemed to be groaning with the weight of a potential avalanche of bottles and a scree of cans behind it that would come flooding out the second they were opened. Everywhere I looked in public there were people drinking at the crack of dawn, drinking at the close of day and at all other hours in between. The graveyards were full of drunks both dead and alive. Gastro pubs, basement bars, kebab shops with back rooms, family run restaurants, high street nite spots, threatening-looking nightclubs, all disgorging alcoholics onto the pavements like a meat grinding machine. Warehouse-sized supermarkets with alcohol sections the size of housing estates. Night buses and taxis ferrying the alcoholically incapacitated, spilling them onto streets that were little better than vomitoria.

Of course, this was nothing more than a heightened sense of reality and I now no longer notice any of this stuff any more than I did when I was drinking.

I had a couple of epileptic fits, really bad night sweats and terrors but during the day I was pretty much normal if a bit vacant and feeling like I'd been poisoned and beaten up. I didn't even take any time off work. During the daytime I read *Straw Dogs* by John Gray. Then I read *The God Delusion* by Richard Dawkins. Then I read *Straw Dogs* by John Gray again. Then I threw *The God Delusion* in the bin.

And then after about a month, the depression started.

There was nothing impressive or mind-expanding about the depression. There was literally nothing good that came from it. I couldn't learn from it. I couldn't grow from it. I couldn't put a spin on it.

It makes me feel depressed now even to mention it. I hate talking about it. Not only is it impossible to convey to people who don't understand, exactly what having severe clinical depression is like, it is also impossible to recall exactly how bad it was yourself when it ends. I remain aware that this period of depression was fucking terrible, that I longed to cut myself, to drag a craft knife up my wrists, to topple weakly in front of tube trains, to tumble, eyes shut off high roofs, to 'accidentally' drown myself in the bath, to walk round shrieking shrilly at people I didn't know: 'Don't you realise how much pain I'm in? Can't you just kill me?' But this vile state of sub-existence simply stops possessing any tangibility when I'm not waist deep in it.

I can only explain it via metaphors, but even these are completely useless as they are not strong enough to convey the malign feelings of hatred, despondency, violence, misanthropy, weakness, degeneracy, self-absorption and fatigue that I felt but at the same time they feel too gauche, too fantastical and too grotesque for anyone to believe in.

Imagine all the inner and outer audio signals of your life running down a cable which is plugged into a 24-channel mixing desk. The talented, trained, sympathetic sound engineer who usually works with you is no longer at the controls. Some loud, fast talking, high maintenance, bipolar drunk is chained to the console in his place. The booth monitor volume control, which represents in general terms how good you feel, has been turned down to somewhere between zero and one. You can pray for it to go back up to six or maybe even seven but it won't happen. Not now and maybe never again. All the first eight channels that your streams of conscious thought are being fed through – the ones you usually have full control over – are being faded up and down at random and having bursts of unusual FX applied to them. Channels nine and ten have tinnitus allocated to them and they are both up to eight. The next fourteen channels though… they're the ones. Lines which are usually dead during waking hours are now live and fully open. They are attached to malfunctioning samplers, spitting out violently loud gobbets of low quality audio. Non-stop. Relentless. Looped. Compressed. Layered. The sound effects to every cinematic gunshot wound to the head you have ever heard are on one channel. The sound the dog made when the car went straight over it that night down Rainhill Road, when it dragged itself away screaming by its still working two front legs. The answering machine message left for you after he killed himself. The sound the cigarette made as it was extinguished on the smoothest part of your inner thigh. That choking sound she made when you said you'd sooner drink yourself to death than dry out for her...

Like most depressed people, I had an inability to break free from destructive, wearying, ruminative loops. I spent every second of every minute of every hour of every day, going over and over the same information time and time again. It was the very repetitive nature of this process that wore me out and made me obsessional. During this period everything internal was reflected onto everything external making existence itself seem sick, ugly and without merit.

These loops were the shackles which bound me. When someone you love dies. When you quit an addictive drug. When you stop drinking. When you split up with your partner. Insolvable conundrums are formed. And these circular traps of language were what I became snared in and couldn't free myself from. The more I struggled the tighter they bound around my limbs and round my neck. These fucking reasonable questions: Why did he have to die? Why can't I just have one more line? Why is it wrong for me to have a glass of wine? Why won't she come back? I didn't have to go to see a counsellor or a therapist to be told that excessive time spent ruminating was time spent doing something akin to self-harm. The point where I started going over past events again and again, remorselessly and ceaselessly, was the point where the logical and linear exploration of an unfortunate or unpleasant series of events got twisted into a loop, a snare, a noose, that was near impossible to escape from; where necessary examination of the past had become a tar pit of depression in the present.

Even if I occasionally had an inkling of what was happening, once I reached this point it was too late to do anything about it. It was like being strapped into some cheap and nasty funfair ride – once I was on, it was impossible to get off again until it was over. And then it was only a matter of time before I would willingly get aboard another ride.

So how should I write about this ugly mundanity? Some

years after the fact in 2012 I became obsessed with the song 'The Prize' by the musician Nick Talbot, aka Gravenhurst. It spoke volumes to me about depression – or rather about how to think about depression at one stage removed. With this song Nick had provided a master class in restraint and subtlety when writing around difficult themes. The lyrics suggested someone who couldn't or wouldn't look directly at a bad event itself but who stared at the perimeters and then to the aftermath: "As the house lights turn/ reveal cigarette burns and the tide line/ of last night's cries of despair/ that emanate from the underpass and echo back to anywhere/ Still the ties that bind us blind us to the emptiness of the prize." I felt that a metaphor like the one contained in 'The Prize' was important to me because it at least allowed for the potential dignity of hope. It contained the fleeting promise of transcendence, a helping hand to pull the listener out of the self-destructive loop of rumination.

One of the best aspects of being a music journalist is the chance you very occasionally get to meet unusually talented, perspicacious and profoundly creative people. And despite usually attempting to keep my social life and my work life separate, I was lucky enough to become friends with Nick, a beautiful and highly intelligent person. One very bright spring morning, sitting on a bench by the Thames eating ice creams, he told me – in the most flattering way possible – that my interpretation of 'The Prize' was completely different to what he was singing about. I'd always cursed musicians for refusing to discuss the concrete meanings to their lyrics but on that day I learned that this reticence was a benefit... that songs were hardly ever written for critics, and were nearly always written for listeners and that a song could lose its power as a tool for the listener when the author's intents were spelled out for them.

Not only was the depression terrible but it went on and on, for way longer than the physical withdrawal effects of the addiction. All I could do to take the edge off it was pay attention to my physical health and hope that this would impact positively on my mental health.

It was a wise decision. Alcohol is a massive analgesic – I hadn't known this – and masks all sorts of secondary problems by softening pain receptors. As soon as my body was cleared of this, I started feeling pain in my kidneys, pancreas, head, joints... all over basically. On top of that, being drunk all the time had introduced a weird equilibrium into my body which was – unfortunately – a pain to disturb in the short term, meaning I had to be really careful not to pick up flu or a virus. Now this might not sound like much but getting actual influenza when I already had something which felt like poisoning and temporary schizophrenia was probably best avoided. So cod liver oil tablets, milk thistle for the liver, Vitamin B complex were what I stocked up on. I ate a banana, an avocado and some tangerines every day. This was something the middle classes knew instinctively but that I had to learn. What's the difference between Shaun Ryder and Jason Pierce? Probably about three hours extra sleep a night and a banana, an avocado and some tangerines.

The pain wasn't unendurable but there was such a generous amount of it... There wasn't a single minute of it that I couldn't sit through again right now, but there were hundreds of thousands of these minutes. And they stretched out far past the horizon. I developed a painkiller habit almost immediately, which was fucking stupid. Take a guess what the major side effect of coming off painkillers is? Loads of pain. Other than that though I tried to concentrate on things that helped get my body flushed out. High fibre cereals, low sugar muesli, dried fruit, green salads, loads of water. Also I used to make up drinks from special sachets of powder which injected a lot of fibre into my diet. I tried to have no fast food and have a cooked meal once a day. I couldn't face coffee for the first few weeks – it just gave me panic attacks – but after that I got bang into having loads each morning. I'd drink litres of espresso until I felt like I could see into the future and control the weather.

Coffee was an alcohol substitute. Since giving up drinking, the major alcohol substitutes I have gone in for have been cake, cocaine, MDMA, Coca-Cola, amphetamines, coffee, record shopping for vinyl, plant food, diazepam, chocolate, cheese, donuts, cough medicine, ketamine, HBO box sets, work and, eventually, the gym with varying degrees of short-term success.

I started going to Alcoholics Anonymous three days after stopping drinking. There was a wide scale upon which people with drink problems existed and I was probably at the more extreme end, so needed to stack all of the odds in my favour. I had no idea if AA was successful or highly regarded as a means of quitting but I felt it wouldn't hurt me to try. I phoned up a helpline and spoke to someone the day after I stopped. She asked if the idea that I was an alcoholic was new to me. I said it was something I'd known for a long time. I reassured her that I was relatively comfortable with the information and that I wasn't going to do anything rash. I received some literature the following day through the post. I attended my first meeting the day after that and at first tried to get to five meetings a week.

When you first give up drinking, you have to rearrange everything about your life to begin with. The trouble was, a lot of the people I knew who drank themselves could not understand on a very fundamental level what I was doing. Even years later I knew people who seemed to think I could just drink weaker beer if I wanted or have a glass of wine with a meal. They would ask me when I was starting again and didn't even seem to realise that wine, spirits and beer were all the same thing to me now. Irritatingly – and odds suggest that this will always be the case – occasionally there were even people who would try to get me to drink again. Not in a very aggressive way but enough that it was unpleasant nonetheless.

I knew that the main reason I might start drinking again would be because I'd persuade myself that it was alright to or that I was better. I would maybe fall prey to the idea that I had been cured, that I had been a drama queen for a while when I decided that I was an alkie, but now I had come to my senses. That there was no way I was like that. That there was no way my drinking was anywhere near as bad as most of the people I met in AA.

Because of this risk I had to learn how to be very self-aware, very, very quickly. This was easier said than done as most problem drinkers by definition have zero self-awareness. I had to make it my mantra and be very clear with myself that by stopping drinking I meant exactly that. No treats, no rewards, no exceptions, no accidents, no 'my dog just died', no 'my friend just died', no, 'it's my birthday', no, 'it's your funeral', no, 'it's your wedding', no, 'I just got the job', no, 'it's such a nice meal', no, 'it's our anniversary', no, 'I'm on holiday', no, 'I'm interviewing Mark E Smith', no, 'I literally can't cope for another second', no, 'it's one of those weeks'... no booze under any circumstances.

This needed 100% vigilance for the short and medium term. Subconsciously the part of me that was desperate to return to my normal routine developed an overbearingly loud and obnoxious internal monologue which marshalled all the insincere guile of a university debating team champion mixed with the smarm of a Millbank spin doctor, and trained it into persuading me to have a drink at all times. At every fucking waking hour of the day. And beyond that. Because drinking is all I dreamed about for five years solid after quitting. I knew that no one would pat me on the back if I said no to this voice a hundred and twenty five thousand times, or even ten million times, but knew that I would lose everything if I gave in to it just once.

This interior monologue retreated. Gradually. But while it was still audible, my feeling was that it was better to stop going to the pub. I couldn't understand why some people would torture themselves with nights out on the town drinking Becks Blue or Kaliber, teeth clamped into rictus grins while everyone round them dissolved into warm merriment.

I discovered that a very small number of good mates would come round and see me at my house or agree to meet me in a café or a restaurant or invite me to their houses. The others, temporarily, could go and fuck themselves. Or permanently as the case sometimes was. If you ever want to know who of your friends will come and visit you in prison or, when the time arrives, in hospital, all you have to do is stop going to the pub for a few months – you'll soon find out.

Going to the pub sober, I discovered, was pretty much like trying to have a wank while wearing a sandpaper glove. I would have derived a roughly similar experience from sitting at home in a trough full of pig shit, tearing £20 notes into confetti and launching it out of the window.

I didn't want to become agoraphobic but I knew I had to cut back seriously on going out. At first all I'd go to social event wise – for about half a year – were birthdays, weddings and funerals. And then it was more a case of showing my face for a bit and then leaving. After that I'd go to the pub on special occasions but always have an escape route planned. If I felt odd or unhappy or drunks were doing my head in, I wouldn't beat myself up, I'd just get in a cab and leave. Some people could be a bit rubbish about it. Really unhelpful actually but I just had to keep on explaining to them in as conciliatory a way as possible that it was not a diss, I just had to leave.

Plenty of people who drank all of the time simply didn't get it. They couldn't fully understand it, so I eventually stopped wasting my time trying to explain it to them. It was such an alien concept to them. I knew that to other heavy drinkers I was always going to be someone who was weak – not someone who was ill. I had friends who were clearly going to die within the next few years because of the way they drank. Some of them could barely get a coherent sentence out, night or day. They twitched, sweated and shook while they were talking to me but all of the time they would still laugh in my face and talk to me condescendingly as if I was in some kind of mad cult that preyed upon the terminally gullible. They felt I was fully deserving of their pity. But that was fine, I had to leave them to their conviviality, their bar tabs, their long, rattling laughs and their inspirational Dean Martin, Dorothy Parker and Tom Waits quotes on Facebook. Leave them to accidentally pissing their pants on the night bus while trying to find the page they were up to in a battered Penguin edition of *Under The Volcano*. I had been given a dishonourable discharge. It was time to say farewell.

But there were times when I had no choice but to go to the

pub, or rather I let people make me believe I had no choice – and those were some of the worst times of all. After about a year of sobriety, I let people think it was just normal me not drinking – they were thinking of me as 'cured' (which in some respects will never happen) simply because I had let them think that way. After ten months dry I had a massive birthday party at the Mucky Pup – the excellent rock pub in Angel where I spent most of my last few years drinking. It was for my 38ᵗʰ and it was fucking horrible. I was nearly in tears by about two in the morning but no one noticed because they were all raging drunk and getting me in a headlock or trying to get me to have a toy fight or trying to get me to have a sneaky drink or laughing at me for my sobriety. I mentioned a cab home at 11pm and it still hadn't arrived by 3am. One girl told me the same anecdote about Joan Jett 16 times. Life, quite literally, was too short. I knew I had to stop standing for it.

Of course, I knew that I'd been all the other people present myself: the guy saying, 'Cheer up!', the person incomprehensible, the annoying guy wanting an argument... But after this happened a few times I started to realise that this was no longer my problem, that whatever I had or hadn't done while drinking – literally none of it was going to be leavened by standing round in pubs wearing a hair shirt. There was no need for me to do penance by being around drunks. It became clear to me that if I had annoyed some people when I was drunk then that was their fault for hanging out in the kind of pubs where awesome drunks hang out. It went with the territory, which is not the case with staying at home and watching *True Detective* with some guacamole.

I lost friends. It was inevitable. I didn't fall out with anyone *per se* but there were people I just didn't see anymore. And of those friends that I kept, some would talk to me about nothing but my drinking from that moment on. People were fascinated by my sobriety and seemed to have no problem with having exactly the same conversation with me every single time I met them. They would stand there grinning while I explained exactly the same information to them again and again and again, to the kind of countenance that suggested I was detailing my membership of the

Flat Earth Society or describing some photographs I'd taken of faeries at the bottom of my garden.

Then people began to talk to me about their drink problems. Sometimes they would want to talk about it when they were sober which was totally cool. But there would also be people who insisted on talking to me about it only when they were really pissed which could be annoying. I developed a rule after a few years that said if anyone wanted to talk to me about it while they were wankered I would speak to them the next day instead. I would always get in touch with them and they never knew what I was talking about when I called them. One mate who'd been crying in my arms the night before laughed in my face and called me a soft cunt when I broached it the following day.

But these people were usually just self-aggrandising Sunday drinkers who wanted to have a bit of drama time. You know the sort of people I'm talking about; they'd probably never gotten over the fact that they had pissed their pants once or sucked their flatmate off when they were blasted. If I'd only ever pissed my pants in public once I'd have it printed on my fucking business cards.

Kicking any addiction – and drink is no exception – is like heartbreak or losing someone you love, as I found out. And I had to go through exactly the same stages in order to recover afterwards. The cruellest stage was the home straight because it didn't happen naturally, it required me to give up on the substance for good – to make my peace with it. Do you know that person who never really got over their first love? Who is always thinking about them even though it was 20 or 30 years ago? I couldn't afford to be like that with drink or drugs. Thinking about your ex all the time won't kill you. Thinking about alcohol all the time quite probably could. Once it's done, it's done. Walk away from it and don't fucking look back.

On And On South Of Heaven (2008)

So, let me tell you how I kept off the drink.

All my life I've heard people voice the opinion that men need to have a hobby. That they need to create something; have some kind of arts, crafts, electronics or science project into which they can divert a lot of their energy. A shed, essentially. The theory seems to be that this makes up for the fact that they don't get to give birth to children. I don't know about that but about half the people I know personally (both men and women) need an all-encompassing creative problem – something to wrestle with over a long period of time. And some of them, like me, will fill their lives up to the brim with appalling things if it isn't demanding or satisfying enough.

I didn't have a project in the first half of my life but then, once over the hump, it became the Quietus, the music and culture website I co-founded and run with my good friend, Luke Turner. I didn't know it was going to replace drinking in my life when I first started thinking about it – I genuinely had no intention of stopping drinking until I fell down dead. In fact, if I'd known the Quietus was going to have anything to do with me stopping drinking, I would have abandoned it at the drawing board stage. And then I would have kicked the drawing board down a mineshaft as a precaution.

My aims when I started it were not very noble. I wanted one last crack at earning a meagre living as a music writer because I knew that I was done otherwise and I'd have to go and get a real job. I don't think I had any ambitions beyond that.

The idea didn't come as a bolt out of the blue. After *Bang*, the magazine that I got my first break on as a music journalist, folded in Christmas 2003, I immediately started looking for an excuse to carry on working with my former colleague and new mate Pricey.

I remember when I first met Simon Price in the flesh earlier that year, after years of reading his music journalism. He looked like a 30-something Marlon Brando would have done back in the day if he'd taken to wearing a lot of makeup, rubber trousers, a pink Chic T-shirt, a leopard print coat and had bunches of hair on either side of his head made from a multitude of brightly coloured strips of plastic. (These bunches have since been replaced with bright red horns.) While his look certainly splits the vote, I remember Wayne Coyne from The Flaming Lips telling me once that they were thinking about doing a show where all of their dancers would be dressed like Pricey. As he pointed out reasonably: "If everyone dressed like him, I don't imagine there would be much trouble in the world." Though, if everyone dressed like Simon, he would probably start dressing like a businessman. I like the way he dresses and I wish I had a flamboyant streak myself but above and beyond that, I love the way he writes about music. He's a true original and one of the best.

In my head I saw my ideal job as me and Simon rolling into work at about midday, listening to some Gary Numan, commissioning some features on disco, synth pop, goth, rave, heavy metal and post punk, doing some writing and then heading out for a show before hitting some horrific nightclub to dance to AC/DC and Donna Summer before being scraped into cabs at 4am. (During the year we worked together, the best days had pretty much unfolded along these lines anyway.) So we worked tirelessly on a pitch for a new monthly music magazine with the working title of *ATOMIC*, which was essentially going to be *MOJO* for people who grew up in the 80s and 90s. Instead of Pink

Floyd, The Beatles and The Kinks on the front cover it was going to feature The Smiths, Blondie and Public Enemy. We really put in the work analysing all the music magazines out there, conducting our own brand of market research, mocking up covers... We even found out how you're supposed to dress when you pitch a magazine to a big international publishing house. (Suit jacket, jeans, converse trainers and Joy Division T-shirt is the required uniform apparently.)

During this research process however, the boomer rock monthly *UNCUT* tried to relaunch itself as a more youthful magazine. The first cover even featured a preposterously airbrushed picture of Morrissey, all torrid, topless and lachrymal. Inside he was interviewed by the person who was number one on our hit list of potential writers: Paul Morley. We realised that it wasn't just a blip on the radar when the following two months featured The Stone Roses and Oasis as their cover stars, in a similar airbrushed, quasi-80s style. Now we could only wait for the ABCs to see if the idea had been successful. When the quarterly magazine figures came in, they were abysmal. *UNCUT* had lost something close to a third of its readers in one fell swoop because of this slight 80s / 90s image make-over. It's not even like IPC had gambled everything on a Klaus Nomi fold out cover, a ten page interview with Hanoi Rocks and a free CD full of Mantronix rarities – Morrissey, Brown and the Gallaghers were core figures to a mainstream music readership like the *NME*'s and, one would have presumed, *UNCUT*'s as well. The trouble was, even the vague 'essence' of the 80s, some male sensitivity and the dangerous homoerotic androgyny of The Stone Roses wearing rain-proof coats had sent literally tens of thousands of readers running for the hills clutching shotguns and copies of *Blood On The Tracks*.

We were still convinced that *ATOMIC* was a great idea but it was clear that everyone else in music publishing would now laugh us out of the room if we tried to pitch it to them, *Unknown Pleasures* T-shirts or not. We dropped the idea, Pricey moved to Brighton to start his new life by the sea and that was that.

I carried on freelancing for a few years and then in early 2007, Sean Adams from music site Drowned In Sound asked me to apply to be the editor of a projected sister site, saying something like, "Would you be interested in running a classic rock site aimed at £50 man?" I told him I was but that I might "tweak" the pitch ever so slightly.

I turned immediately to my friend Luke Turner for advice on how to put the pitch together, partially because I trusted his judgement and partially because he was my former commissioning editor at Playlouder.com and understood the world of music websites – something I had little experience of. When the proposal actually started taking shape and I was offered the job I asked if he'd run the site with me. While the proposed site now included elements of the *ATOMIC* pitch, as a web-based publication its scope had got much wider very quickly.

Thankfully Luke agreed to leave a comfortable job at the Natural History Museum to do this. He'd already had his moment of clarity and run sensibly away from the music business as fast as his classic brogues would carry him. I was very happy indeed to see him make the return trip.

In theory it should be a nightmare running a site with two editors with equal say but it hasn't worked out like that. Aside from giving up drinking, asking Luke to be co-editor has been the most important professional decision I have ever made. The website simply wouldn't have worked otherwise. He is one of my best friends – something very important to the success of the site. If we were simply business partners he would have ended up caving my head in with some heavyweight SunnO))) vinyl years ago as large periods of the site's history have been very stressful, I haven't always been in the best of mental health and, because of this, nor have I been the easiest person to get along with.

For the first few years of the Quietus' existence I saw a lot more of Luke than I did of Maria. I remember once when she was pregnant we went to hospital for an antenatal class and I got my phone out of my pocket. "This isn't the time to be texting Luke about The Fall!" she upbraided me angrily. I was only getting my phone out to take notes but it was a fair assumption to make as Luke and I were in almost constant contact back then.

It has been too easy for me in retrospect to construct a simple narrative that goes like this – "I really needed to stop drinking and sort my life out in order to prevent myself from dying, so I poured all of my spare time and energy into setting up and running the Quietus." That's still what I tell people now for the sake of brevity when they ask me about the history of the site. However, it wasn't that straightforward. Nothing ever is.

I can't speak for Luke but in my heart of hearts I didn't really think the website would last that long. Most new internet ventures of this kind fail well within a year of launch, as in fact the Quietus very nearly did. But the money was OK, we'd had a good idea and I certainly didn't have any other options open to me. I was also certainly half crazed with drink and drugs in the early days of setting up the site and not really in possession of a long-term plan for it or for myself. I didn't need a long-term plan as I was working on the assumption that I was probably going to die soon.

So despite being my project for sobriety, the Quietus was initially born in a cataclysmic blaze of alcohol. The first thing Luke and I did with our first month's wages was to go and watch Wire in an art gallery in Belgium. Which sounds really civilised. Except it really wasn't. On our way out there we tried to fool ourselves that we were following in Jonathan Meades' footsteps, trying to locate the dividing line between Northern and Southern Europe, but it didn't take much to scrape this veneer of intellectual curiosity away.

At least we managed to go and look at a church before we submitted to the merciless grip of ethanol. In Leuven's town square, *aprés* train, pre-drinks, we entered the magnificent St Pieterskerk. An entire gigantic tree trunk had been carved into a towering pulpit showing the unlucky St Norbert being dismounted dramatically by a lightning bolt. A weeping but eyeless wooden Christ, with arms outstretched, loomed in the shadows like a partially remembered adversary of Tom Baker's *Dr Who*. A harrowing Dieric Bouts triptych showed St Erasmus, praying serenely as his innards – tied securely to a winch – were wound out of his pale, skinny frame by two sneering brutes.

We got into town at midday and by 2pm were done with sightseeing and sat in the first of many bars. This was when our own innate Northernness came into play. To be Northern is to have your Northernness amplified with each step taken in a Southerly direction. By 3pm we were dishevelled. By 4pm we were disreputable. By 5pm we were almost there but not quite properly drunk as furniture had not yet been knocked over. Dostoyevsky defined the condition of being properly drunk as the point at which the drinker starts yelling abusively at his companions and everyone in earshot, and by that rule, at 5.30pm we had arrived.

From 6pm onwards everything is a horrific psychedelic blur – brought on no doubt by our attempts to sample every alcoholic drink we encountered that had a religious connection. After trying one bottle of everything brewed by monks we sluiced down syrupy Belgian beers called Judas, Satan and St Peter as well.

I remember standing at the bar waving my arms about maniacally, shouting: "Of course Poperings Hommelbier was in the fucking Bible. Give me two of them, two more bottles of Barabbas, a yard of Leviticus and a bag of salt and vinegar crisps."

Later in the art gallery we stumbled around waiting for the gig to start. One of the exhibitions was a giant pink chair. It never occurred to me to not sit on the massive piece of artwork, it just took me several attempts to get on it because it was about 12 foot tall. My joy at finally sitting on a chair that made me look like a sixteen-month-old with a beard was short lived when a security guard came into the room and asked me to get down in a tone of voice reserved for English idiots. He pointed at a large sign on the wall written in French, which clearly said something along the lines of: "Don't sit on the massive pink chair you English twat."

I can't say that the website meant that much to me at first. It nearly all fell away to nothing before we were given the chance to achieve anything anyway. After half a year of tinkering with stuff behind the scenes, running it as a beta site and then just two more months after it officially launched, the inevitable happened and the funding was pulled.

The team that looked after the Quietus was very small and they were very supportive of us. We never had any contact with our soon-to-be-but-never-were paymasters – things just didn't last that long. Initial startup money had been sourced, with ongoing funding to be provided by a potentially lucrative deal with the advertising department of BSkyB. But that evaporated about two months after we launched and we were cut loose.

"But what about the millions of pounds that were guaranteed for the project?" I asked one of my superiors. He suggested that I could take BSkyB to court if I wanted but he wasn't going to be joining me in the endeavour.

There is no real point in playing 'what if' but my gut feeling is that the Quietus wouldn't have lasted very long if things had gone according to plan. It ended up being a good thing for Luke and I and the website that the money fell through.

I had a feeling the funding was going to disappear almost from the get go. I'd been round the block a few times and was naturally very pessimistic so I'd already started preparing myself for what seemed like the inevitable. When I saw surveyors walking round my offices measuring things, I thought, "Oh, hello – what's going on here then?" But for me, this was a blessing in disguise. I had given up drinking a month before the funding was pulled – I'd had to if I wanted to stay alive and stand any chance at all of winning my girlfriend back; but this also happened at just the right time professionally.

So our website became independent at exactly the same time as my last, so far successful, attempt to quit drinking. And slowly, this effort to build something Luke and I could be proud of helped me not only stay sober, but also to start rebuilding some of my self-respect and sanity.

When I hear people say things like you should never mix business with pleasure or you should never go into business with your friends, I immediately presume they simply associate with bad people or have no true friends. The Quietus has been a product not just of me working with Luke but with my oldest and closest friend Stu who has taken many pictures for the site, and my good pal John Tatlock who has written many incisive pieces for us. John also helps Luke and I to run our record label, the Quietus Phonographic Corporation, which was set up in 2013 in order to alert people to the amazing music of East India Youth, AKA William Doyle, whose austere and romantic electronic avant pop came to my attention when he thrust a self-produced CD into my hands at a Factory Floor gig. Although I don't socialise much anymore, so don't always get to meet newer writers on the site, a sizable chunk of the contributors and all of the section editors past and present are good friends as well.

So by the winter of 2008, having been sober for about three months, I had this really massive project to throw all of my energy and newly acquired free time into. The site was only half built (and still is, the fucking thing doesn't work properly and it drives me round the bend), it didn't have advertising on it, we didn't have offices, we didn't have backing, it wasn't worth anything in financial terms and no one really knew who we were. But on the other hand we had a great team of writers – plenty of whom mucked in to help us out – and I used my redundancy money to pay for content in the short term.

But the decision to go it alone wasn't an instant one. On the last day in our nice offices in West London after the money had run out, Luke and I were putting all of our stuff in bin bags and I was getting rid of the bottles of Jäger, red wine and Jack Daniels that I had hidden everywhere. My former boss, who had a sideline in managing rock stars, was there locking up. One of his charges was Mick Hucknall and he kept an emergency wardrobe for him there in case the flame-haired soul singer had to fly off to do an impromptu gig in Russia or something like that. He said to us, "Look this is some of Mick's old stage gear. Why don't you take it?"

Inside the wardrobe were amazing Ozwald Boateng suits with linings that would have made Colonel Gaddafi flinch, three pairs of hand-cobbled, leather boots, a rack of flamboyant purple-patterned shirts that suggested ketamine psychosis in the designer, a lot of stationary, and packs and packs of unopened black cotton briefs. And cases of Mick's very, very, pleasant olive oil. You can say what you want about Mick Hucknall, but he is certainly a tall man and definitely slimmer than I was then – Luke had to take most of the suits. I could only really fit into his boots and pants (and the shirts if I left them unbuttoned). And it should also be noted that he owns an olive grove that produces fantastic oil.

That was on the Friday. We said cheers, took handfuls of gear and left for good. I said to Luke, "Look, just go home for 24 hours. Have some nice food. Go out for a drink. Chill out. Let's meet up on Sunday and decide what we're going to do."

A couple of days later we met up again. I was wearing Mick Hucknall's pants, his boots, one of his shirts unbuttoned over a SunnO))) T-shirt and I had jotted down a lot of ideas about the future of the Quietus on his Post-It notes using one of his biros. "I have sought advice from a higher power", I said. "I think we should continue." Luke agreed and we went ahead like a pair of heavily armed, psychotic teenagers in a mall after firing the first shot. There was no point in stopping now that we'd invested all this time and effort. We had no back-up plan. We had lost relationships – both of us had ended up single just weeks earlier. Our credibility and any future we had in the music industry were destroyed. We were, at that point, a laughing stock. So there wasn't any discussion – we just met up, both dressed like Mick Hucknall, and said, "Right. Where can we get some free office space from?"

My man Chris Etches – a kinetic Welsh force of nature with a thing for capes, designing apps and releasing gothic electro records – came through for us and our new home was a tiny desk in his work garret in the old Truman Brewery in East London. We were up and running as an independent by the Wednesday of that week. Everyone in the industry and some people on message boards knew, but no one else did. I believed that if we were to survive we had to act like nothing had happened, so right from the off I said that we would publish three features a day, two or three reviews and a bunch of news. And from the outside, I'm guessing it looked like business as usual.

At first, whether the public needed or wanted the Quietus was a moot point – our readership wasn't exactly big – but my need for it to work grew exponentially week by week as it began looking more and more like I might be able to hack not drinking. I became paranoid at the idea of having to leave the music industry; I was convinced that it would knock me off the wagon. On top of that I'd simply spent too long working in factories and behind bars to go back to it, and working in any kind of large shared office space simply made me degenerate and misanthropic due to the heavy ingestion of mind altering drugs that I required to get me through the day. On top of that, I was such a mediocre lifestyle journalist and news reporter that my other options as a writer were all but used up.

I guess I'd always been borderline psychotic when it came to work I didn't like and I didn't see this ever changing. The last temp job I'd had just prior to starting the Quietus was vivid proof of this. While drunk and desperate, I'd accepted a job (arranged for me by well-meaning friends) as a 'film writer' only to find out that the role was actually that of an anodyne corporate copy-editor, CMS operative and picture caption writer at the huge UK headquarters of a very large international communications company. I was fast approaching my bottom, as they say at AA; I was run ragged and losing the plot. I was staying up all night drinking and, when I could afford them, using drugs to make it through the day. It was hard to settle down to work in the oppressively large open plan office because the massive, in-house management consultancy situated several floors above us justified part of their astronomical annual fee by constantly rearranging our seating plan and the ergonomics of our work area. This constant sense of being meddled with by bored rich idiots situated out of sight, on another floor, simply reinforced my already prodigiously inflated sense of paranoia.

The place was littered with the expensive detritus of their utter stupidity and mundanity. One day they erected a circular-shaped, free standing curved partition wall in the middle of the room which formed a tiny cupboard-like space big enough for one person. You could step into it through an opening and it was slightly smaller than the diameter of my outstretched arms. It said LIBRARY in large letters on the outside. The inside wall was lined with pasted on photographs of the spines of real books. The thing that made me most angry was the fact that they had photographed a shelf of *Reader's Digest* abridged classics to line the interior wall. Even if the space had contained real books, who in their right mind would think, "Do you know what? I'm not going to eat over-priced sandwiches from the in-house Costa in my allotted 30-minute break today. I'm going to stand on my own in a circular, unlit, furniture free cubicle the size of a Ryan Air bathroom and power read *The Prime Of Miss Jean Brodie* which has been helpfully edited to take the racy bits out."

Things came to a head when they removed my kitchen. Up until that point there had been one nice place in the whole air-conditioned, charmless glass and steel morgue and that was the kitchen. This was simply because you had some small amount of autonomy there being that it contained a fridge, a kettle, a sink and some cutlery. Some of the white tiles had brown, tea-stained splashback marks, I had a Dr Who mug in the cupboard and by comparison it felt almost homely in a shared student house kind of way.

I came in one day and it was gone, however. The entire structure and all of its contents had been removed overnight. The following week they constructed something called The Imaginarium in its place. It was like a bigger version of 'the library' but with no photographs of book spines, just grey, matte PVC covered partition walls.

Distressed with anger and in danger of kicking the thing to pieces I stamped back to my desk and typed out an embarrassingly nonsensical and half-cocked email to the management consultancy people. It ran along the following lines: "Please be aware that strictly speaking, there is no such word as 'imaginarium'. I'm only pointing this out to save you any further embarrassment before you rebrand the toilets in the same manner. Being that we don't live in Ancient Rome or Victorian England we do not have a librarium, simply a library. Perhaps the word you're looking for here is 'imaginary' which also, interestingly enough, means totally made up. This is why in London, Athens, Rome, Istanbul, New York, Cairo and Paris they have libraries, museums, art galleries and universities, while in Fort Myers, Florida and Anchorage, Alaska they have imaginariums (or imaginaria, if you will). By the way, I'm not charging you for this email, I wrote it on my lunch break so on this occasion I'll be waiving my consultancy fee. The next time you fancy making a word up, perhaps consult one of the many writers who work on the floor below you. They may be able to help with etymology."

My hands were shaking when I sent the mail but in my mind I was already walking to the pub to embark on a catastrophic fortnight-long drinking binge now unencumbered by a job. And sure enough, they sacked me the next day.

It took me a long time to realise that they were looking for an excuse to fire me. That a partially mad, chisel-enraged, swivel-eyed drunk wasn't necessarily the person they wanted working for them.

But the Quietus became a success within a few years. Although the word success does need some qualifying. It didn't earn us any money for a long time and still, at the time of writing, doesn't earn me a living wage; but a lot of people started reading it and some of them even seemed to like what we were writing about. All sorts of odd things started happening. I was 40 and had been, pretty much, an embarrassment my entire adult life but now I was having to get used to the occasional accolade from people I really looked up to: fellow journalists, authors, musicians, artists and filmmakers. Being praised was one thing but then there were the awards as well.

Like any angry drunk with an amphetamine tautened hair-trigger worth his salt I used to hate the idea of awards ceremonies with a berserk passion. Until I actually started winning awards that is; and then I developed a more nuanced appreciation of their role. The Record Of The Day website used to run the annual Music Journalism And PR Awards and it was genuinely quite gratifying each time the Quietus or any of our writers won anything.

On the night of the 2011 ceremony, when we won the best

website award for the third year running, I arrived to see legendary music hack Nick Kent – wearing a vest and a comically large sleng teng hat – standing insolently at the back of the basement venue with Bobby Gillespie who was chewing gum and wearing sunglasses. The Primal Scream frontman probably had a flick knife style comb in the pocket of his jeans. Gillespie, to be fair, looked dead smart in well-fitting black togs, but he ruined the cut of his suit by slouching with limbs twisted into uncomfortable positions, like a posable emo doll which had been run over by a steam roller. "Why can't they stand up straight?" I hissed at Luke – nerves jangling because of a litre of espresso and five pints of Coca Cola.

Kent and Gillespie fired up a joint indoors. "For fuck's sake!" I raged, and moved away from them to stand next to Martin Fry from ABC instead. If I had a gun to my head I'd have to say that I rated *The Lexicon Of Love* by ABC above *XTRMNTR* by Primal Scream but they're both personal all-time top 100 albums for me and there isn't that much between them. The thing is though, trapped in a cellar as we were, Fry was exactly the kind of man I wanted in my corner. He looked good in a suit. He seemed unflappable, like he wouldn't try any funny stuff, even if his number was up. One look at Gillespie and you could be sure that if he felt cornered, he'd fly at your eyes like a crushed black velvet rockabilly attack monkey.

I should come clean and confess that me and Bobby G had history. I once ran into him in the toilets at a Jesus And Mary Chain gig in 2008 and made the mistake of asking the innocuous question, "Hey Bobby, why aren't you playing drums?" He snapped at me, "Why aren't *you* playing drums?" For a second I could visualise myself in my mind's eye, much bigger than I actually was, running through the venue roaring and smashing people out of the way before leaping onstage, knocking the Mary Chain sticksman out and then attacking the drums like a 60ft-tall, cyborg Ginger Baker as the entire venue fell down around me. "Well…" I shouted, "I'm just going to go in this cubicle and do a line. And then WATCH ME GET ON STAGE AND PLAY

THE DRUMS!" But it was even lamer said out loud than it looks written down.

In the cubicle my hands were shaking so much I could barely get my drugs out of my pocket – that fucking pointy-toed psych-rock leprechaun had got one up on me. Outside the door, I could hear Gillespie's mate goading him: "Goan Boaby. Goan…" And then the singer yelled: "Hey – are ye in The Magic Numbers? Because you're big enough and ugly enough. YE FAT BEARDED CUNT." A crossbow bolt fired straight into my Achilles' heel. Straight into one of my legion of Achilles' heels. The utter calumny of it. I yelled: "What the fuck?" and wrenched the door open just in time to see them running out of the toilets giggling like characters from a shoegaze episode of The Bash Street Kids. Nothing hurts more than being belittled by a short middle aged man wearing jeans, winkle pickers and a waistcoat.

Not long after that when I was living near him in North London, the karmic balance was restored somewhat. He was cycling along the pavement on a pushbike that had been built to look like one of the chopped hogs from *Easy Rider*. Over the road he caught a glimpse of the Sonic Boom T-shirt I was wearing and while momentarily checking it out, cycled lazily into a lamppost and fell off into the road. A bus had to break hard to avoid running him over as he cowered on the tarmac. I started walking down the road in the manner of John Travolta in the opening scene of *Saturday Night Fever* and I had to physically restrain myself from pretending both of my hands were guns and blowing smoke out of their imaginary barrels.

Later in the evening when Bobby Gillespie took to the stage to present Nick Kent with his award, chemicals leaked violently without warning into the unorthodox idea part of my brain. Time seemed to slow to a crawl as I felt the weight of the award I had collected earlier – a dinner plate designed to look like a London 'Blue Plaque' – in my hand. I gripped it like a discus and started to imagine the swing of my arm and the graceful arc of the trophy as it sliced through the air like a speeding porcelain kingfisher of death, straight towards his head. I tried to think of him rapping on 'Blood Money', him dancing to 'Country Girl', the word "syphilis" and his duet with Kate Moss, but within a fraction of a second all I could hear was 'If They Move, Kill 'Em', 'I'm Losing More Than I'll Ever Have' (Andrew Weatherall's white label mix), 'Shoot Speed Kill Light', 'Kowalski', The Orb's remix of 'Higher Than The Sun' – Gillespie! You fucking pointy-toed alt-rock oompa loompa! You've won again!

I left immediately for home. What kind of prick would really rain plates down on Nick and Bobby's parade? Not me. They'd earned the right to dress and stand however they liked; I unfortunately hadn't and would never be offered the chance to. Nick Kent was writing incisively about rock when music journalism was arguably at the height of its impact and importance, when most of the field was still wide open and there was still acres of new ground left to be broken. When everything was still left to be said. When I was still in short trousers. Bobby Gillespie – try as he might – could do nothing to strip the shining lamina off the brilliant stuff he had achieved with the Jesus and Mary Chain and Primal Scream. I became a music journalist in 2003, just in time to witness the liquid age of European innovation slowly solidify into the age of refinement. Through dubstep and grime into stasis.

On my way home from the awards in a black cab, I wound down the window so rain spattered onto my face. I felt the linen of my suit between my finger and thumb as we drove past Christ Church Spitalfields and the Geffrye Museum. I started working out in my head how long it would take me to phase out all of my heavy metal tops and slowly introduce shirts, perhaps even get another suit or two fitted. I knew I had to start dressing for the job. Leave the really old men to dress like rebels. Look like a refined man in the age of refinement. I had to start looking like I meant business before the desperate fighting started. Even if the entire industry only lasted for another four or five years. At least then I'd look good when the ship went down. Not like some frightened middle-aged man wearing a High On Fire T-shirt.

Within These Walls (2010)

The day in question was only different to the days either side of it in one fundamental respect.

My quotidian work life rumbled on. Luke and I were now running the Quietus independently, out of a cramped room in a warehouse space above a clothing sweatshop in Tottenham, North East London; a space that we shared with Tim Burgess of The Charlatans, the group Factory Floor and the musician Kenichi Iwasa. Massive demolition units had moved into the street and were in the process of knocking down the vacant office blocks around us. Our landlady was maintaining the pretence that she was not selling up, that everything was fine, that we should just carry on as normal. Even on the day that workmen accidentally punctured two large holes straight through the wall to our office with heavy machinery, she made out we had nothing to worry about. Maybe she had convinced herself that the owners of this giant development would be just fine with an office full of baleful and twitchy music journalists, the lead singer of the Charlatans, an industrial techno group and an experimental Krautrock musician together with a textile factory supplying Primark all housed in a fucked warehouse right in the centre of their soon to be constructed Ballardian maze of luxury flats for well-to-do folk and buy-to-let bastards blundering into Tottenham Hale for the first time in their lives, but she hadn't convinced us. Yet again I was to be regurgitated to another part of London by the unstoppable peristaltic twitch of gentrification.

There was a grimy and migrainous pulse to existence in Tottenham at that time. The destruction of the rest of the street had got rid of the crack dealers who used to ply their trade outside at night, but things were still definitely getting worse. Brick and concrete dust covered everything. The walls and floor shook constantly as giant machines that looked like a herd of yellow metal brontosauruses tore down reinforced concrete walls next door. The blast of pneumatic drills outside sounded like heavy machine gun fire. The noise was cacophonous and even more brutally oppressive than the Baader Meinhoff bum dungeon assault techno that Luke liked to listen to all day long. The cockroaches, mice and rats that lived elsewhere along the street had now migrated into our building, in preparation for their Alamo. Factory Floor were desperately trying to get their debut album finished and when they were not recording their drummer Gabe sat in the kitchen smoking B&H, shooting rodents with a rifle while attempting to listen to Classic FM over the tumult of collapsing buildings, his flatulent and maudlin dog Vince at his feet.

As normal I caught up with my emails, commissioned some articles and published my features on the Quietus for the day. Then I checked the battered booklet in my bag. There was a meeting in a different part of London that I liked going to. It would be on in an hour. Just enough time to get there comfortably by bus and still get a seat. I was happy that for once the working day was ending before 11pm so I could pack up and leave for AA.

After I stopped drinking in August 2008 I went to Alcoholics Anonymous a lot at first – most days in fact for about half a year. I don't go that often anymore and I haven't done any of the twelve steps but I'd still say the programme was a crucial aid to me quitting.

I guess even before I joined the fellowship I already had an inkling of what AA would be like. I'd seen enough Ken Loach films, endured enough episodes of *Casualty* and watched my fill of *Eastenders*, so I was prepped. Generally speaking, it was as I'd imagined it – a neon strip-lit, magnolia painted room with trestle tables and stackable chairs – usually in churches, village halls or community centres. Careworn people in comfortable clothes, chatting, sipping tea, rolling cigarettes. The 12 commandments and the 12 traditions would be unrolled and hung on the back wall. The yellow card ("Who you see here / What you hear here / When you leave here / LET IT STAY HERE!") would be placed prominently at the front, resting against a small tub for the collection of voluntary subs at the end of the meeting. There would be a literature table full of pamphlets, information sheets and books and a box containing chips, or commemorative engraved metal tokens, for those who had hit a notable anniversary in sobriety – including the most important one: 24 hours. There would always be one or more copies of *The Big Book* there – the text written in 1939 by Bill W, to help alcoholics.

Chapter Three of *The Big Book* says: "Most of us have been unwilling to admit we were real alcoholics. No person likes to think he is mentally different from his fellows. Therefore it is not surprising that our drinking careers have been characterised by countless vain attempts to prove we could drink like other people. The idea that somehow, someday he will control and enjoy his drinking is the great obsession of every abnormal drinker. The persistence of this illusion is astonishing. Many pursue it into the gates of insanity or death."

Insanity and death. Those were two of the things I had an inkling I was going to hear a lot about when I first went into the rooms.

Then there were some other things that didn't surprise me when I did hear about them, but were shocking nonetheless: violent Dads, insane mothers, child abuse, trouble at school, unemployment, prison, the madhouse, fights, regretful sex, unplanned pregnancies, regretful abortions, drunk driving, car accidents, the death of friends, rape, murder, depression, suicide, chronic illness and hospitals. Cradle to the grave drinking.

I had been prepared to pursue the chimera of controlled

drinking right through the gates of death myself. When I gave up I was close to dying and had nearly checked out accidentally once earlier the same year. But I'd made my peace with death. I had come to believe that alcohol was the only thing that made life bearable. And in a lot of ways it was.

There was dirt, horror and disfigurement everywhere I looked. But after one stiff drink I could leave the house; after two drinks the fear started lifting and after the third drink I'd feel like an artist. Or to be more precise, I would see the world through the eyes of an artist. And after five drinks, well, I could take my pick of them. On a good day I felt like Picasso. But there were all kinds of days. Imagine being Gustav Klimt in Hull, the golden light of the low winter sun at 3pm in the afternoon radiating along The Avenues. Imagine being Walter Sickert in Manchester, the violent brown and black smudges radiating from your feet and along canal towpaths. Imagine being Vincent van Gogh in St Helens, the sky ablaze with stars. That is something close to victory, something close to beating death.

They laughed at me and called me a piss artist. And how right they were. I was an aesthete with a broken nose in a stained shirt and inside-out boxer shorts, drinking the world beautiful.

When you drink constantly, you become numb, slipping down into a sub-life, a waking coma. You become a chaotic ghost that exists almost at one step removed from everything else. You float through the film of your own life. You see the sublime in the augury of fried chicken bones and tomato sauce cast upon the upper deck floor of a bus. You can divine a narrative among the finger-drawn doodles on the misted windows. You can feel your destiny in hundreds of individual condensation droplets on the glass turning red, then amber, then green.

Everything that you'd worried about a few hours previously... Where will I get the money from? What if he beats me up? Am I seriously ill? Am I dying? Have I got cancer? What will she say when I finally get home a week late? Will she cry when we eventually go to bed together? Will she pack her things and leave the next day? How near is death? What will it be like? Will I scream and cry? What is it like to die? And now, after some drinks, there is just the sweet sensation of your life passing you by with no struggle and no fuss. The rope slides through your fingers with no friction, just warmth as a balloon rises higher and higher out of sight. I have bottles and bottles and bottles and my phone is out of credit. A Mark Rothko night. A Jackson Pollock night…

This is the eternal holiday of the alcoholic. Once you create as much distance from your everyday life as you naturally have from orange tinted Polaroids of childhood caravan trips or stays in seaside hotels and Super 8 film reels of school sports days, then you start to experience your quotidian life like it's the sun-bleached memory of a happy event. You feel nostalgia and warmth for boring events that are unfolding right in front of you. You feel wistful about experiences that most people would find barbaric or gauche or unremarkable. You experience the epic, the heart-warming and the hilarious in post office and supermarket queues. You develop permanently rose-tinted glasses.

But there's no getting away from it, after a while the strategy starts failing. You start seeing everything through the eyes of Francis Bacon, through the eyes of Edvard Munch, through the eyes of HR Giger… Your vision becomes stained and cracked.

It took me 45 minutes on the bus to get to the church hall where the meeting was. I said hello to a couple of people standing outside smoking before entering.

It is pretty tough stopping drinking but it's not like I want a pat on the back for it.

I see alcoholism as a self-inflicted leisure injury to some extent, disease or not. But going on the wagon is nothing compared to coming to terms with what you are like sober. The trouble with stopping drinking is that the only thing it solves in your life is you being drunk or hungover and ill all the time. When you stop drinking, everything you drank to avoid dealing with is still there, as bad as ever. Mental illness, debt, depression, the impulse to self-harm, the impulse to commit suicide, anxiety, social dysfunction, eating disorders, body dysmorphia, stress, anger, violent rage… I started drinking when I was 13 and was drinking every day by the

time I was 15. I stayed pretty much constantly drunk until I was
37. When I stopped I had no real idea what I would be like.

Alcoholism is debt consolidation for your life. Submit to
alcoholism and your life becomes incredibly simple. Drink
becomes the only thing you care about – and you will end up just
fine with letting all the other stuff slide to the extent that it doesn't
even matter if you die or not. The only real problem with this
arrangement is what happens if you decide to stop.

Picture a reservoir surrounded by mountains. You have
been tasked with draining the massive body of water away to
repopulate the area. But once the water has gone you are faced
with the former town that was initially flooded and the now
wrecked buildings which need to be pulled down. Call several
construction firms. People have been fly tipping here for years.
There is tons of rubbish here. You will need help to clean the
area up. There are corpses wrapped in carpet and chains. It was
the ideal place to dump bodies. You'll need to call the police and
the coroner's office. The press are on their way. There are rotten
and half eaten animal carcasses that need to be cleared up and
disposed of. Environmental health need to be involved. You have
never seen so many mangled shopping trollies, broken children's
bikes and unwanted cars. The clearance job will be massive. There
are burst canisters of toxic waste that have long since leached
into the ground. It will be years before you can do anything with
this land. The water was merely the stuff that was making this
area look picturesque. What you have left in its place is an area of
outstanding natural horror. It probably feels like you should have
left well enough alone.

Before claiming a seat by putting my coat on the back of it,
and even before queuing up for a brew, I went into the gents to try
and freshen up – to wash some of the construction site dust off
me. I scrubbed my hands hard and splashed freezing cold water
onto my face – prodding the dark purple streaks of flesh under
each eye with a fingertip. I stood for some time looking into the
mirror as the water dripped off my face.

What did I look like? A middle-aged man with long hair in a

heavy metal T-shirt. The beard of someone who slept behind a hedge on an A-road roundabout. Face permanently blotched red down one side with hundreds of burst capillaries after spending three days awake doing amphetamines in 1996. A Monday night which culminated in nurses shouting: "Shave his chest, shave his chest!" A nose broken 17 times and eventually surgically rebuilt. Forehead like the cover of *Unknown Pleasures*. Right eyelid drooping down over a partially sighted eye, scarred and damaged beyond repair.

Before I started writing on the internet it was possible to delude myself that I looked a little bit like a chunkier Thurston Moore with stubble after a heavy night out, but since entering the coliseum this luxury has been hacked to pieces completely by strangers who are able to share their opinions on my looks freely. Here is a selection of the things I was called by readers of my site in 2010: "Romeo from The Magic Numbers" (actually a fine-looking man in my book), "Hagrid", "Ted Kaczynski", a "syphilitic mutant who is creating hordes of lesbians with his terrifying looks", a "fat mutant who should be put in a cage", "beardy troll", "fucking Tollund Man", "long haired heavy metal retard", "potbellied, middle-England, ITV1, bearded ponce", "hideously ugly, midlife crisis suffering, hormonally imbalanced, Iron Maiden fan, extra from *Lord Of The Rings*" and, worst of all, "Justin Lee Collins". Most of the time it was water off a duck's back, but if someone put some real effort into it and caught me unawares on a bad day, it could be temporarily quite upsetting. And once I started doing TV and documentary work, the game was over. I simply couldn't escape from the fact that I looked like a partially domesticated long-haired sloth with galloping obesity, crammed into an Anaal Nathrakh T-shirt and performing simple tricks for plantain, cheese toasties and Haribo.

George Orwell said we all get the kind of face we deserve by the time we turn 40. I had mine hammered irreversibly into place by my 25th birthday. Ostensibly I looked like the same person, but somehow as if reflected in the back of a rusty soup spoon instead of a mirror. I had become used to what I looked like. Or rather the part of my brain that was supposed to care about these things had hyper-atrophied into petrified uselessness. I was, after all, middle-aged – the point at which you're supposed to stop giving a fuck entirely about what you look like and just settle for being content at still being alive.

I queued for tea and was delighted to find that the evening's comestibles included a slice of Old Jamaica Ginger Cake and Fig Rolls – a truly delightful combination, I'm sure you'll agree. The man on tea service picked up a light blue mug. I stopped him "I'm really sorry about this… I know it sounds stupid but I can't drink out of blue mugs. Can I have a white mug please?"

Half of the pleasure of drinking tea comes from the ritual and the aesthetic of the exercise – the taste of the drink itself being close to ephemeral. The excellence of a brew can only be plotted on a tightly formed bell curve not on a linear graph, meaning that the things that separate a fantastic cup of tea from an atrocity are very subtle. Blue and black mugs discolour the liquid by means of contrast, making the drink seem weaker, more watery and milkier, whereas the white mug provides the perfect background for a well mashed drink.

The man smiled in a kindly way, "No one knows how they like their tea like an alcoholic does. No problem."

When he poured my mug from a dented metal urn it was perfect and a thimbleful of milk revealed its true mahogany glory. I took a seat toward the back of the room.

I was comfortable with going to AA now that I'd been going for nearly two years but still, the back of the room suited me just fine – it's not a Kate Bush concert, you're not missing anything if you don't sit in the front row.

Comfort was not on the agenda the first time I went to AA however. My first visit to the rooms might as well have been my first day at senior school, or my first day in prison, for all the stress it caused me. I went while visiting friends up north and it was terrifying. A bare concrete room with old school chairs, bare lightbulbs and spiders in the corners. A retirement age man with a nose like a red, purple and blue blood sac Mumbled brutal things as other broken people looked at their feet. When I stepped outside into the freezing cold night after the 60 minutes were up I had to sit on a garden wall for ten minutes, staring at the ground under an orange sodium light. I was unable to stand properly because of anxiety and I was still dizzy with fear walking away afterwards. It struck me quite clearly that there might not even be any point to giving up drinking, that it could even make things worse in some ways.

It's bad form to talk about the meetings or AA at all. Tradition 11 says: "Our public relations policy is based on attraction rather than promotion; we need always maintain personal anonymity at the level of press, radio and films." I'd like to apologise for speaking about AA here, even if it is just in very general terms. I would never repeat what anyone else said there; I never talk there myself, I just sit and listen. I wait for the reassurance of identification and nothing else.

"I was like that once. I was that bad. I never want to go back to that again."

My first trip to an AA meeting in London was with my thirsty friend Jeremy. On and off we had drunk together in a very serious manner for about five years before he went and did the unthinkable and quit. I love Jeremy. He is my brother. If he hadn't stopped first I doubt I would have done. I didn't even think it was possible. When I told Maria that I would stop I looked to Jeremy who had quit 12 months before me and I knew that it was possible. It was like he said on his second year of sobriety: "I love not drinking. I wake up and my first thought isn't that I want to cut my throat any more. And some mornings, maybe even most mornings, I'm happy to be alive."

When I decided to stop drinking I knew that on top of AA I would need someone who lived near me who didn't drink, and who I could talk to – Jeremy was that person. The vast majority of people – no matter how sympathetic – simply didn't understand what I was talking about as a recovering alcoholic. I needed the ear of a recuperating thirsty bastard to chew. It was an absolute necessity.

We spent a lot of time together after I gave up drinking; a lot of that time was enjoyable but not all of what we got up to was particularly healthy or wise. Despite him helping me through my difficult first year of sobriety, I repaid the favour by nearly killing him. When I first stopped drinking in 2008, I carried on taking illegal drugs and, despite easing my passage into sobriety, this behaviour is something that I now have mixed feelings about, as bit by bit I transferred my obsession with alcohol onto narcotics. Occasional binges on MDMA, cocaine and ketamine were no longer hitting the spot for me as a sober person, so I started getting into legal highs. As soon as I tried mephedrone, a grainy amphetamine with darkly psychedelic overtones known as plant food which was satisfyingly painful to snort but smelled like a charnel house, I knew that I had a new hobby and I encouraged everyone I knew to take it up, Jeremy included.

I went through pillowcases of the stuff, taking it during the day at work and in the evening at gigs and house parties. I smelled like someone who worked in a chemicals plant and every time I took my hands out of my pockets, a synthetic, glittering snow shower of crystals would float to the ground.

And once you're at the front of the queue for a new drug – not even leaving it for a year or two to let word filter back down about what the pitfalls are – you'll rush headlong into everything. 2cb. Benzo Fury. Champhetamine. Naphyrone. BZP. GBL. Just stop talking and pass the fucking baggy here.

And it was during my brief thirst for this crap that Jeremy nearly died.

There are plenty of reasons why I shouldn't tell anyone about this, not least because Jeremy is a writer himself and if you tell another writer's story you might as well punch them square in the face. But mainly because I'm simply not a good enough writer to do that terrible fortnight in 2010 any justice.

I don't even deserve to call myself a writer. Well, not according to Graham Greene anyway. In his quite bracingly charmless 1971 autobiography, *A Sort Of Life,* he recalls recuperating from appendicitis on a hospital ward, when he got the chance to observe several deaths at close quarters. One of the unfortunate souls was a ten-year-old boy who was admitted because of a broken leg but who later died unexpectedly because of complications.

Greene threw more relish into recalling this incident than a Bond villain explaining his plan for world domination, making his point effectively if nothing else:

"... to shut out the sound of the mother's tears and cries all my companions in the ward lay with their earphones on, listening – there was nothing else for them to hear – to *Children's Hour*. All my companions but not myself. There is a splinter of ice in the heart of a writer. I watched and listened. This was something one day that I might need: the woman speaking, uttering the banalities she must have remembered from some woman's magazine, a genuine grief that could communicate only in clichés."

After about three months of sobriety, Maria eventually took me back, and when my sister Catherine and her husband Paul emigrated, Jeremy and another friend, Leo moved into our shared house. And it was while I lived with Jeremy he nearly died three times in one week after falling off the wagon – something that was no doubt precipitated by the fact we were taking massive amounts of untried and untested experimental amphetamines round the clock until he had a psychotic episode. The second and third incidents were fucking savage and happened in the actual house. I don't want to state the obvious but you really don't want to live in a house where someone you care about dies unnecessarily in unpleasant circumstances. It isn't very nice. Getting him sectioned wasn't particularly nice or easy either but in this case was the only option available to me. Completely unbalanced after reacting badly to a mail order pill and still patently determined to kill himself – to join the majority a good four or five decades early – I knew he wouldn't survive the inevitable fourth fall.

Once the wheels were in motion he ended up in the evaluation wards of the secure psychiatric unit of Homerton Hospital within the day. It's actually quite difficult to get someone sectioned and I had to argue with the assessors until I was blue in the face to get them to agree to keep him for a period longer than 24 hours.

Thankfully they settled on a trial period of four days – much to Jeremy's chagrin when he was sober enough to realise what was going on. The stay was then extended to a week and they finally reassured me that, should they need to, they could keep him in for a much longer stay.

The day after he was admitted, I went back to visit him on the ward. At first it was quite upsetting. If I had a splinter of ice in my heart, I was having trouble locating it. He didn't seem to have hit his bottom yet. He was furious with me for letting him get locked up, potentially indefinitely, when he had believed he was only going in for overnight observation. He wouldn't stop going on about getting out in time to watch a football match down the Hospital Arms pub. "I've decided, it's OK", he said. "I'm just going to start drinking again when I get out. Take it slower. Maybe take less drugs as well but it's going to be OK. I've decided it's going to be OK."

He walked off to have a cigarette in the smoking room.

"Don't drink the water," whispered an androgynous youth near the water cooler. "They put heroin in it."

A shaved and drooling manatee in hospital robes shuffled past, slack mouthed and seemingly unencumbered by any comprehension of where he was. I could feel my lower lip wobbling and my eyes brimming.

After a few more hours of having the same angry conversation with Jeremy that I'd been having with him all week I started getting ready to leave and said to him: "You know. When you get out of here and start drinking, you'll die before the end of the year because you've got nowhere left to go. There's nothing below mental hospital in this scenario, just the morgue. And when you die, I'll steal your story and write it. And the women... the women will throw themselves at me because of the power of my story – except of course it's your story. And you will not be able to enjoy having all these women throw themselves at you because you will be dead... You will be dead and unable to enjoy the company of women. Or you can stop drinking and taking drugs, get well, get out of here and write the story yourself. And the women… the women will be yours. The choice is yours. If you die I'll steal your story. I really will."

By the end of the week it felt like he was about to turn a corner. He'd stopped talking about going to the pub as soon as he got out and had started entertaining the idea of going back to AA.

On my last visit, we were chatting casually until it was time for the football to start and then we went and sat in the communal TV area with its suspiciously stained sofas and large, cheap wall-mounted flat screen behind a scratched, bolted-in-place sheet of Plexiglass.

The match pre-amble seemed to last for ages and then the cameras switched from the studio to the pitch as the teams filed out. At first I couldn't place the song they were playing in the stadium as the teams lined up facing one another. It was some sort of trance-y UK hip hop thing: "I wake up every day it's a daydream. Everything in my life ain't what it seems."

It was a few more seconds before I realised it was Dizzee Rascal: "Some people think I'm bonkers but I just think I'm free. And I'm just living my life. There's nothing crazy about me."

Unable to stop myself I started giggling. I looked round the room but it seemed like everyone else was too doped up to realise what was going on. I started laughing nervously and nudged Jeremy: "Bonkers!" He clicked what song it was and started singing along to it: "Bonk-bonk-bonk-bonk-bonk-bonk-bonkers!"

And we sat there laughing. And for the first time in weeks a weight like an anvil lifted from my shoulders and I allowed myself to believe that there was a chance that things might start improving slightly.

He did go back to AA again; this time successfully. He has, of yet, not written his book, but I have a feeling he will do.

Back at the AA meeting I took a seat with my perfect cup of tea, slice of cake and biscuit; and not long afterwards Jeremy came in and sat next to me. And then, after the meeting we went to a cafe nearby.

This day that I've described may sound dour or slightly

depressing to you but to me it wasn't – it crackled with possibility. I was alive and for the first time ever I didn't resent being in that position. After two years of sobriety, life was starting to offer up opportunities that I had discounted as impossible decades earlier. Today was different to the other days that surrounded it in one fundamental respect.

I told him: "Maria and I were talking about it this morning. We've decided to try for a child."

Going Underground (2010)

I'd never given any serious thought to me becoming a Dad. What would have been the point? Obviously some people who drink a lot bring up kids – I'm not interested in pointing fingers – but it wasn't something I intended to do. So the thought had never crossed my mind.

My sister used to tease my mother: "He's never going to give you grandchildren – look at him." My poor sainted mother and the infernal stress I've caused her. When I rang her out of the blue to say that Maria was expecting, I initially thought she'd had a heart attack when she dropped the phone. "On top of everything else I've even killed her now... I hope she was happy for the split second before she passed", I thought. She was so overwhelmed she couldn't speak. I had to promise my Dad I'd call her back 24 hours later when she might be more calm. But then who can blame her? The news was so unexpected.

When Maria told me she was pregnant, we were just leaving the house to drive to Green Man, the music festival in Wales. Maria – as she often did – was driving the van full of snappers, journalists and, if memory serves correctly, a professional hula hoop dancer whose unenviable job was to try and make Four Tet's DJ set seem more exciting. The idea that I was going to become a Dad didn't really set into concrete on the long trip to the Brecon

Beacons. I felt very serene, like I'd just taken a diazepam. We pitched our tent and then after a bit of work – DJing and radio stuff for me, photography for everyone else who wasn't a writer or a hula hoop dancer – I turned in. Maria fell asleep quite quickly with her head on my chest. I tuned in to the sounds of the festival. I could hear music coming from about six different sources – one late stage still playing middle class rave, some dub rolling in from a serious sound system elsewhere on the campsite, a nearby transistor playing pop, some idiots with acoustic guitars. These sound banks drifted in and out of clarity on the wind, punctuated by fireworks, shrieks, laughs, conversations whispered nearby and shouted far away. Everything that would normally have irritated me to distraction just washed over me. I just enjoyed feeling the dimensionality of the noise all around me.

When I woke the next day Maria had already left to take shots of the campsites and festival ground while it was still relatively quiet. My neighbours were stirring and by the sound of it, had a Trangia going and were using it to fry something – bacon and eggs judging by the smell.

A female voice – as clear and strong as a rung bell started singing the Ce-Lo Green song that was at number one in the charts: "Maybe I'm crazy/ Maybe you're crazy/ Maybe we're crazy/ Probably." Little by little, other voices joined in providing harmonies, ad-libbing, vamping. My curiosity got the better of me so I peered through the tent opening and there was Charlotte Church and ten of her mates sat round in deckchairs right outside my tent singing over their breakfast fry-up and champagne.

I lay back down laughing to myself as I listened to them in a daze for another half an hour.

There was nothing crazy about Maria's pregnancy thankfully. It just seemed like the most normal and natural thing that had ever happened. Which is easy for me to say, I guess. We moved out of the room we had in a shared house and into a small flat in Stamford Hill when she was eight months pregnant and while that was unavoidably very stressful, everything else couldn't have gone more smoothly.

Again, if I'm ever tempted to think of myself as unlucky I just have to remind myself of Maria's pregnancy and labour to know that when it really counts, I'm about as lucky as they come.

I went to antenatal classes at University College Hospital. During the second class there were a few other men present but it soon became clear that one of them was blind drunk. He was cracking nonsensical jokes, slurring wildly. The heavily pregnant woman who was with him, who was also drunk, was the only person laughing.

"For fuck's sake!" I raged to myself. "Not only are we in a hospital for fucking antenatal class but it's only..."

Ten thirty in the morning.

He was blind drunk and it was ten thirty in the morning. Because who would do that right? What kind of utterly debased wanker is drunk at this time of the morning? I was hit by equal amounts rage and shame and stared intently at my feet until the session was over.

I think I acquitted myself well as the birth partner of a pregnant woman but it's not for me to say, you'd have to ask Maria. I certainly put in the overtime trying my hardest to prevent unnecessary lifting, building, running, bicycle riding, mountain climbing, acrobatics and base jumping by Maria who doesn't really cope amazingly well with being told what to do – especially by me.

At one point during the pregnancy Maria's mother asked me to stop her from doing so much. I told her that, with the greatest will in the world, she might as well ask me to somersault over the block of flats we lived in. I told her: "You're lucky to have such a strong willed daughter. You have to trust she knows her own body and what she's doing. But she's certainly not going to stop being so active on my account." If anything, all of this physical exercise during pregnancy probably helped her to have a fairly straightforward labour.

I do have one piece of advice for you, if you're reading this though and you or your partner is heavily pregnant: Don't rent the DVD of Gaspar Noé's *Enter The Void*. Still, four years later, I have no idea what I was thinking that night. I'm saving *Eraserhead* for if we go for a second child.

The labour lasted for almost exactly 12 hours and went without complication. Some people say that childbirth is beautiful; others think of it as horrific. I lean completely to the former but it isn't the primary word that I would choose to describe it. Lots of things in life are beautiful but they don't really affect you fundamentally one way or the other. I think that childbirth is the most organically psychedelic thing that I have ever been witness to. It ruptures your life and before it heals again, it allows you to momentarily see things afresh. As though it were you being born and not the child.

When Little John finally arrived, I was grateful to Maria for gripping onto my forearms with such force that I could still see the outlines of her hands some four days later, because it kept me in the room, such was the sense of unreality to me. The iPod playlist we'd made a fortnight beforehand arrived at Mogwai's 'The Sun Smells Too Loud' and I heard my son cry for the first time.

When I was given John James Atticus Doran to hold – a tiny bundle, who looked uncannily like a cross between a squirrel and Mark E Smith – I realised the answer to the question I'd been asking myself for the previous two and a half years: why had I finally managed to stop drinking? It was because I needed to get ready for John's arrival.

(If you're Irish or American you probably won't bat an eyelid at the fact that my son is called John Doran – this is my Dad's name and his Dad's name as well, with the line going back to the 19th Century; not only that but my Mum's Dad was called John and so is my father-in-law. However when you try explaining this to people in London, they mainly look at you like you've called your firstborn Spatula Flange Skywalker.)

After another four hours, Maria's Mum and Dad arrived up from Kent so I took the opportunity to go and get something to eat. I walked up Tottenham Court Road, past some pubs I used to drink in during the 90s. I could still feel the tractor beam pulling at my feet as I went past. The clamour of internal voices was still there. They demanded that I go in for a celebratory pint but finally sounded querulous and unsure.

"Just fuck off eh?" I snapped angrily at The Northumberland Arms much to the surprise of a man walking past me, who turned on his heel and jogged off rapidly.

I carried on for a couple of blocks and treated myself to the biggest pizza I could find. I ate it as quickly as I could and went back to the hospital to see what I could do.

I've always been a socialist but it was easy when I was a drunk because my need for people to do things for me far outstripped my ability to do things for them in return. The balance shifted in the right direction after I stopped drinking, although in some cases I still had to learn what I had an aptitude for as an adult. But if my baby was to receive according to its needs then I would have to work hard in other ways that I had never contemplated before. I would have to work hard to establish what my abilities actually were.

If I had to list what fatherhood gave to me in the first few years, I guess I would say the following: It brought me pure unadulterated joy. It also brought me a mix of euphoria and near hysteria brought on by lack of sleep. It brought me a short-term level of tiredness which reduced me to a state of near imbecility. I would say that becoming a father also stopped me from being afraid of dying, almost overnight.

It was something close to torture to be separated from John for any length of time during his first few years but occasionally I'd have to go on trips to festivals and conferences abroad to work.

After returning from one such trip when John was two years old, I noticed that an interloper had moved onto my turf. He was much slimmer than me and younger as well. It looked like I was being replaced by a younger model. Literally.

He was called Cardboard Daddy. His torso was a stiff, white A2 sized oblong of card, with lanky limbs made from folded out then trimmed and glued together cereal packets, plain sides out. His head was the kind of off-white paper plate with crimped edges that gets used at children's parties. He had round, blue, full fat milk carton lids instead of eyes and strands of shoulder length blue wool as hair. He had a smirk drawn onto his face and the SunnO))) logo on his chest. He was sitting in my seat, wearing my headphones, plugged into my stereo, with my favourite mug at his side and my copy of *Private Eye* open on his lap.

Maria had made him for Little John; to fill my role while I was out of the house. Now I would argue that I actually did a lot more than simply sitting in the corner listening to music that no one else wanted to hear, drinking tea, reading magazines and wearing SunnO))) merch but I had come to learn in life that perceptions count for an awful lot.

So each time I returned from a work trip, Cardboard Daddy would be folded up and put on a shelf in the small utility cupboard with the vacuum cleaner and the tools. But then after a while something disturbing happened. I got home from a day's work at our new office in Kings Cross and saw that Cardboard Daddy was out again and sitting in my chair, reading the copy of the *London Review Of Books* which I had bought but hadn't even had time to put a crease in myself.

"And so it begins", I thought. "You get in from work knackered and all you want to do is to sit down, have a brew, listen to Bolt Thrower and read the *LRB* but you can't because some sexy cardboard cuckoo bastard is sat in your chair."

And then Maria dropped the bombshell: "Little John wanted to see Cardboard Daddy so we got him out."

How can it be that I was being replaced as a father figure already? And by someone made from cereal packets?

When I became a parent, all kinds of novel ideas about influence came into play.

Would I be able to influence my son in a positive way? Would I know when it was time to let him make his own mistakes? What kind of position of authority could I talk from given various incontrovertible biographical facts about my own life – especially those concerning drink and drugs? How would I influence him on certain important issues more than his peer group? When my duty to influence him positively on certain matters came into direct conflict with me getting on with him as a friend, would I have the mettle to do the right thing? At what point did parental influence start having a negative effect?

To be honest, I felt that all children were so markedly different from each other that there wasn't a neat way to answer any of these questions ahead of time. The only planning I could do was to keep on reminding myself to be pragmatic; to respond to difficulties and challenges in a positive manner as they arose and not get locked into any pre-determined proscriptive or authoritarian course of action that I felt I had to stick to no matter what. Through most of my childhood and teenage years my own father had warned me, in graphic terms – literally on a daily basis – about the horrors of alcoholism and drug abuse. Of course, it wasn't his fault at all I became an alcoholic with several drug habits but his determined, crusading plan to steer me safely away from these things served absolutely no positive purpose at all.

What I hadn't considered, as the parent of a two-year-old, was that I would have to think seriously about those things right away. I had been living in a fool's paradise where I imagined my child, who was of course an angel, would not give me any kind of serious grief until the age of 14, and before then would simply look up in awe to me as this amazing font of wisdom. However, if I have learned one thing, it is that children are so much sharper than nearly anyone gives them any credit for.

It came as a shock when I was larking about in an attempt to make him laugh one day when he put up a hand to halt me and shouted: "Mummy! Stop!"

(He has never called me Daddy. He calls me Mummy and then when I protest he half-heartedly calls me Mumdy instead.)

"Mummy stop dancing!"

"Daddy you mean…"

"Mumdy – stop dancing. You are a very silly man."

So much for me being an unquestionable authority figure to him until the eve of his 15th birthday.

Good for him though, I thought. I didn't want to influence him for the sake of it, there's no point. People are always asking me what music I'm getting him into – no doubt keen to hear that he has a very youthful penchant for Norwegian black metal or dystopian techno, but I've got no interest in that to be honest. I don't want him to grow up to be a music obsessive, I want him to be happy instead. If I try to force him to listen to the Ganja Kru and Coil he will no doubt rebel by developing a love for Coldplay in his teenage years anyway.

Perhaps this attitude seems odd, coming from a music writer. I don't know. In this field it can sometimes be hard to see the line that divides the desire to promote music and the desire to manipulate/shape the environment it exists in – and doubtless some would even argue that this distinction doesn't exist. Even by simply observing the music making process, you already affect this act of cultural production in a very subtle way, so to actively seek involvement, to covet co-authorship, to claim ownership, to mercilessly hype and to attempt to manipulate listeners is to become too violently involved in proceedings and too likely to alter the creative process – usually in a negative way. I have very strong ideas about what I think makes for good music but it's important to say that I know these ideas are not universal truths and that I do not think other people, who have different tastes and approaches to me are wrong (unless they like The Libertines). Some people reading this will find the idea that I'm not interested in influencing the direction and the impact of the art form I'm primarily concerned with, risible. Surely I must want everyone to feel the same way as me? But the truth is, I don't. I gave up this unhealthy belief a long time ago and as soon as I did my professional life became a lot simpler and (vaguely) more relaxed. Manipulative behaviour is a hallmark of the chronic but high functioning alcoholic. It is the main thing that stops them from ending up friendless, jobless and homeless. I have come to fully understand that 'Pipes' by Katie Gately is never going to be playlisted on Radio One. And I fully appreciate why as well. This doesn't denigrate it as a piece of art in any way.

It is a healthy way to be because, on the very odd occasion anyone tells me that they have listened to something because of my recommendation it always comes as a pleasant surprise.

Why would anyone listen to a music journalist in the first place? I find it extremely puzzling. They all have such fucking appalling taste in music – me especially. If ever there is an entire profession populated exclusively by people who were bullied at school for their awful taste in music and are now engaged in an unsatisfying project to get their revenge on life, it is music journalism.

I've never, ever seen anyone on the tube or the bus reading a magazine or a newspaper article that I have written. I know that water coolers up and down the land are not surrounded by people discussing my articles on Electro Chaabi, Stara Rzeka or Frisk Frugt. It is best to simply write the stuff and be glad it is expunged from my head. I am happy to let someone else worry about what happens next.

This is not to say that I never influence people at all. It is just that it happens in ways that can't be predicted. Just after John was born a new green grocers opened in Hackney and blown away by their reasonable prices and excellent high quality selection, I tweeted effusively about the establishment. The next day I returned to the shop and it appeared to be full of people in Mayhem and Godflesh T-shirts. One guy in an Electric Wizard T-shirt and a giant beard came stumbling out of the door holding a bag of satsumas and said: "Jesus Christ mate, the fruit in there is excellent."

But I was shocked the night I got in from work, a few days after my foreign business trip, and found Cardboard Daddy sitting in my chair, entertaining both my girlfriend and my son. I couldn't be 100% sure but I thought Maria had just been laughing at some amusing bon mot the flat, blue-haired fucker had just made.

"Don't worry, I'll sit over here", I said pointing to where I never sat.

They appeared to be pretending that Cardboard Daddy was tired or ill and they were tucking him in, under a Thomas The Tank Engine blanket. Making a right fuss of him.

And then, as if things weren't already bad enough, I heard Little John say: "I love you Cardboard Daddy!"

Maria let out an involuntary gasp. I heard her whispering to Little John, "I think you should go and tell Real Daddy that you love him as well or he might get upset."

Little John walked over to me and said, "Mummy…"

"Daddy, you mean…"

He started again, "Mumdy… I love Cardboard Daddy."

He walked back over to the slim line intruder and I heard Maria entreat him, "No! I think you should tell Real Daddy that you love him otherwise he might start crying."

Little John walked over to me giggling and said, "Mumdy. I love… THOMAS THE TANK ENGINE!"

I kept my composure in a stoic manner, ruffled his hair and said, "I know you do mate."

Then Maria and him disappeared out of the room to deal with some imaginary disaster on the Island Of Sodor.

My son is a great child and I love him deeply – more than anything else in life. I can already tell that he won't suffer fools gladly when he is older – his old man included. And even if this means that sometimes my life won't be made any easier, my heart is already reassured that he will never be a follower and will always think for himself.

The warm feeling I had evaporated instantaneously when I saw Cardboard Daddy sitting in my chair with a blanket over him, smirking at me.

I pointed out of the window: "Have you ever seen what the rain does to a cardboard man? Now that is something you should see…"

Maria poked her head round the door. "Did you say something Daddy?" she asked.

"No! Just clearing my throat…" I said.

Maria came in and picked up Cardboard Daddy and carried him out of the room, I could see his grinning head over her shoulder as she carried him into the bedroom where he now lived on top of the bookcase. When did he get moved into the bedroom? Why hadn't I noticed?

"Don't get comfortable Cardboard Daddy", I hissed after

they left. "I've got moves you haven't seen yet, you insufferable bendy shit heel. I'm not going to stop until you're in the recycling and the balance of power has been restored."

The following day John started coming down with some kind of cold. Having a third human being in close proximity at all times had a noticeable effect on illness levels in the flat at first but these skyrocketed the day he started at nursery. On that fateful day, John essentially became a viral go-between; a courier of toxic gifts to us; a deliverer of presents from a potent chemical warfare lab. What normally happened was this: he would pick up a bug going round nursery and get ill for about eight hours; then Maria would get ill with the same thing for two days; then I'd contract it and feel like I was dying for three weeks.

He became a bit agitated in the evening when it was time for him to go to sleep and the only way I could get him to lie down in his cot was to give him one of my hands to hold onto so he could put it under his head like a pillow, leaving me to stroke his back with my free hand. This made me feel good as it was obvious he wanted me there even when he was asleep, even if it was not too good for my back. On one of these occasions he was coughing and making strange little exclamations so I thought I would tell him a story. Whisper it until he drifted off. I didn't really know any kids' stories so I just used to tell him about different heavy metal bands. In this instance I decided to tell him about the time I went to Slovenia with Bullet For My Valentine.

The job was for *Metal Hammer* and it was to cover the filming of a video shoot in the 13-mile long Postojna Karst cave system in Notranjska. It was thought to be the second largest cave system in the country; and was definitely the most extensive one that was accessible by members of the public.

Like a lot of things in Slovenia, the entrance to the cave was naturally ostentatious and surreal, looking as if it had been created for a very expensive Hollywood action movie. In bold, large lettering, the phrase 'Immensum Ad Antrum Aditus!' had been chiselled into the rock above the maw. 'Enter Traveller Into This Immensity!'

I started whispering to Little John: "The Slovenian Minister For Caves met us! He was a funny fellow and obviously as drunk as a lord but he wouldn't share his bottle of whiskey with Daddy. The caves were so big that to get where we were going we had to take an underground train. The train looked like Thomas The Tank Engine! The minister looked at the way we were dressed and said: 'You British idiots! You come to Slovenia to go five miles underground where it is below zero, and you wear Iron Maiden T-shirts…' He insisted on driving the train standing up and singing in Slovenian. He drove it far too fast and screamed, 'Duck!' when we were about to go under a low roof. And at one point he shouted: 'Many people have had their heads bashed here! HA HA HA!' We passed through a cathedral-like domed chamber that had an antique chandelier hanging from the natural ceiling by a very long chain. Orchestras played concerts in there, sometimes to 10,000 people."

Bullet For My Valentine were there to shoot a video under a domed roof of stalactites. It was a great time to travel with a band when they were just starting to go abroad. Not because of any bullshit rock & roll mythology but because the enthusiasm and excitement could be overwhelming and infectious. Two of the band had Dads who were coal miners back in Wales, they owned and ran an independent co-operative pit. They said their Dads were really made up at the opportunities that being in the band was giving them. Very nice lads. I played a lame trick on Moose, the drummer. I said that every time he hit his snare, the giant 30ft long stalactite above his head was wobbling slightly. If you watch the video now you can just about make him out glancing nervously upwards while hitting his kit.

But while they were going through the time-consuming process of constructing a stage, assembling the instruments and putting cameras on dolly rails, one of the minister's men offered to take me and the press officer Matt on a two-hour walking tour.

My son had stopped gabbling but he still had tight hold of my hand: "We walked through passage after passage, and after a while our eyes started playing tricks on us. When you see nothing but stalactites and stalagmites for half an hour, they start to look fantastical as your depth perception falters. There were rocks that looked like angels, and stalactites that looked like totem poles with faces and even some translucent natural screens that looked like rashers of bacon hanging from the ceiling. And then we came across a pool where the baby dragons were."

The caves are home to a completely local breed of trogloditic salamander called *Proteus anguinus*, or the Human Fish. Their name came from their soft, baby-like skin, which was translucent but looked pink because of the visible blood circulation. Not only were they completely blind but their faces were entirely smooth, with their eyes, useless and atavistic, completely bred out of existence.

According to the 17th Century chronicler Valvasor, Slovenian people hundreds of years earlier had always been too afraid to explore these caves because they believed the salamanders were baby dragons, whose mother was just round the corner no doubt, and ready to create merry havoc with the human nest invaders.

I lowered my voice: "These creatures were so beautiful. About six inches long, a bit more pink than you and swimming round gracefully. It was so strange. They all looked freshly born, but some of them could have been over a century old. They couldn't see us but they knew we were there. We walked on so as to not disturb them. When we got to the deepest part we could reach, where the caverns' lighting system stopped, our guide told us to make ourselves comfortable and said, 'I'm going to turn off the lights.' And the blackness was total but it wasn't horrible, it was comforting, like floating in space."

In the dark, the ten minutes stretched out to an eternity. The blackness seeped into my skull switching off internal thought loops one by one. The background static and chatter of my brain subsided to absolutely nothing. I felt very happy. I know the experience had a profound effect on Matt as well. He went back on his own to visit again afterwards, and I would love to return if given the opportunity.

My son's hands are unbelievably smooth. Silk is too coarse

a comparison. I hoped my hands didn't feel too strange to him. I was fascinated with my Dad's hands when I was very young, they were hard and rough like breeze blocks, calloused, with raised ridges of scar tissue from numerous minor factory injuries, and his hectic splinter self-removal procedure, which he took grim enjoyment in. On top of this they were constantly stained brown with varnish and ochre with pipe tobacco. It was like holding the hand of a giant, brutally unfinished statue. He turned 80 recently. His hands are softer now but still nowhere near as delicate as my pampered media mits.

I wondered if I would be there when it happened. I really hoped it wouldn't be for some time yet and I really hoped I was. Sitting next to the bed. Holding his hand on top of starched white sheets. If I could talk him out... If I could just do that one thing for him. Keep him company. Take his mind off it. I wouldn't say anything important. I didn't know if there was anything important to say. Maybe I could tell him about my trip to Slovenia. Not about Bullet For My Valentine but the nearby Predjama Castle, which was literally built half way up a cliff face. The castle proved an impenetrable fortress for local robber baron and Robin Hood type, Erazem Lueger, in the 15th Century which was good because it was where he was surrounded for months by Austrian troops. They couldn't get into the castle and neither could they find the secret tunnel that led out down through the cliffs and into the caves. Erazem came and went freely despite the army blockade. He would stand on his balcony and shower the troops below with fresh cherries every day to show his disdain for them.

Unfortunately the bastards eventually got him. They fired a cannonball at the castle wall and despite the colossal odds, it hit him as he was sat on the toilet. I saw the castle at sundown and thousands of bats flew out of the windows, apparently a nightly occurrence.

The entire area was littered with the uncanny. We saw a functional jousting strip and a centuries old piece of wooden siege machinery, just rotting in a field. I would tell him about the underground train and the stalactites and tell him about how peaceful it was there. And then someone would eventually say, 'It's done. He's gone.'

My son's hand finally loosened its grip and his breathing became more shallow and smooth. I waited for five minutes to check he was asleep before tip-toeing out of the room.

It's up to us to shape stories out of the chaos. I have to impose a narrative, to make some kind of sense out of it. We have to end up in the deep perfection of the low dark. Still and at peace – that is a good place to end the story.

On the plane on the way home to London after the job, I got really angry with an idiot from the Bullet For My Valentine's record label. He'd picked up one of the salamanders and put it in his pocket. It was dead before we even got to the airport but I guess he wanted it as some kind of souvenir. To get it on the plane he forced it through the slightly too small aperture of a can of Coke he was carrying. And that's where it was left, snapped and split, inside crushed metal packaging, discarded by someone who was already bored with it, left on the floor of an Easy Jet Airbus 319 en route to Stansted.

Cameras Ready Prepare To Flash (2011)

A couple of months after I stopped drinking – after I was properly detoxed – I remember thinking that in the short term I was going to allow myself as much Coca-Cola as I wanted. I decided that there were going to be no immediate limits on cake, chocolate, donuts, toffee and whatever other sweet things I desired. The trouble was, I didn't put any time frame on this indulgence, and what was supposed to be a temporary treat became a way of life. And things got much worse after I became a dad. The energy I needed for fatherhood – getting up at odd hours, staying up all night doing my writing work when everyone else was asleep – I got from the most ridiculous of sources. I didn't even have a sweet tooth when I was drinking but by the time Little John was ten months old I often 'accidentally' left a tub of Ben and Jerry's out overnight so I could pour it onto my cereal in the morning instead of milk the second I got up. It was grinding my immune system into the dirt. I needed to face up to the fact that I was getting ill because of it.

There were tell-tale signs. My head only had to touch the pillow and my body immediately started jettisoning liquid. Litres would pour through my back and gallons off my scalp. I had become a malfunctioning flesh water bomber sucking up reservoirs of liquid during the day just to dump the entire payload the second I fell asleep. Each night, every few hours I would wake up on glistening, sodden sheets, with my head throbbing, mouth gummed shut and internal organs aching due to dehydration. And the night sweats slowly became the diurnal sweats when exercise was thrown into the mix. And by exercise what I mean is things like walking, standing up, typing and making sandwiches. Also it had got to the stage that I couldn't ignore the pains in my chest any more. It felt like Slash was plucking the guitar solo to November Rain on my ventricles and aortas. Running became this thing that I used to be able to do badly and comically but now could no longer even risk thinking about. And occasionally it simply felt like a sadist was squeezing down on one of my major organ's four cavities between thumb and finger.

Fate intervened and I was shamed into going to the doctor's.

When I took my son to a check-up at the baby clinic, the health visitor decided the fact that it was me that had brought him in (even though this was something I did regularly) and not Maria, was obviously a cry for help. "I can tell" she said imperiously looking down her nose at my Slayer T shirt featuring a skeleton on a crucifix against a blazing sky, "that you aren't very happy. That you're stressed out and are having trouble coping with life."

I gritted my teeth and acquiesced sweetly to a doctor's appointment realizing that to angrily defend myself would simply prove her right.

A few days later Dr B told me: "It's good you've finally come in. Your cholesterol levels are dangerously high."

I exclaimed that it was amazing she could tell that much just by looking at me but she said: "No, it's from the blood tests we did last year. Didn't you get the letters we sent?"

Then there was a brief and animated discussion after which Dr B agreed once more to attempt to update my postal address on the surgery's transcendentally shit computer system.

"Well given my family history of madness, drug dependence, alcoholism, lung cancer and heart disease this is almost like good news!" I said jovially.

"Yes... About that..." she said and booked me in for a whole raft of other tests.

Although often attributed to GK Chesterton, it was actually the Belgian poet Émile Cammaerts, who said: "When people stop believing in God, they don't believe in nothing – they believe in anything."

When it was time to give up drinking one of the many thoughts that was vying for dominance at first was the idea that no one would ever take me seriously again. I was sure that no one would find me interesting or engaging either. Too much of my self-worth had become tied up with alcohol; I was pointless without it and no one would ever want to get to know the real me. Of course, for those friends that counted, nothing could be further from the truth. It didn't occur to me at all that the wives and husbands and girlfriends and boyfriends and workmates, flatmates and best friends of alcoholics were probably all too keen to reconnect with the boring sober person fully dried out who didn't wet themselves on public transport, didn't shout at police cars, didn't dive out of windows apropos of nothing, didn't burst into tears during wildlife documentaries and didn't set themselves on fire during conversational lulls.

But this paranoia was a strong one. Stopping drinking, in the short term, really only helped foster a vacuum which nature found very, very abhorrent.

I became prey to ill-advised drink-replacement mania. My self-worth had formerly been derived from booze but now that I was sober it seemed there were a multitude of things vying for the role. And around this time my self-worth was entirely based on Häagen-Dazs strawberry cheesecake ice cream.

But after my trip to the doctors, I said a tearful farewell to the gallons of sugary, brightly coloured gunk that had kept me afloat over the last few years.

Just in case I felt like wavering and ditching my new diet, a few days later London sent me a clear sign that I should persevere. I was on the 106 headed for Bethnal Green on a bright Saturday morning when a woman collapsed right in front of me. There was no noise. She just vanished from view and rematerialised face down on the deck with her Caterpillar boots in the wheelchair bay and her dyed red hair near the rear doors.

Perhaps if she had fallen with a resounding thud, there would have been immediate and decisive action. Instead a ripple of faff spread through the double decker followed two seconds later by an aftershock of ambulance calling and pulse checking.

A woman with a baby in a buggy and a toddler in hand was the first to shout to the driver to pull over. She dialled 999 and answered the operator's questions quickly and precisely, asking other passengers for assistance when she needed it.

Generally the parents of the very young are hypersensitive to danger and the immediate responsive action it requires in a way that other people simply aren't. She injected just the right amount of urgency and command into what she was doing as if she was whipping a butter knife being pressed into a plug socket out of sticky little fingers. She pretty much had the situation under control before anyone else realised or registered what was happening.

"Where are we?" she asked.

As people started shouting things like, "In Hackney!", "By the Shell Garage!" and "Near Paddy Power!" I scanned the shop fronts out of the rear window looking for the actual address to relay to her.

She seemed to be answering a very long list of questions.

In front of me a man was having a phone conversation with someone called Sharon. Despite speaking in the most measured, persuasive and conciliatory way to Sharon he broke off occasionally without warning to bellow instructions to the woman making the 999 call – or to be more precise, to bellow at the person she was on the phone to.

"Look Sharon I ain't an evil man... You know that I am a moral man... All I can say is that I made a mistake... BLOODCLAART! THAT'S ENOUGH WITH THE QUESTIONS! SHE HAS PASSED OUT JUST SEND AN AMBULANCE! Look Sharon... I just need to come round and see you face to face so we can talk about it… I feel like we can both learn from this experience… SHE NEEDS AN AMBULANCE! WHY ARE YOU ASKING IF SHE'S WITH ANYONE? DO YOU WANT TO KNOW WHAT COLOUR COAT SHE HAS ON? JUST SEND A BLOODY AMBULANCE! I could be round in fifteen minutes Sharon…"

Outside of the window I noticed how nice the weather was for the time of year.

It was exactly the same weather in 1987 when the brakes failed on the yellow Datsun Sunny with no insurance. As we rolled down the hill in Thirsk it picked up speed while everyone inside flapped wildly. We rolled onto the dual carriageway and into the back of a speeding Ford Sierra, taking off the rear left wing and the hatchback door. We barely moved but the other car span off the road and straight through a fence.

It was exactly the same weather in 1996 when Joyce stroked out at work. She slumped from her chair silently onto the cheap office carpet and instead of leaving her on the floor I pulled her upright so she was leaning against the wall. I'd always hated having to work with her but at that moment I was overcome with anger on her behalf. The utter fucking indignity of life, leaving her like this, face twisted into some grotesque parody of its former self. The angry girl who wore the beret was standing over her shouting: "It's alright Joyce… you've just had a facial spasm… it's nothing… Don't worry Joyce… Don't worry about it." I never saw Joyce again.

It was exactly the same weather in 2002 when the boy landed on the pavement in front of me on Leyton High Street.

For a second I started to believe that maybe I could cheat death, illness and accident simply by moving to a town where the sun never shines. Stockport, Carlisle or somewhere like that.

The rapid response paramedic arrived literally within a couple of minutes. She asked us all to get off the bus. As I stepped over the prone woman I peered downwards. She was completely still apart from her eyes which were vibrating rapidly behind closed lids. It was like these small organs were escape pods trying to jettison a crippled vessel. I felt bad for her in a very abstract, shallow way. I hoped that she would be alright even though it wasn't looking that good for her.

I couldn't cheat death by moving to a rainy town. Now that I had reached a certain age, preparation for death had become paramount. I could no longer flinch it. There were no blinkers for me to wear. I could no longer drink enough to forget about it. It was impossible to ignore. All I could do was walk calmly toward it. The only nobility left on offer to me was to live like I was ready to go at any time.

This was not how I used to live.

When the boy landed on the ground in front of me on Leyton High Street in 2002 it was almost comical at first because I didn't understand that he'd been hit by a bus. He just lay in front of me like he'd fallen out of a tree. He looked directly at me and it was a full second before a crazy paving, cracked ice pattern of blood appeared all over his pale face. He let out a massive exhalation – Hsssssssss! – and as he did a large bubble of blood inflated from his nose. There was such a sense of unreality to what happened that I just stepped over him and carried on walking. I was barely aware of the commotion that erupted behind me car horns blaring, people shouting…

I reached the pub just as the doors were opening and I managed to drink five pints before what I'd just done fully sank in.

I was far from alone in developing a post-booze sweet tooth. There are a couple of major reasons why anyone who has just quit drinking a lot every day will probably develop an obsessive craving for sugar. It is an easy short-term way to manipulate the mood in the absence of alcohol and the body craves the massive amounts of calories and sugar that once came from lager, wine or cocktails. But with the sugar finally gone from my diet, the inevitable happened and I became really depressed.

Which was why when the possibility of a night out reared its goggle-eyed and haggard face a few days later, I wasn't sure it was such a great idea. When The Lex – a gig venue and club near Kings Cross – asked me if I wanted to DJ there on a Sunday, my knee jerk reaction was to think, "Oh great! I can get some drugs in, make a night of it…" which was immediately followed by the plummeting despondency of the realisation that I simply couldn't do that anymore. I couldn't even drink my fill of Coca-Cola any more. However I was flat broke and an invitation to DJ was one of the only things that would get me to leave the house in the evening, so I said yes.

It's odd at first, DJing sober. Despite running a modestly successful club night in London for four years and DJing in some pretty big clubs and venues it was not a skill I'd ever needed before.

I started the Big Sexy Land night in 2005, the same year my friend John Tatlock was just starting to dabble in production and had made me a bootleg of Gary Numan's 'Cars' and Sir Mix-a-Lot's 'Baby's Got Back' as a birthday present. London was drowning in rocket powered MDMA crystals and we'd just got our hands on a cracked version of Traktor, so a club night seemed inevitable.

My flatmate Manish christened the night in honour of the debut Revolting Cocks album and though I still like the name, it wasn't without its problems. Unbeknownst to us Big Sexy Land was also the name of a chain of sex clubs on the continent. While most of the nights were amazing there were a few real stinkers. One of the worst was when there was only one punter, a European who sat in the corner glowering at us for two hours while we gamely played post punk and acid house until he stormed over to us angrily demanding to know when the live sex show started. Ironically if he had come back the following month he would have got what he wanted. A couple graduated from raunchy dancing, to stripping and simulating sex and were about to get to fourth base when I had to get the bouncers to politely ask them to put their clothes back on. I was cool with them having sex but the spectacle had pretty much stopped everyone else from dancing.

The motto of the club was Non-Stop Neurotic Cabaret as a kind of a tribute to the low levels of psychic disturbance that all the founding DJs (and a good portion of the ones who joined us later) were often governed by. (It was a toss-up between that

and The OCD Soundsystem.) But really the overall levels of disc
jockey mental health at the club would have probably been better
if there were fewer stimulants flying round. How we ever got
past our first six months is beyond me. The bar was set pretty
low on our first night. I was so infernally spangled that I spent
ages trying to send a text message to someone on the remote
control for the video screen and a man from the crowd had to
come into the booth and explain to me what I was doing wrong.
Then when I'd actually written a text, instead of pressing send
on my phone, I pressed the big silver stop button on the Technics
deck, killing the music. I was so flustered that again someone from
the audience had to step into the booth and lead me through the
relatively straightforward process of starting the record again.
And that's when things really started going downhill. The official
line is that we ran out of records nearly two hours early due to
inexperience but the truth was that I simply couldn't remember
what I'd already played and was rapidly heading towards a *Father
Ted* incident except with 'Shack Up' by A Certain Ratio instead
of 'Ghost Town' by The Specials. We ended up running down
the road to beg Jeff Transmission, who was working in a nearby
nightclub, to come and finish our set for us.

Thing is, we didn't really cut down on the narcotics, we just
got used to them and did a lot more practice. By the time we
moved to the basement of The Albany on Great Portland Street
I could pretty much execute a good DJ set while half asleep –
which was a very good thing given that my eyes were pointing
inwards at their sockets during quite a few of these nights. One
of the best sets I ever played was carried out despite everyone in
the club looking like a giant pair of chattering wind-up teeth with
a single giant eyeball on top. And no amount of experimentation
into combining those levels of ketamine, MDMA and cocaine
ever reproduced those reality-boggling effects again.

I had some of the best nights of my life doing that club and it
was certainly worth the few misfires we endured. Probably the most
ill-advised thing we did was try and launch a Manchester spin-off
night. Certainly the omens were advising us that it was a terrible

idea. Around the time we were discussing our new venture, John and I went on a fact finding mission to watch Prince in London. This involved an all-day drinking session before heading over to the 02 Dome for the show. More facts were then gathered at the 02 Indigo nightclub, where Prince was also playing an intimate club set. John, who, by 2am, had reached dangerous Three Mile Island levels of funkiness was busting some spectacular dance moves. Encouraged by our friend Richard, he demonstrated how he could go from dancing, into a 720 degree spin, then stop facing exactly the same way and carry on dancing as before – all in one fluid motion. However no one was watching when he did it the first time so he angrily shouted at everyone to pay attention, did it for a second time and broke his own leg. This was how, a week later, when we were going to view a potential venue for our Northern Big Sexy Land off-shoot, not only was John on crutches but when we got there, in the middle of the deserted street directly in front of the club's door, there was an ambulance on fire. I distinctly remember looking at John – whose face was all crimson because of the blazing vehicle we were stood next to, covering his mouth with a scarf because of the noxious black smoke coming from the tyres – and saying: "It'll probably have a friendlier vibe when the students are back in town." We opened the night there; it lasted for three terrible months before we wrote it off as an awful mistake.

It was a long time after I stopped drinking – probably about four years – before I realised that I'd been using DJing as a really big crutch to help me socialise when sober. Whenever I had to go out, I engineered the situation so I got to DJ instead of having to mix with people. Work gatherings at the pub, house parties, after hours get-togethers in clubs… there wasn't a situation where I wouldn't try and make it a prerequisite of my attendance that I be left behind the decks. I knew with a job to do, I would then be too busy to have to talk to big groups of people who were drinking. Manipulating people into drinking and taking drugs with me was the hallmark of the first half of my adult life; getting them to let me be the DJ – whether they wanted it or not – was shaping up to be my MO in the second half.

Admittedly, transferring all of my obsessional behaviour onto sourcing obscure records and playing them to small groups of people in ever more bizarre situations ("You're making pancakes tomorrow morning for Shrove Tuesday? Would you like me to come round and play you Peruvian psych while you eat?") affected different groups of my friends in different ways. A lot of my friends were fine with it. My good friend Anthea, especially, started having parties at her flat – rambunctious, colossal, mind-fryingly joyous events – that were pretty much started as an excuse for me to placate my ever expanding mania. She was dead cool about it – a really good friend. However, god knows how I must have looked to some other people.

I remember calling round for Kev and Tom from the band Real Lies one Saturday night with some records and my DJing laptop under my arm. They lived in a big detached place next to a reservoir in Manor House and threw low level parties that went on constantly, it seemed, from Wednesday afternoon until 9am Monday morning each week. When I got there they were having some kind of medicated bacchanal that involved them wearing no tops and false moustaches. They were all flopping about in the hallway when I walked through the door like basking seal cubs, their false moustaches laden with MDMA crystals and their eyes like oil covered liquorice wheels. They asked me to come and sit with them and watch a DVD of Arsenal goal highlights from 2002 while a late 90s R&B compilation played in the background. They were extremely welcoming ("John! Go upstairs and get yourself some MDMA. It's in Kev's room inside the porcelain weasel.") However after a while, unable to relax or contain myself, despite the sudden burst of serotonin and despite the bonhomie of my hosts, I jumped up and started fiddling through my vinyl and shouted in a state of agitation: "Have you ever heard 'What I Say' by Miles Davis? It's like a fusion band playing drum and bass." I queued it up, pressed play, and what followed was the longest twenty one minutes and ten seconds of my life. All of them did a good impression of pretending not to be dismayed but I suddenly had a clear image of what I was: a fat 40-something with a beard insisting that a load of young people having a really good time on a Saturday night suddenly stop and listen to jazz instead. I have never felt as old as I did right then. As soon as it ended I packed up my gear again and left never to return. There was something special going on in that house, as the music of Real Lies attests. All shimmering early mornings huddled by the reservoir – the neon roar of Hackney, Haringey and Hornsey just about audible in the background, blissed out young geezers and their friends seeing in a new day listening to R&B and house, the Pet Shop Boys and Aaliyah and thankfully not a five-minute fucking oboe solo in sight. Leave that for your 17th album boys.

I had deferred maturity for an unthinkably long period by staying drunk every day and becoming a music journalist but after I stopped, eventually this extension of childhood – this *illusion* of extended childhood – simply shattered and fell to pieces around my feet.

If obsessional, ritual behaviour about music was a symptom of an illness – and I was starting to realise that it was – I was glad to have it… I just had to be more careful how I controlled it in front of other people.

After this realisation and the birth of my son, most opportunities for socialising tapered off. But I wasn't sad about this fact; I felt the opposite if anything. I felt relieved. Social gatherings, by the sheer dint of being now few and far between, started to take on quite a sheen. They very rarely happened but when they did, they lit up my life like a massive coronal discharge.

Maybe I'm just a limited writer but I find it hard to do justice in words to the beauty of time spent with good friends that I have a lot of affection for simply because, by its very nature, it must seem boring to other people, or at least mundane or unremarkable. Golden age, peak-time congregations lack the dramatic tension of the true horror that life can throw at you. All I know is it's hard to pin down that glorious feeling you get when there is a series of smooth clicks, as cog after beautiful golden cog slips into place. The right people. The right place. The right time.

I reckon that if you happened to tot up all the best nights out I've ever had, there would be an odds-on chance that John Tatlock or Stu Green, or both of them, were there (probably wearing flamboyant trousers and helping me into a cab). I met John in 1985. He was playing guitar in the only St Helens band who could steal my affections away from GNARL, called The Volunteers. I was very impressed by this and the fact he wore a dead priest's overcoat. And this sense of fashion might not have improved noticeably for either of us over the following 25 years but what constituted a party did end up meaning more than a bottle of Thunderbird and some low grade acid in The Royal Alfred car park.

That said, we did used to put a lot of effort into going out. Around my 26th birthday we went out in Brixton one Monday night and took a bunch of these cheeky, Yves Klein International Blue-coloured pills with a long tail pitched somewhere between *Mad Max Beyond Thunderdome* and *Predator 2*. I came up like a bottle rocket the second I stepped over the threshold of the Dog Star on Coldharbour Lane, where there was some kind of night for gay goths on. 'Let's Dance' was thundering out of the system and hardcore gay porn was being projected all over the walls and the ceiling. Only a few steps inside I bent down to retrieve my drugs out of my shoe but the second my head reached waist level a giant rush threatened to knock me over and I'd have to stand up again. All over the walls giant stiff penises were ploughing in and out of anuses and mouths and bursting into psychedelic supernovae and fireworks. "Jesus! Bowie! Cock! Christ!" was all I could say. After a few seconds I tried again but my head flooded with the red hot lava of a thousand lovely Krakatoas. I don't know how long I was there, going up and down right in front of the door like a giant saucer-eyed, Ministry T-shirt-wearing drinking bird, staring slack jawed at the throbbing celluloid cock mural, but eventually a kindly bouncer came over to me and said, "Look mate, if you go over there and sit down, you'll find it easier to get your drugs out of your shoe and then I can let some more people in." John helped me over to a table as we waded through shin-deep pools of Nile Rodgers brass and bass. He nodded at the wall: "My God! It's full of cocks."

And then in Manchester on the Saturday night of John's 40th

it was just perfect. We'd hired out a room in Castlefield where we set decks and laptops up. Richard had his first ever lot of MDMA and it was beautiful seeing this rapturous look playing across his face. When Damien started playing the theme music from *Cheers* I thought he was about to start crying, or at least attempt to tell me how much empathy he felt for Cliff Clavin.

I met some friends I hadn't seen for years and we stood round talking about how great it was having kids. I made a handful of new friends and we did exactly the same thing. It doesn't matter what your lot is like in life, sometimes you need a night out like this to remind you that being alive isn't always like being herded through a giant Ikea with a massive meat grinder instead of an exit at the other end.

At one point, someone at the other end of the room pressed a finger down on a black button and the flash on a camera flared up. A bank of thick golden light rolled along the walls and splashed over me and my friends, temporarily illuminating us as the shutter snapped open and then closed.

But there were no drugs, no friends, no ice cream and no Coca-Cola at the Lexington club in Kings Cross when I turned up for work with two flight cases full of vinyl and a laptop full of WAVs. I was manning the decks upstairs after the bands finished; on at 10.30pm and off again at 4am the next morning. To be fair, the crowd were sweet. A lot of the requests were good and everyone was up dancing. No one asked for Madness or Pink Floyd.

Within ten minutes, all thoughts of drugs had left my mind. It may sound like a cliché to you but to me it's a truism: dance music helps cure you of your ills, temporarily at least. Disco, if you let it, will cleanse your soul. And at about 2am, to repay the indulgence of the revellers, who'd stuck with what I'd been playing all night, I decided it was time to break open some stone cold classic house, techno and disco and head into the home straight of the set (I knew the only people left after 3am would be psychotic drunks) and I started off by playing 'Move Your Body (The House Music Anthem)' by Marshall Jefferson.

As soon as those tumbling, hesitant, melancholy yet uplifting piano chords chimed out, people started shouting and screaming in sheer joy and going crazy dancing. There was only one person in the room who didn't seem to like it but his reaction was pretty extreme. Doing that I've-just-shat-an-anvil walk that Liam Gallagher does he elbowed his way roughly across the floor to stand in front of me shouting, "What the fuck is this shit? Why can't you play something that everyone likes?" He was seemingly unconcerned that he was framed by 249 people behind him going fucking nuts. And then without waiting for a reply he started making the wanker sign at me.

Under any other circumstances I would have ignored him. There's no accounting for taste (or lack thereof) when it comes to drunks and you can't accommodate everyone. Moaning about your lot while DJing is idiotic. It's not like it's a hard or unenjoyable job making people dance. There will always people who go out in order to have a bad time. But then, ignoring all this, I thought, "You know what, we're talking about Marshall Jefferson here. I'm simply not standing for this level of ignorance from someone who looks like he could be a member of King Krule with rickets."

I texted the head of security – a Russian gentleman with infinite patience and hands like JCB scoops who looked like *RoboCop* with an ill-fitting human skin pulled over his metal chassis – to say: "We have a young man up here disrespecting 'The House Music Anthem' in a most unpleasant way. I think he could do with a quick breath of fresh air to consider the further trajectory of his night out." The young man was helped rapidly outside into the cold air to consider the error of his ways for a few minutes while everyone else was left to enjoy the tune. I went straight from that into 'Get Down' by Connie Case and 'Weekend' by Class Action (Larry Levan Mix). There was a flash of pure phosphorescent light which rolled across the contours and ridges on the surface of my brain. I levitated above the decks and then burst through the roof of the Lexington soaring up into the air over Kings Cross to where the air was crisp and tiny raindrops stung my eyes. I watched the golden lights of London spidering away from me into the distance toward the dark halo of the Home Counties.

Pretty Ugly (2012)

Arranging a loan. Declaring bankruptcy. Drawing a will. Consolidating debts. Taking out a mortgage. Sorting out any one of these financial arrangements is a cakewalk when compared to the logistical (and moral) complexity of buying drugs.

But even if you discount where narcotics are grown and manufactured and the toll paid by producers, traffickers, law enforcement professionals and users, few commercial decisions you ever make will be as problematic or politically suspect as the purchase of illegal drugs.

This was something I gave no thought to when I first bought them in the mid-80s. And to be honest it had only just begun to dawn on me some 28 years later, on the last occasion I paid for them.

In many ways my first and last drug-related transactions felt the same to me. Superficially I was very much a different person of course. I was no longer a rake-thin teenage goth in an Alien Sex Fiend vest, bangles and makeup; instead I was a middle aged dad who looked like an extra from *Game Of Thrones*. But fundamentally I felt the same – harassed, depressed, doing something I was vaguely aware I shouldn't be doing and couldn't really afford to but not feeling entirely in control of the process either. I was certainly still buying them mainly for the wrong reasons. How much had actually changed in the intervening years?

Perhaps this feeling of *déjà vu* was down to the fact that the times themselves – 1985 and 2012 – felt so similar. Certainly the political spirit of Thatcher's second term in office and David Cameron's austerity Britain were uncannily alike; both periods made you feel like there could barely be a worse political administration in power with no viable alternative to speak of – and that was just for starters. Beyond this, mainstream music felt just as worthless to me – as if culture had resigned itself into merely being a minor distraction against the domestic affairs of the day. Chart music may not have been specifically designed to anaesthetize and distract but these were two roles it seemed to fulfil with ease in the face of such an uninspiring political environment. Or maybe it's just that when a person is so stressed out and sick with worry about what they're seeing on the news every night, the music they hear on Radio 1 can't help but seem vacuous, superficial and hollow. Another aspect of the uncanny similarity of these two years nearly three decades apart was that radical ideas around social equality seemed to be flourishing with greater vigour than any kind of radical aspect to popular music.

No doubt radical ideas were always being generated but it was during times when people felt genuinely desperate that they seemed to gain most mainstream traction. This was certainly the case in the mid-80s when I was finishing up at school and preparing to go to college. You could feel that there was a sea-change in behaviour and belief systems happening. People get misty eyed about the 80s – and it probably was great if you were upper middle class and lived somewhere like London – but as far as I'm concerned socially the decade was fucking awful. Forgetting for a second the violence and tribalism (two things that affected me most deeply), racist jokes were the norm – on TV, in clubs, in pubs, in schoolyards, on the radio. Women were often treated abominably, as little better than common property. In my experience, it wasn't that uncommon to see people of colour being screamed at and spat at in the street. Yet, the amount of people who irritably resisted the perception of change to their 'freedoms' demanded by the so-called politically correct was quite stunning. (In 2012, people once called politically correct were now witheringly dismissed as Social Justice Warriors, but the sentiment was identical.)

And in 2012 it felt like the normal social concerns of the left – class issues, sexism, homophobia and racism – had expanded to include such areas as transphobia, intersectionality and privilege. It felt, to me at least, like equality itself was slowly becoming a more completist project.

My gut reaction to most of these new ideas was initially one of mistrust. And this seemed to be the case for many people. But one of the scant few advantages of getting older was the realisation that I had seen the dynamics of these arguments before – and the adverse reactions to them. I understood that people who refused to acknowledge that there was anything wrong with treating trans people with contempt and as second-class human beings for example, were thinking and acting in a similar way to those refusing to curb their homophobic, racist or sexist language a generation or two ago.

During this year, 2012, there was an important political concept – one that was very pertinent to me – slowly penetrating through my thick skull. The idea was simply that if men wanted to engage seriously with any concepts of equality they needed to stop hating themselves first. And this was simply because men who hate themselves and are lacking in self-respect are almost always never strong enough to simply take it out on themselves – they are always on the lookout for other people to forcibly share their misery with.

Every dickhead I'd ever seen belittling a woman in a public space; every creepy fucker I'd had to sack for writing misogynist drivel (ie literally every writer I'd had to sack); most of the literate writers I'd had to deny work to in the first place and a notable chunk of the illiterate ones; most people I'd had to block on social media; everyone I'd ever met who was violent; everyone I'd met who was a bully; most career drunks; most career drug users – and shamefully these last two groups included myself – most of them were people who lacked self-respect... as far as I could tell. And all of them, to a man, simply couldn't keep this sense of disgust to themselves.

It feels like that as a society we have always told men that they can have whatever they want and that they can be whatever they want as long as they try hard. It feels like men are told this every single day of their lives by their parents and the media and most producers of culture until the day they graduate from university... and then, blinking in incomprehension, they end up working in Foxtons in a £110 suit while marinating in cheap lager and hatred, going home each night to frozen meals, YouPorn.com and ultra-violent first-person shooters on the Xbox, wondering exactly whose fault it is that they haven't ended up as Ryan Gosling or the guy who invented Facebook.

At the end of the day it is primarily men themselves who stand to benefit from being encouraged to seriously consider improving their sense of self-respect. Once you look beyond the already obscene levels of suicide among young men; once you factor in the number of deaths by misadventure, understandably ruled as such by UK coroner's courts wishing to spare grieving families even more pain; once you look at all the premature deaths of males with alcohol and illegal drugs being the primary cause or playing a significant contributory factor – you're no longer looking at 'depressing statistics'. You're looking at a fucking epidemic.

And other than working on our self-respect, it's clear that the one really huge job left in the whole equality project is for us – men that is – to shut up and man up *as far as educating ourselves goes*. After all, when it boils down to it, women tend to be alright and people who aren't alright, tend to be men.

And mea culpa, I've had my own fair share of problems with the shutting up and listening / reading part of the equation to be honest. Every fibre in my being tended to scream that this self-education – any new idea in identity politics – was for different, 'other', more terrible men. Y'know, those blokes over there with the hair gel and the football tops by the pool table; it wasn't something that I needed to worry myself with.

Except of course I was wrong to think of myself as exempt. And it was in recognising that I was an addict that I finally saw sense. I came to understand that the very refusal to undertake a fearless inventory of what constituted my core beliefs and actions was ultimately proof that I probably wasn't the right-thinking socialist feminist I lazily perceived myself to be. Anyone who is comfortable with their beliefs is comfortable with testing them vigorously. Anyone who presumes that a new development in identity politics, for example, doesn't apply to them, without at least thoroughly researching it and thinking it through, is probably very uncomfortable at the idea of having to check their core beliefs at all for fear of what they may find.

I remember exactly when it was that I first came across the idea of privilege; it was in a series of digital articles from the *New Statesman* that I read in 2012. In rough terms, these features contained the idea that people should be aware of ways in which they have social, cultural or economic advantages in life as a result of their class, race, gender and sexual orientation. It was an idea that I initially reacted strongly against. This was probably because I had other things – namely scoring cocaine – on my mind. But as I realised, nearly too late, all of these things were actually tied together.

When I came crashing off the (narcotic) wagon in November of 2012, I realise now that I did so as an enemy of feminism, socialism and everything else that is right in the world. Because if you're a Dad in your 40s and you suddenly decide that you can't be doing with a carefully planned and girlfriend-negotiated drugs dabble once in a blue moon and that you have to start doing lots of cocaine and amphetamines at home in secret even though you don't have that much money, you can reasonably be thought of as a lot of things, but feminist isn't one of them.

I had patted myself on the back in the past for being appalled at men who spouted sexist drivel only to shamelessly play the "How can I be a misogynist when I've got a mother, a girlfriend and a sister who I really respect?" card. But wasn't I really doing something very similar? Wasn't going back to heavy drugs, given what I knew about myself and addiction and given how poor my health had become, the same thing? Because whether I realised it or not I was essentially expecting a woman to pick up the pieces for me if it all went wrong. Almost certainly not my sister and probably not my mother but definitely my girlfriend. (The same went for socialism. By surrendering to my addiction I was subconsciously trying to reverse the ratio of how much I received according to my needs and worked according to my abilities, in my own lazy favour.)

I don't really know where it came from but the idea of getting myself some chisel to take while I was putting in my (usual) long night shifts writing while Maria and Little John were in bed, had been incubating within me for some time. It had effloresced in my head like a cancerous bloom. It had become so tangible that when I allowed the idea to condense into a probability rather than just some sordid daydream, I got a rush so hard I had to sit down, just by thinking about it.

No matter how hard I tried, I could never quite get rid of Jimmy The Saint's number. It was always there somewhere on a phone, in an email, jotted down on a piece of paper, in a text message. There would always be someone who'd resend the number if I asked them sweetly enough.

And once I relented and thought: "Well, I'll only take it at night after they've gone to sleep and I'll make sure it's locked away at the bottom of my wardrobe where he could never get to it in a million years" – that was it. I was fucked.

Two hours later I was stood in a car park in Hackney waiting for the embellished Honda Civic to pick me up. I asked for the six for five deal and Jimmy The Saint agreed to drive me to the cash machine. We hit traffic and as it was something I'd been trying to get my head around, I asked him what he thought of the idea of privilege but his lack of a reply suggested that he either hadn't heard of it or had but wasn't interested.

He was much better than me at hiding agitation, irritation

and anger because he simply nodded while I trampled over the boundaries of the dealer / client relationship shouting: "I'm not saying white guys… heterosexual white guys… heterosexual, middle class white guys…"

Jimmy The Saint chipped in: "Able-bodied as well innit."

I carried on: "Thank you Jimmy. I'm not saying that heterosexual, middle class, able-bodied, white guys don't have advantages in life… we probably do but that's not the whole story… there are other things to factor in! It's not the whole picture! It's like, I might be middle class now but I'm terrible at it… I've got no money… I can't dress smartly… I don't even know what hummus is made of. I know it's got lemon in it… And I can't pronounce quinoa."

Jimmy The Saint shook his head: "All sounds like first world problems to me, innit… And you'd *better* have some fucking money when we get to Sainsbury's."

He saw a green light changing to orange, slowed down gently and stopped at the junction despite having just enough time to make it: "And it's keenWAH blood. Everyone knows that."

I carried on: "I went to a school where the pass rate was one O Level per two and a half students. I got beaten nearly blind when I was 14. I HAD AN UNCONVENTIONAL UPBRINGING! I'm an alcoholic who got thrown out of Hull University…"

Jimmy The Saint just shrugged and said: "We're here."

I got the £200 out of the machine and jogged back to the car, and we set off back toward the vicinity of my flat.

I carried on: "I don't feel like I've got any privilege. Why could I never get any writing work outside of heavy metal magazines? I had to start my own magazine just so I'd be able to write. Other than that I had to write for free – no one would pay me. I'm fucking flat broke and I can't get any work. Everyone gives me these awards but I'm desperate for work! I mean, I'm better than half the people writing about music for some publications and better than all the music writers on others. So why can't I even get a fucking down page Skrillex review into a national newspaper? Is it because I'm not jolly fucking hockey sticks?"

Jimmy The Saint thought for a bit and then said: "Nah. It's because you only listen to that shit music that everyone hates. And you've got no social skills innit. And you look like you live in the woods. You want to write about Rihanna mate."

I was about to say something but he butted in: "You told me you said to the man at that broadsheet that he wouldn't recognise a good album if it was fired out of a bazooka into his head."

I gritted my teeth: "That was ten years ago, I was very depressed and I had been drinking very heavily... these papers and magazines are stuffed to the rafters with Oxbridge fuckers, I'm sure of it... and they're probably just as rude as I am. I might well be white, male, heterosexual..."

"And able-bodied..."

"...and abled-bodied, thank you, but I think there's more to it than that."

Jimmy The Saint – who delivered all over London to Fleet Street and lifestyle magazines and almost certainly knew more journalists than I did – ignored what I was saying and carried on: "Didn't you tell the man from the *Guardian Guide* he looked like Harry Potter and wrote like a 13-year-old sending a text message? He doesn't give you work because you're rude. Rude and an idiot, if you don't mind me saying so. You can't compare a potential boss to someone who plays quidditch."

I rubbed my temples and said quietly: "He does actually look like a teenage wizard if you meet him."

Jimmy The Saint was now warming to the theme: "What was the name of the publication where you said to the editor it should be easy for him to roll-up his magazine and jam it up his arse because the paper was so cheap and shiny? And the guy from the *Observer*... didn't you call his music section a comic? And what about the guy from *Kerrang!* whose throat you threatened to slit because he changed something you wrote and you had to beg him not to call the police? And the *NME*... the *NME*... Ha ha ha!"

I shouted: "THAT'S ENOUGH JIMMY! I CAN WALK FROM HERE!"

He pulled over to the kerb and said: "Look John, you know I

appreciate the business but you can't be doing too badly if you can afford my services. Everyone you've mentioned that you've fallen out with who won't give you work – apparently – well, what's the common theme there? None of them are black lesbians on crutches are they? But seriously blood, I think you need to work on your social skills. And if you're feeling a bit uptight, don't do any of this white after you've had a double espresso. And stop spending so much time on social media reading about political buzzwords – you're obviously not cut out for it."

He passed me a baggy containing six chunky wraps and I climbed out of the car. I leaned back in through the window and said quietly: "Privilege doesn't recognise mental health factors though."

He replied: "Then how come it's always insane white men editing magazines and writing the big features. Why can't the insane women get a look in? Mental health has nothing to do with it. Look John, it's good to have you back on board but would you get away from the fucking motor? You're making me look like a drug dealer."

After he drove off I felt weak and had to hold onto a lamppost for support while gently muttering to myself: "They forgot to factor in mental health problems and other environmental issues. They forgot the mental health..." After a while the throbbing in my head subsided enough for me to shuffle home slowly fingering the six wraps inside the baggie in my pocket.

I think it's fair enough to say that I love drugs. I was born to take them. From my first experience of an adult strength pre-med and an armful of morphine when I was 14, I knew they were for me.

It was only after stopping drinking in 2008 that I really threw myself headfirst into drugs, despite having 22 years' of heavy narcotic use under my belt, suggesting the alcohol had only been a way to warm up for the main event.

When Maria got pregnant though, I tapered down on my use dramatically. We moved into our small two bedroomed flat in Stamford Hill and got ready to be parents. It really had to be a red letter day for me to get on one after that. A Dethscalator gig, a GNOD gig or maybe the birthday party of a close friend at a push. And then after Little John was born it became even more of a rarity. At first I'd go out once every two or three months and stay out all night round at a friend's flat, getting loaded, listening to music and then not come home until I was straight at some point early the next day. My big night out for the quarter.

But once I was back on board with Jimmy The Saint in the winter of 2012 I hit the powders and potions so hard it was almost as if I were trying to make up for lost time. Over the next six weeks, I powered through an absurd amount of cocaine, a rigid and physically punishing amount of speed, a rakish amount of opium, tons of MDMA, as much crystal meth as I could buy (thankfully not that much), a pillowcase-full of mephedrone and some horrible horrible grass.

And the worst thing about this binge was I didn't even enjoy it.

The speed made me feel like I'd been hit by a truck. The MDMA was cancelled out by the cocaine. And I don't really even like cocaine to start with, I'm just addicted to it. The opium was cancelled out by the SSRIs and the speed, the crystal meth wasn't very good quality and grass is the worst drug ever invented – it made me feel so paranoid and insane, I'd have to take loads more speed just to feel normal again. Weeks of joyless, surreptitious, anxious snorting, smoking, eating, swallowing and dabbing slid by in numb silence and then finally, in the last few hours of the six-week binge I got to where I wanted to go. On the morning of Christmas Eve, after lying in bed all night twitching, sweating and shaking with the last of the drugs that I could afford to buy slowly working their way through my system, I looked through the window at dawn's first light and the sky was on fire. The firmament was the colour of raw, flayed flesh punctuated by clouds that looked like explosions of gold, swarming with ants. I reached for my iPod, put my headphones on and pressed play on L. Pierre's *The Island Come True*. "It's so beautiful" I thought, preparing to experience as much of the tail light rush as I could, before falling fast asleep two minutes later.

Toward the end of that six-week binge I recognised the extent to which I'd been lying to myself and determined to stop completely. I had crossed several Rubicons that I said I'd never even approach. My trouble was I could no longer just do a little bit of drugs once or twice a year, like some trendy Dad with a Primal Scream T-shirt and some Basement Jaxx CDs who liked going to Fabric on his birthday. It wasn't in my nature. I'd reached a point where I had to choose between getting high and being a Dad – as the two things were, for me, seemingly incompatible. And this was no choice at all when it came down to it.

Christmas isn't the ideal time to quit taking drugs, but then again, when is? I crawled through the holiday period on hands and knees feeling like Satan had kicked me in the heart with an iron-shod, cloven-hooved roundhouse – straight to the sternum. I felt like he'd taken a three day postponed rave shit in my liver and pissed all over my over-heated pancreas with a sizzling micturition that sounded like a hot dog vendor's frying onions. No doubt it would smell like that too if someone sliced me open. My heart was bruised and radiating a painful network of burst veins and damaged arteries, like a roadmap of poor life choices.

And the depression? Jesus Christ I was lugubrious. I felt like the b-side to a Tindersticks 7" played at 33rpm. I felt like the typeface on the lyric sheet of an unloved, late 90s Morrissey album. I felt like wearing a black armband even though I wasn't a footballer or a Victorian undertaker.

A few days later I was completely drug free and floating on my back in the sea looking up at a cloudless blue sky.

The surface tension was incredible as barely any of me was below the surface. To my right the viscous seawater merged into a gloopy, ski-slope-like meniscus which arced vertiginously up into the base of a towering cliff. The structure was formed from opaque pelagic plastics which were sludgily fused together by partially bio-degraded Evian and Volvic bottles. I must have been near the North Pacific Gyre, tens of thousands of years into the future. I was floating by the new continent of discarded plastic.

My head was heavy and started sinking below the surface.

As my eyes went under I realised that my head was now in Hell. "Ah! I see! In the future, everything under sea level is in Hell." I peered down into the crimson depths. There was a sprawling factory complex for the mass production of spiders down there. Looking at the clientele milling about I would say it was an unfashionable backwater of perdition, mainly populated by folk who could count themselves very unlucky to have ended up there instead of in Purgatory: no win no fee lawyers, low ranking pirates, alcoholic priests, celebrity chefs, old school park flashers...

"What are you crying about? This place isn't so bad, apart from the spiders", I shouted down to someone weeping under a blackened and leafless tree. He looked up, all pissy eyed and said: "It's true, it's not so bad. They started subcontracting a lot of essential maintenance work to the lowest out-of-house bidders. It soon became financially unviable to have a Hell that was terrible for everyone. This is late capitalist Hell. Don't get me wrong, it's pretty grim but most of the time it's just annoying, none of the really terrifying stuff works properly any more... and if your tastes run to the bleak, misanthropic or masochistic, well, you'll do OK here. Imagine being in one of those HR Giger theme bars with a pretty full on hangover listening to early 90s hardcore. If you don't think too much about the 'eternity' aspect of it, it's not so bad."

"Hardcore punk or hardcore rave?" I asked.

"Whichever one you dislike, that's what you hear," he replied.

"Sure, but what's the real problem here?"

"I really hate spiders."

There were spiders everywhere, it had to be said. They were probably quite cost effective to produce and they did horrify a lot of people.

There was a roll of thunder and I yanked my head up above the surface. Larry Grayson was walking towards me across a beach of nurdles. He was weeping mermaid's tears, which rolled down his cheeks, and cascaded down his messianic robes and scattered by his feet. "Larry, I'm cold", I told him. He looked up and solemnly addressed someone out of sight: "Shut that door. It's freezing down here."

We had a long conversation about what was happening but I couldn't really understand anything he was saying to me, such was its profundity. Grayson was the only one off the telly that I trusted as a child. A truly beautiful man of sensitivity and charm, surrounded by ignorant brutes. "They're all down there aren't they?" I asked Grayson, who simply nodded, eyes brimming with plastic tears.

"Is he down there as well?" I asked him. My teacher with the carnation, the powder blue crushed velveteen suit and the stupid haircut had to be down there. He had an odd way of punishing boys that one. A soft punishment that would leave you wishing for the cane instead.

"Take a look for yourself" said Grayson and my head started sinking under the surface again.

Back in Hell, I drifted high above the plains, looking down on the lost but something was wrong with my balance, I was pitching and yawing. Tipping forwards. Threatening to come tumbling to the floor of this horrible blood red world. I didn't want to go down to Hell... I wasn't ready...

I woke up, just as I came rolling forward out of my Mum's electric riser/ recliner chair. I was on my hands and knees with my chin on the carpet and my son was stood next to me, hitting me delightedly with a toy train. My Mum was giggling. I was at an absolute loss as to what was going on.

"Larry?" I asked weakly.

After a few moments I realised that it was December 28 and I was round at my parents' house in Rainhill. We had driven up from London yesterday for the annual Christmas visit. She told me that she was watching me for some time before I fell out of the chair. I would nod off, my head would loll slowly backwards until a combination snore / shout – caused by a blocked nose and sleep apnoea – would make me jolt upright awake before I would start slowly lolling backwards asleep again. But then Little John joined in the torment. Growing bored and wanting someone to play with, he used the electronic controller on the side of the chair to tip it forward sending me crashing on to the floor. This function of the chair would normally be used by a pensioner to help them get up into standing position.

"So I'm not in Hell?" I asked gingerly and my Mum shook her head.

Spiders and Satanic matters were two things that always plagued my dreams when I was trying to kick a habit and I did understand why that was. Spiders were an abomination and the very idea of them was enough to get me to do almost anything. On top of that Satan was a powerful metaphor for the exertion of self-will. He symbolised the rejection of society's norms and the bold statement of belief in man as a self-sufficient entity in charge of his own destiny. Someone who identified with Satan probably believed in free will and opposed governance by the church, the state, the judiciary, teachers, police, social workers, librarians, bus drivers, park wardens, people in call centres... Lucifer helped man oppose The Man.

The trouble was, I didn't really believe in free will any more. I'd spent my entire life banging my head against a brick wall convinced that I could knock it down through application of will and all I had to show for it was a totally fucked face and concussion. And every day I woke up staring at the same completely unchanged brick wall. About 95% of my life was already mapped out for me by genetics and environment with the only real daily choice I was making being the choice between eating white or brown bread. I didn't really believe I was in charge of my own destiny to any remarkable degree and there wasn't any striking evidence to suggest that I should do. And as for the other 5% of my life that actually did present me with genuine chances to completely change my fundamental fortunes... Well, I would probably be in a better position to recognise those all too rare opportunities when they arose and maybe even make the right decisions when they presented themselves if I hadn't just boshed three grams of MDMA, a fat line of ketamine, a nose-up of crystal meth and was not whooping blind with poppers. Drugs may well have been a symbol of free will to some but for me they represented yet another form of control. There was no free will involved in being a 41-year-old desperately trying to score speed on a Wednesday lunchtime.

Maria came into the front room: "What are you doing on the floor?!"

My Mum said: "Don't forget we're Skyping your sister, Paul and Olivia in Tasmania in half an hour. Go and get a shower. You don't want her to see you looking like this."

I nodded mutely and headed upstairs for the bathroom, hoping against hope that a shower would make me feel better. But it didn't. The kind of cleaning I needed would have to go deeper than the pores. I leant face forward, splayed against the freezing cold tiles as the weak but red hot sprinkling of water ran down my back.

I'd gotten past the stage where a shower was going to make everything OK. I wanted to get up and walk away from how I felt but I couldn't. I just had to stand there and wait for it to pass. And the worst thing was, this time I knew exactly how long it was going to take. I wanted the screen to go white, like it did during a movie denoting the passage of time before a new scene started some weeks or months later. But there was no fade cut. No edit. No time passing montage. Just real time crawling forwards. Months staring at the clock thinking, 'Life's too long.' And the horror squatting on my shoulders pushing all of my life, personality and experience into an ultra-dense ball, deep inside my body, somewhere just out of reach.

Spiral Arms (2013)

I had barely gotten used to the idea of taking no illegal drugs again for the rest of my life before I became swept up in an ill-advised plan to cure myself of all my other ills in record time as well. Pining for narcotics was making me feel glum, so to take my mind off it, I decided the project I needed was to stop drinking caffeine and to stop taking antidepressants – at the same time.

I had been taking SSRI drugs for eight years. These selective serotonin reuptake inhibitors were prescribed widely to people with anxiety, depression and some personality disorders. Combined with several courses of cognitive behavioural therapy or CBT, they had done me a lot of favours over that period but with each passing year I was getting more and more worried about SSRI discontinuation syndrome: the dreaded cessation effects. In 2013 I began my plan to stop taking these pills by following a relatively rigorous reduction programme. I tapered down slowly over the course of ten weeks. I went from taking 30mg of Escitalopram a day, to alternating between 30mg a day and 25 mg a day; then to 25 mg a day; then to alternating between 25mg and 20mg a day and so on, using a craft knife to divide each tablet up into portions. I even kept a record of where I was up to on Google calendar. Although, given that one of the side effects of

coming off these serotonin manipulating drugs was poor short-term memory, perhaps it was inevitable that this careful 'scientific' method would eventually fall apart and give way to some proper cargo cult, vegetation myth madness, which is what happened as soon as I got below 10mg per day.

I was initially determined not to move on to the next phase of reduction until I felt like I had acclimatised to the level I was on. But instead I got so bowled over with enthusiasm for the project I started viewing it as a race to the bottom. Once I hit 10mg a day I ended up taking none at all less than a week later. In the last stage, even though I could tell that something odd was happening to me it didn't become really unpleasant until the day I went from taking 5mg to taking nothing at all. The experience was sort of like falling out of a plane, in that the plummeting bit was more weird and uncomfortable than anything else; it was the last few metres and hitting the ground which was utterly objectionable.

At first I was fine with the memory loss, the headaches, the constant fatigue, the permanent anxiety, the fainting, the sensation that I was being tasered on the surface of the brain every 100 seconds, the vomiting and depression. But then after 72 hours I was unable to shake the panic-ridden feeling that these side-effects were permanent and I was always going to feel that wretched. The first day I started to think that I might not have gotten away with it – about three days after taking my last portion of a pill – I was on my way to a wedding in West London. My friends Ros and Simon were tying the knot in Hammersmith and having a reception in a nice working man's club near the river. As soon as we left the house at 6pm, Little John – who was then two and a half – became vocally concerned that the trip wasn't part of his daily routine. As I was pushing him toward Seven Sisters tube station he started shouting: "Oh no! Daddy! It's dark! Where are we going?!" I tried to reassure him that we were going to go on a train journey – his second favourite thing to do after going to see the dinosaurs at the Natural History Museum – but this didn't placate him at all. "NO! Not a train at night time!" he started shouting instead. To be honest, I shared his suspicion of the journey ahead.

I had interviewed Nicky Wire of the Manic Street Preachers earlier in the week and while catching up over Dad chat he said something about fatherhood that chimed with me. When talking about the song 'This Sullen Welsh Heart' he said he really worried about the effect his ruminative personality would have on his kids. I told him that I believed that the people who really fretted about this stuff were the kind of people who made great parents. That said, I did identify with the song's opening lyrics ("I don't want my children to grow up like me / It's just so destroying, it's a mocking disease / A wasting disease").

I'd lost count of the number of times that year I'd gone into John's room at 7am to get him up and dressed for the day, only to hear him say: "I had a bad dream... I was on a train. There was a terrible accident." Each time I dug my nails into my palms and thought: "This is normal. All children have bad dreams... you haven't poisoned him. This isn't your fault." And I would scoop him up and say brightly: "Never mind mate! It's only a dream! It can't hurt you. Let's go and read your dinosaur book..."

There wasn't an accident when we got onto the tube but something uncanny did happen.

After changing at Kings Cross for the Hammersmith and City Line, I started to become convinced that I'd made a terrible mistake in coming out, that something bad was about to happen. And despite spending a full half an hour prior to leaving the house getting together everything Little John might need for the trip such as spare clothes, books, Spiderman pyjamas and plastic dinosaur models, stupidly I forgot to pack food. By the time we reached Great Portland Street he was looking forlornly at an empty packet of sultanas he had found in the pushchair and was asking for biscuits.

A kindly looking man in a tweed jacket asked: "Does he like oranges?" When I nodded he fished one out of his rucksack and handed it to me.

"That's very kind of you. Say thank you, John."

I started to peel the orange slowly. The skin was extremely tough and proved quite difficult for me to get to grips with. For a few seconds I thought he had handed me a fake orange. The sort of thing you might have on a film or television set, in a bowl – so it wouldn't go off under the heat of the lights.

One of the main side effects of stopping antidepressants had been an aggravating increase in my tinnitus. I was now constantly aware of the sound – which was not so much like ringing in the ears as brain piercing squalls of feedback and jagged waves of nauseating power electronics – and it didn't take much in the way of stress to ratchet it up a few notches. The noise of the old train clattering along steel rails, the whine of its engines and my hearing impairment seemed to be combining in an evil three-part harmony. But there was now also a fourth element that I just couldn't place. The environmental noise seemed to be producing actual music. I didn't mean *musique concrète*. I didn't mean organic machine rhythms making industrial music. I meant that the train was making what sounded like the noise of a piano or a string quartet playing a slow, drawn-out drone. My head started going south, flooding with a chemical that made my eyes go cold and my mouth start salivating.

"Orange", said John. I tensed and the merest application of extra pressure caused my thumb to press straight through the pith into the flesh causing a geyser of juice to squirt into my eye. It wasn't a fake orange. With blurred vision and a swimming head I pulled out a couple of segments of fruit and handed them to the boy. I felt faint so I leant my head against the pole I was holding on to.

The second my head touched the steel, the musicality got much more noticeable and undeniable, as if a second similar instrument had joined in to a structured drone. I looked round the packed rush hour carriage but it was obvious that no one else could hear the music or if they could, they were extremely unconcerned by it. I looked at the manual brass ventilation grille.

"Subliminal music is being pumped through the 'ventilation ducts' on underground trains on the Hammersmith And City Line by Transport For London", I thought. "But why?"

With shaking hands I reached over and slid the metal grille

shutter switch from the 'open' to the 'closed' position but it didn't stop the drone. In the same way that they played classical music in Zone 3 and 4 tube stations to repel teenagers looking for somewhere to shelter from the rain, it was obvious that they had now started playing avant classical drone music on rush hour tube trains at near subliminal levels to stop people from… to stop them from… *what?*

I looked up at the inviting, bright red passenger alarm handle.

"Oh God! I've become one of those mad people who has panic attacks on the tube and has to pull the handle between stations", I thought. "I could do with getting off this tube. Maybe I should just pull the handle and worry about what happens later…"

I noticed there was a poster next to the alarm handle warning people not to use it in between stations. "What exactly is it for then?" I wondered angrily.

Then it hit me. "Tim Hecker!" I said out loud jubilantly.

"It's Tim Hecker!" I thought. "Or is it early Growing? Or Ben Frost? Or is it Nils Frahm… OF COURSE IT'S NOT NILS FRAHM YOU TIN-EARED CUNT!"

Before chastising myself: "Let's just take this down a notch or two."

I took a deep breath, handed John some more orange and rubbed my temples with my free hand: "It's Tim Hecker. But why are they playing Tim Hecker on the tube? Is it to stop people from freaking out?" I thought.

"It's not doing a very good job", I hissed to myself and a man looked up from his copy of the *Evening Standard*.

I looked round, now in a near panic. Why couldn't anyone else hear it? The track was more like an outtake from *Ravedeath 1972* – or perhaps it was from the piano-based follow up which he released later the same year. That was more likely than something from *Virgins*, it wasn't as annoyingly ecclesiastical and pompous, this was a looser, braver piece of drone music. The musician had more trust in his audience, giving the notes enough space to fill the…

"*Dropped Pianos!*" I muttered triumphantly when I

remembered the name of the EP. The man looked up from his paper and glared at me momentarily.

"Wait. What am I doing?" I thought to myself. "Am I reviewing a piece of music – that may or may not only exist inside my own head – under my breath on a packed commuter tube train?"

"Madness!" I said out loud sharply.

"Orange Daddy", said John. I handed him more segments.

I kept on waiting / praying for the sound to fade away, but instead, by the time we passed through Latimer Road, there were several notes of acousmatic music playing in unpleasant polyphony, combined in a weird chord structure that I didn't recognise, a jarring yet bravely non-standard tonal cluster. "Hmmm, probably non-Western", I thought to myself. It was throbbing in time with the engine and the repetitive clattering rail rhythm now. I looked at the black tunnel walls outside the tube windows. How long had I been down here? How fast were we going? Where were we actually headed? Had I ever been anywhere else? Had I always been down here?

Another note joined into the weird chord, I could taste something metallic in my mouth and two terrible cog wheels slid together for the first time in a long time. "Oh God. I'm having an acid flashback. Please. Not here. Not now…"

A lot of people don't believe that acid flashbacks exist – that they are just anti-drugs propaganda, dreamt up by narcs and swallowed by saps. But then those people invariably haven't had very bad psychological experiences on drugs. If you've had a proper bad trip – and I don't mean a weird trip or a down trip or a paranoid trip or even an unpleasant trip, what I mean is that you have willingly walked through the gates of Hell, and experienced the leisure version of acute paranoid schizophrenia for the duration of eight or nine hours but time stretched to feel like one hundred years – you probably understand what I mean when I say that I see the acid flashback as a form of shell shock or post-traumatic stress disorder.

(It embarrasses me to even consider this possibility. My own paternal grandfather had terrible PTSD after serving in the trenches of the First World War. If he was in the cinema with my Dad and there was a loud explosion on screen or if they were in the street and a car backfired, he would often go diving for cover shouting about bombs. How pathetic of me to be part of a generation that didn't need to go to war but endeavoured to destroy its sanity with drink and drugs regardless.)

A small rivulet of sweat the consistency of hot olive oil flowed down my face along my nose and then dripped to the floor. "What is in the orange? What did the man put in the orange? Why is the music coming through the vents? Why did I bring the boy into this never ending tunnel? Why didn't we stay at home and watch *Dinosaur Train?*" I looked round the crowded carriage but everyone was reading the *ES* or their Kindle or chatting to their neighbour.

Except there was someone who wasn't. A young nervous looking man in a wax jacket. Earlier he had headphones on and his eyes were closed but then it was suddenly clear that something had happened. His eyes snapped open, he pulled his headphones off, his mouth gaped in shock and he reached slowly down for the zipper on his big grey canvas holdall.

When he unzipped the bag the music got louder and this time people registered it, looking up in surprise. In the bag was a Dr Marten's boot lying on a large store bought electronic keyboard. It still took me another two or three seconds to process what was going on. "Oh dear!" said the young man in a flustered manner taking the boot off the keyboard and then fumbling to turn it off as the polyphonic synthesized racket died down to nothing. An elderly lady laughed and her companion said: "What are the chances of that?! I wondered where the music was coming from!"

The young man tutted: "I can't believe I left it switched on! The batteries will be half flat now!"

Everyone laughed and I gripped the handle on the tube until my knuckles turned white and we reached Hammersmith.

Even ten minutes later I was marginally ashamed at the level of melodrama I had managed to conjure out of a switched on synth in a canvas bag. Stopping taking any kind of medication after an extended period was always going to be odd, I just needed to give it time to settle down before leaping to any conclusions about my long-term psychiatric outlook. And in the meantime I needed to get my game face on. Of course it was tempting to think: "The last year I spent any time not on drink, drugs or strong medication was probably about 1986 and I was a teenager, so I wonder what I'm actually like, 100% sober?" And then, after literally just three days leap to the conclusion: "OMG! I'm completely fucking insane!" I was probably no more depressed and psychically distressed than any 40-something man who worked too much, slept too little, did no exercise and spent too much time on the internet.

Later at the wedding, there were other children there playing and John joined in with them, tentatively at first but soon building up a head of steam. They charged around the perimeter of the dance floor before diving onto their bellies, howling with laughter each time they made the circuit of the room and hit the deck. He ran round faster and faster and the energy and light that poured out of him momentarily seemed brighter than a thousand suns. And then at 9pm in the back of a black cab, dressed in his Spiderman pyjamas, tucked into his lowered pushchair, he fell into a deep, contented sleep immediately, unaware of the neon signs, the ambulance sirens, the street lights, the motorbike engines, the car horns and the chaos of London on a Friday night all around him on the streets outside.

I became unfit for purpose when I was this depressed and my judgement became appalling. Every time anyone talked to me I just felt like licking my finger and putting it in a plug socket or jumping in front of a bus just so I could get out of replying. One night, when I should have just gone to bed early I stupidly agreed to go and watch the rock band Savages in Hoxton. I really like their music and was trying to arrange an artistic endeavour between them and another group as well as to cover them extensively on the Quietus. The band kindly agreed to get me and two other people in on the free list.

I never realised it at the time but in retrospect it's clear that when I was that low, I was simply looking for an excuse to thrust myself into a mood which was far worse than the one I was already in. And on that night I was cruising round, looking for trouble.

The first problem happened when my friend Natalie Sharp, the musician known as the Lone Taxidermist, turned up to the gig wearing face paint. The bouncer on the door told her immediately she couldn't come in. I actually like the majority of security people I deal with in London. Most of them seem on top of their game and I certainly hadn't seen any of them severely injure or hospitalise punters like I had done in Hull.

The bouncer said: "This venue doesn't like to encourage arty stuff."

Nat, kind of brilliantly, just repeated this phrase really slowly until he looked flustered and let her in.

There was a big queue to get in to see the band. When I got to the door a vaguely hobbit-esque promoter in a bright red polo shirt told me that I would have to pay to get us all in. I paid us in, but childishly stayed to argue about it with him. He had the upper hand. I was a complete dick for not letting it go and should have just gone inside to watch the show. However, when I was in that frame of mind, I was a guided depression missile, relentlessly seeking out a bad time until I was locked onto one and primed to explode. The bands were all paid, the venue was packed, there was press in and a bunch of bright young things in attendance; if he wanted to cream extra money off the guest list, there wasn't much I could do about it. He waved a big bunch of his mates through for free while saying to me: "Why not write it off as a reasonable business expense, yeah?" And then rubbed his thumb and fingers together in the internationally accepted hand signal for money in front of my face.

If I thought about it for the rest of my life I wouldn't be able to explain why this annoyed me to the point of distraction. Whether it was the Loadsamoney hand gesture, the AQI pronunciation, the completely reasonable suggestion that eight quid times three was not that much cash in the greater scheme of things...

I left immediately and when I got home Maria asked me how it was. I replied with a grunt because I couldn't say: "A hobbit shoes fusspot in a red shirt made a funny hand gesture at me and I became so demented I had to come home." And I sulked and sulked and sulked until it was time for sleep.

I felt subbasement low for well over a week but then snapped out of it on hearing a really good album – the first I'd come across in weeks. And after ten days trapped in a loop of cephalic chaos this album was the only thing strong enough to sort me out. Because despite the art-terrified bouncers, the Del Boy indie promoters, the stupid journalists, the sulking journalists, the lazy, drunk and drugged journalists; despite the hyping hipsters; despite David Cameron, Bobby Gillespie and Tony Parsons; despite weaponised ebola, international terrorism and spiders; despite global dimming, Sharia Law and Kim Dotcom; despite the deathly sepulchres of academia, the merciless bindweed of critical theory and hate-filled message boards; despite the labels and the lawyers; despite the boredom and decadence of a dying culture... despite all of this and more, young musicians still fearlessly strode through this valley of carnage and excrement for little or no reward or thanks with only madness, despair and death as payment. And against all odds and all of our best attempts to stop them, a handful made it through every year untainted, with the thunder still clapping in their chests to deliver the fucking goods.

And that is the genius of music. There is literally nothing you or I can do to stop it. It thrives in the most hostile of conditions.

(The band by the way were the Fat White Family – and the album is called *Champagne Holocaust*.)

But even music was just music and not a magic potion. After three days in this lucid interval, I slipped back inside the featureless expanse of depression once more. I lasted exactly one more month antidepressant-free before throwing the towel in. I simply felt incrementally worse each day until I got to a stage where I couldn't remember ever having felt that bad before. There was an LSD-like sensation of the Earth disappearing beneath my feet, leaving nothing but bottomless void underneath me. How deep could I go? There was no limit to how bad it could get, was the implication. There was much more of this waiting in the wings was what I was feeling. I was on the ladder and the ladder went all the way down. This ladder only went down. There was no up left. It had been removed.

It's funny how you can pick up ideas without even noticing it and have them stay with you for the longest of times. In 1977, during Queen Elizabeth II's Silver Jubilee celebrations, when I was six years old, I saw the Red Arrows performing aerobatics. As they flew overhead in formation, the Folland Gnat planes left vapour trails behind them in red, white and blue. I was very taken with the coloured smoke and how it left very well defined patterns in the sky. Later that day I imagined I was a plane, with my arms outstretched and my hands leaving vapour trails behind me as I ran down the road.

At some point after that I started imagining that my individual fingers left coloured jet trails behind them as I ran along. Without noticing it happening, it became something that I would think about all the time, imagining the trails I would leave behind me on the way to school or the shops and then down motorways en route to family caravan holidays in North Wales, Devon or Yorkshire. In my mind, the smoke trails never dissipated and I imagined that I could see dense three dimensional highways of colour at waist height down roads I used frequently; becoming thicker and more tangible with every repeat journey. I thought, 'What if the Earth completely disappeared – what would be left behind? How many caravan holidays would I have to take before you could see a rough outline of the British Isles? Could I leave some kind of real trace behind me?'

At some point – probably around 1982 when I joined secondary school and after reading *Cosmos* by Carl Sagan – the imaginary smoke trail that I was leaving behind me suddenly took on a dramatic new form. For reasons I can no longer remember I decided that the vapour stayed put in real universal terms, marking out exactly where I had been in the bigger scheme of things. I figured that even if I took the same route to school and back every single day, the pattern I was creating was not just a loop but one of much deeper, three dimensional complexity because of the rotation of the Earth, the movement of the Earth round the Sun and the movement of the solar system inside the Milky Way. I would wonder what kind of weird – but presumably more or less geometrical – pattern I was leaving in interstellar space.

Probably when I started drinking I thought of this less and less but when I did I would spread my fingers if no one was looking and imagine blue, red and white trails coming from my hands and spiralling up into the sky behind me and then away to god knows where. And even though I thought of it less and less as I grew up, when bored on long journeys I would still try and work out what frequent trips up and down the M62 were doing to my interstellar trace.

Recently I realised that if I wanted to know what pattern I'd made in my own infinitesimally small bit of the universe I would have to factor in how the Milky Way itself was moving inside the entire universe.

But without designating relative observation points, it simply has no meaning. One's path through true space depends entirely on the frame of reference, the state of motion in which the observations are taken. It's not entirely arbitrary, in that some possible frames of reference which use the position of stars or the centre of our galaxy as an observation point are kind of natural but others are, frankly, perverse.

I hoped I was leaving a beautiful three dimensional pattern spiralling out into the void, carving out at least some kind of notional pattern behind me but it turns out that, according to one frame of reference, where there is no fixed universal observation point, I'm not even moving. I'm simply inertia in boundless nothingness.

Even by its own unpleasant standards the depression eventually became untenable. So I took a half day off work to go to the doctor's – my first time off ill in ages – and not really knowing what to do before the appointment but needing to get away from the internet, I went to watch the film *Gravity* in 3D. The (fabulous) Rio in Dalston helped to recreate the terrible conditions of an accident in the unforgiving vacuum of space by giving us 3D glasses and leaving the heating turned off. It was a great film to watch at the cinema of course. The people who called it bunkum were kind of missing the point by a large margin and were probably the kind of people who complained loudly at weddings about the drinks being "sparkling wine not champagne, actually". There was an amazing scene very early doors which was essentially a close up of Sandra Bullock's hyper ventilating face, dominating the entire screen. She was stock still at the centre of all things, as the rest of creation span vertiginously round her.

I'd been building up to taking action about the depression for a few days. The weekend before my trip to the doctor's, while visiting Crystal Palace with Maria and Little John, I had been hit by an urge to vault a fence and to wade out into the lake to join the anatomically incorrect statues of ichthyosaurs, like some melancholy Virginia Woolf-reading palaeontologist on Blue Tuesday. I thought about Christmas coming up. I thought about how, when I was a kid, my Dad would spend the entire Christmas break from his factory in bed with the curtains drawn, crippled with depression, staring at the ceiling in silence, his ears screaming with tinnitus. All I could see was me doing exactly the same thing while John was growing up. Decades of sprinting in the opposite direction had left me in exactly the same position my Dad was in. At that moment I truly understood what he had gone through and the realisation was crushing.

My experiment with not being on any kind of medication had failed. For the time being at least. I tried to tell Maria but what came out of my mouth was a dry strangulated gargle of nonsense. "Jesus Christ! I can't even talk! It's like I've got stones in my mouth", I thought. She asked me to repeat what I had said so I tried again, this time enunciating each word very slowly and more clearly: "It's no good, I need to get some help." The admission was a blessed relief.

After *Gravity*, I killed time until my appointment. My doctor's surgery was completely surrounded by scaffolding and full of builders drinking mugs of tea so I had my consultation in a portacabin.

I found myself saying to my doctor: "I had this idea that I could fix myself, if I had a check list and worked my way through all the things that were wrong with my life. Drink, drugs, depression, illness, weight... everything... even the way I dressed and my haircut, how I acted on the internet and how I spoke to people I didn't know. I really thought I could get myself sorted out. It's weird though, ever since I was about 14 I've always been able to control my mood with something or other. The last month was my first time ever with nothing. And I thought, 'Is this what I'm like? Is this what my bedrock personality is like? Is this what I'm all about – all this anger, nihilism, self-pity, violent thoughts, bitterness and mean spiritedness? Maybe it would have got better, but I'm not sure I can wait to find out at this time. It's like I haven't moved. Or I've come back round full circle to where I started from. You don't need to worry, I'm never going to hurt myself or anyone else but there would need to be some kind of alleviation; some kind of respite eventually. Nah, I'd never drink again – it's fucking horrible. I hate it. It would probably be drugs... It would definitely be drugs. If I carry on like this I'll find some way of putting myself in a void before Christmas."

And I walked out of there with a new prescription for the same tablets that I just spent months trying to come off and some sleeping tablets for the insomnia.

Slaughter In The Air (2013)

I was on holiday in the middle of nowhere when she died. In a way it was like it never happened. Even days later it was as if she was still lurking in the shadows like some bogeyman: part Steve Bell cartoon, part *Spitting Image* puppet, part Emperor Palpatine. While she was slipping away unnoticed I was in a hotel restaurant near Birnam Wood, Perthshire. She would have liked it there. The walls were covered in photographs of her, Tony Blair, the Queen and family, Sean Connery in a kilt, Ewan McGregor wearing chinos with a sweater knotted loosely round his neck with a quote about how seriously he took being Scottish, Annie Lennox and some spam-coloured lummox with an ABH haircut and a rugby top.

Maria was always delighted to be in posh restaurants in the same way I was usually deeply uncomfortable in them. I had hyper-atrophied table manners and had to concentrate on not eating with my fingers at all times – a battle I often lost. My grandparents wouldn't have stood for the way that I now ate. Both sides of my family were aspirational working class immigrants from Ireland who had moved to Liverpool early in the 20th Century. My Dad's Dad – Daddy-gran – was a merchant sailor and may have looked uncannily like Popeye, down to the pipe, cap and bulging biceps covered in nautical-themed, Indian ink tattoos, but he knew every last rule there was to know about positioning of cutlery and the setting of a fine table. And he may have left school at 13 but he also liked to read Byron and Shelley. Maybe less so after he got home from the trenches of World War One with gangrene (in a leg that got whittled away over the years), shrapnel wounds and shell shock. The PTSD became his unintentional bequest to some of his nine children; the youngest, my Dad, included. It manifested itself in them in the form of alcoholism, prescription drug addiction, obsessive compulsive religious mania, a whole raft of mental illnesses and perhaps, most debilitating of all: the virulent contagion of nihilism.

My Dad's dad died when I was eight and I didn't hear him speak much before that but I did hear him say this: "They were bloody cowards. They took some valley boys. Crying for their mothers. Could barely speak a word of English. Only enough to pray. They knew all the words to 'Our Father'. Their nerves were shot. They couldn't carry on. They should have been sent home but they were shot dead crying for their mothers and buried in ditches by the road side."

Bombs went off in families but it could be decades before everyone caught the flak.

I got told this stuff on a daily basis from as early as I can remember. Some of it Frank McCourt would have baulked at putting in *Angela's Ashes*, for fear of it not being believed. I mean, who coats their children in thick layers of goose fat and brown paper for the entire winter? (This was one of many baroque stories that was wheeled out when I made requests for branded sportswear. Even I had to admit that my Dad had me on this one though and I'd have to settle for some bizarre looking track suit bought from a unit on an industrial estate in Prescot for a few quid instead of the brand new Sergio Tacchini I wanted. I'd sigh on sight of the single stripe piped onto the arms of the monstrosity thrust upon me. My Dad would say: "Your Mum will sew a few more stripes on it for you and you can draw your own logo on in pen." Only a man who had been brought up to think of goose fat as seasonal underwear could employ such barbaric logic.)

There was no time for learning about cutlery for my Dad. During the German air raids on Liverpool during World War Two, his friend who lived next door was killed along with his family. My Dad was evacuated to the countryside to stay on a farm when he was eight but he was left to sleep in a stable, was fed leftover scraps of food and was never washed – it was during summer so there was no excuse for this. So his sisters went down there mob handed and took him back. They'd sooner he was blown to bits than made to live like an animal.

During our meal Maria looked out of the window at a row of gleaming classic cars dating back to at least the 1930s and announced: "Look at those posh cars!" The restaurateur chortled to himself as if at some *faux pas*: "Well! I've heard them called old before but never posh..."

The next day we drove down the East Coast and I passed the time keeping a tally of the number of UKIP anti-immigration bill boards I saw in consecutive coastal towns after we hit England. We stopped for tea in Whitley Bay and it took us a while to find anywhere open among the shuttered and boarded-up buildings and crumbling tenements. Whitley Bay, the seaside town they remembered to close down.

The next day, when we got there, Stockton-on-Tees felt like a once-great town that had been punched repeatedly in the face but never offered an explanation why. It looked reminiscent of any British working class town that had been dealt a series of body blows by out-of-town retail development and pedestrianisation. It was wreathed in road works, traffic jams and vacant units.

As we pulled onto Yarm Street a hassled looking man with neck tattoos broke into a faltering jog next to the car and shouted through the open window: "Coppers?"

"What?" asked Maria, perplexed.

"Coppers love. Coppers! Can you spare any coppers?" he said, just about keeping up with the car.

He didn't wait for an answer but carried on jogging onwards with a limp – like a man with a grim appointment to keep.

I was visiting the town's last remaining record shop, Sound It Out, which revealed itself to be an Aladdin's Cave of great music. It was a pleasure to meet Tom, the keeper of the vinyl, and the other staff who were on duty. I ended up restricting myself to ten purchases but could have come away with 20 pieces from The Fall and Killing Joke sections alone.

I knew about the shop because of an excellent documentary called *Sound It Out* by the filmmaker Jeanie Finlay and I'd been after an excuse to visit since watching it. It didn't disappoint and in fact was a really moving experience. ("It's like being in the film!" I thought to myself excitedly and then couldn't work out if it was a stupid thing to think or not.) While I was there a hip young kid bought an original 12" copy of Joey Beltram's 'Energy Flash' and a pair of excitable and evergreen rock chicks came in to discuss how many points you would get for the word 'fellatio' while playing strip Scrabble and the just announced Gary Numan tour. Tom put a copy of the new Numan album *Splinter* on order for one of them and a copy of Bowie's *The Next Day* on vinyl under the counter for the other until payday. They both left made up.

Everyone who came in was talking excitedly about Record Store Day and all of them – bar people coming in to the shop to sell old vinyl – seemed to know each other by first name. Even Tom's Mum and Dad popped in to see him. After two hours browsing in the shop watching people come and go, it was clear this place was as much a community centre as it was a place to source very reasonably priced records.

Tom was working round the clock to get the shop ready for Record Store Day, expanding the shop into a back room with new shelves which had been acquired from the town's recently closed down HMV – another unit boarded up. When I asked if they were getting geared up for the event everyone groaned.

RSD is genuinely the thin black line between success and failure for many shops in the UK so they have to treat it with utmost seriousness. They were right in the middle of an order check and with only a week left to go nerves were beginning to fray a little. "Metal?" shouted Tom. "We've got enough room for one Bolt Thrower, all the Mayhems twice, three Judas Priests, all the Aerosmiths twice and one Cannibal Corpse", came the reply.

The next day we ended up driving from my parents' house in Rainhill to the nearest soft play centre, in Earlstown seven miles away, so Little John could have some exercise. As we parked up I realised the industrial unit with the kids play centre in it was near the flat that my old friends Mike and Debbie lived in twenty years ago. The flat was on Chemical Street above the barbers and opposite a junkyard, whose contents were piled high above the lip of the rusted corrugated iron walls, and threatened to spill onto the damp pavements below. When I walked over to have a look, the flat looked like it had been burned out in the intervening decades. All the windows at the rear were boarded up and one of the three at the side was as well. While I was staring up, I saw movement behind the curtains but then a man in overalls started striding angrily out of an adjacent lock up toward me so I beat a retreat back over the road to the soft play centre. I felt momentarily guilty. Mike didn't talk to me for four months once because I laughed about the name of his road. He thought I was being a stuck up prick because I'd moved down South but really I was joking about the amount of drugs we used to do there. Someone had tagged 'DOPE' in big, blunt letters all over Earlstown's walls and doors. But then, why not? Someone had also gone round lashing up professionally made green plastic posters with the address of their 'Growise Hydro' business, situated in a nearby shop unit. Weed looked like the only commercial enterprise that was taking root in Earlstown at that moment.

As we drove back home, my Mum saw the sign for Haydock along the East Lancs Road and said: "Do you remember when you had that terrible job?"

"The roofing thing? That wasn't so bad." I explained to Maria: "It was a factory yard called Hoogovens Aluminium. We made the roofs for other big factories. Ten-hour shifts outdoors."

My Mum said: "It was so hot that summer that you were working in just your trousers, do you remember? I begged him to take some sun cream to work with him because he was getting really burned but he said he wouldn't have been able to put it on in front of the other men. They were horrible to you weren't they?"

I ignored Maria grinning.

The men in that yard were alright really. I think I was probably being a bit precious. Most of the people I met in factories up north were alright really. I learned how to do cryptic crosswords in the aerosol factory in Hull. These guys in Haydock would take the mickey out of me because I was the youngest and had long hair. It wasn't like in Hertfordshire. I worked with some proper recidivists, thugs and racists down there.

I instantly felt bad at having this thought – fuck knows how someone with a cockney accent would have gotten on working in Haydock or Hull in 1993. Then I remembered the broken pint glass and felt less bad. The chant: "Southern jobs for Southern boys." Imminent violence in the afternoon outside a pub in Welwyn Garden City, 1996. "Why don't you fuck off back home you Scouse monkey?" But I was less than 500 yards away from the flat where I lived.

My Mum said: "You always worked though didn't you? Even if you had to cycle for miles."

I shrugged and nodded but I felt like a fraud. I worked every day because it was the only way I could afford to go out and drink heavily every night. I tried it on the dole. I gave that a good test drive when I was a teenager. I was climbing the walls after a while, raiding the copper jar for a can of Special Brew, borrowing money for a bottle of sherry, smoking nibs out of overflowing ashtrays. I couldn't handle it at all.

My Mum carried on to Maria: "A lot of very clever men ended up taking very poor work up here in the 1980s and 1990s. The competition was so fierce for the jobs... not like when I was young. You'd could leave one job in the morning and have another by the afternoon."

The job at Hoogovens was a cakewalk compared to other roofing jobs I'd had over the years. Even earlier, in 1993, my mate Riki Day and I ended up working with a freelance roofer in North

Hull. Ex-squaddie with dreadlocks. Dead hard. Pretty far out guy. Smoked a crazy amount of weed. We were putting the roof on a five-storey factory framework from a kind of cherry picker or platform crane, that would sway about everywhere with us skidding about on top of that. On this industrial estate they used to process vegetable oil and margarine. It always felt like there were huge clouds of oil in the air, like you were always trying to find your way through a giant fog of fat. We would sometimes see some guys wandering round in what looked like NBC suits but we'd just be there in jeans and Revolting Cocks T-shirts. And it wasn't just up the cherry picker where we'd be skidding round all over the place. On all the metal walkways and gantries, there would be stalactites of congealed fat dripping down. All the footpaths inside and outside were slick with fat. Literally everything you could see was covered in thick, processed vegetable grease. When we knocked off and made our way home we'd have solid white oil in our hair and it was near impossible to wash this stuff off you.

It was terrifying up that cherry picker. We didn't last that long. Even Riki Day was scared and his party trick was taking his eyes out with a spoon handle when he was drunk and pointing them round in different directions to freak people out. And when a dude who takes his own eyes out for a laugh is scared, then I'm scared as well.

On the way back to Rainhill, we drove back through St Helens and I could only mark how much it had changed by checking off all the absences and presences. The far side of town had gone. It was all just roundabouts and chain fast food stores. The last of the mines closed in 1992. The industry had been going downhill but went into a tail spin in 1985. It wasn't like a coal mining monoculture that you'd see in a worthy but cliché-ridden British TV series or film from the mid-90s but some of our immediate neighbours when I was growing up were coal miners and there was a giant slag heap on the field at the back of my estate. You say the words "slag heap at the end of my road" to some people and they look at you like you've just announced that you were suckled by wolves in a hillside forest until the age of 18. The slag heaps had gone now but the new roundabouts on the link road had mining-themed civic sculpture denoting the dignity of labour and all that fucking nonsense. From the M62 at the junction for my parents' house you could see a big, cigar-shaped, mopey-faced sculpture about five storeys tall. No disrespect to those involved in commissioning The Dream but it looked like Primark Escher and it really wasn't as good as the Angel Of The North.

Most of the really big factories had gone bar the enormous Pilkingtons glass works in town that looked like something out of *Dune*. Beechams was gone. Ravenhead Glass was gone. United Glass was gone. Triplex was gone.

The building where I played euphonium and trombone in a brass band had gone, replaced by the catering college. From production to service, the transition was nearly complete. If you gave it a few more years Stockton-On-Tees would look exactly like St Helens except maybe with some different crappy civic art that was of no use to anyone celebrating the no-longer-existent shipbuilding industry.

Then I ticked them off one by one as we drove through Thatto Heath and Nutgrove in the thickening drizzle and dwindling light. The pub where Steve and his mate who died at Hillsborough drank. Gone. All the other pubs where you'd get beaten up for being queer. Still there. A club I drank in and had all but forgotten. A burned out shell, scorched to the brickwork. My high school – a hive of duffers, thugs and lads who weren't credited with a hope in hell – that had an average GCE / CSE pass rate of one measly fucking result per 2.5 pupils. Gone – closed the year I left, replaced by Barratt Homes. Rainhill Psychiatric Hospital. Gone, replaced by Barratt Homes. Houses presumably not filled with the thousands of former inmates. No care for them in this community.

The off-licence where I used to buy Special Brew and Thunderbird wine when I was a teenager. Still there but now with cashiers stood behind thick, bulletproof Plexiglass.

The alleyway where I was beaten nearly blind when I was 14 by a gang of lads from about three miles down the road in Prescot: still there.

And then just as we were nearing my parents' home Maria spotted St James' Methodist Church. She said: "Oooh! Isn't that the church you and Stu Green were arrested on top of?"

"WELL!" I shouted, tapping an invisible watch on my wrist. "Is that the time? We'd better get a move on! Dad will be wondering where we are! Do you know what I fancy for lunch? Cheese on toast…"

"Eh? You did what?" said my Mum.

Maria grimaced apologetically and put her foot down.

AFTERWORD

My book ends here. But it ends with a flight of the imagination. Ill advised, poorly thought out, risible and almost certainly the by-product of a manic episode combined with a burgeoning mid-life crisis. But a bona fide flight of the imagination nonetheless.

The idea had been with me for months but I only realised what I was doing, in March 2015. As I laid the large fold-out road map of the UK on my living room floor and started placing small star stickers (stolen from one of my son's Thomas The Tank Engine magazines) over various towns and cities, I tried to pin down where this idea had originated as I marked Salford, Eastbourne, Plymouth, Manchester, Bristol, Stockton-on-Tees, Durham, Sunderland, Sheffield, Taunton, Liverpool, Rochester, Cambridge, Leeds, Bradford, Birmingham, Totnes, Nottingham, Northampton, Worcester, Brighton... Every star represented a stop on a reading tour round England I was going to undertake in May 2015 to promote my book *Jolly Lad*. Each of the small, colourful circles of paper had been placed over the site of a gig location; either in a prison, a library, a school, a record store, a church, a university, a gig venue, an arts space, a theatre, a bookshop or a cinema. Each marker stood for an opportunity I was taking to collaborate with various artists, poets, musicians, writers and filmmakers along the route.

The actual business of phoning up and booking all of these various venues started in earnest in December 2014, sparked off by the completion of the first readable draft of *Jolly Lad* I had managed to produce. In all likelihood I was swept along by the sheer, unexpected euphoria of actually breaking the back of the writing because just months earlier I nearly had to shelve the idea.

In the spring of that year I decided I needed something to distract myself from the heavy bouts of depression and agitation caused by quitting drugs. I recalled my experience of throwing all my energies into making the Quietus a good website and a viable job for myself and how this had helped me stay off the ale. I decided that writing a book was exactly the kind of distraction I needed this time.

At first the going was terrible because I was already quite ill with stress. It was quite noticeable given that one of the symptoms was my beard falling out. Now drug free and on a very healthy diet I could no longer pretend that the blinding headaches, fatigue, poor digestion and violent mood swings I was suffering on a daily basis were simply down to my lifestyle. An exclusion diet and blood tests suggested that I had developed no fewer than 18 food intolerances and allergies.

Despite this I decided to try and combine the three-month sabbatical I had taken from work, starting in September, in order to write my book with another attempt to come off the antidepressants that I'd been on for a decade. Despite tapering down gradually over three months, when I graduated from taking a tiny dose to finally ingesting nothing at all the effects were just as harsh as they had been the year before. I'm legally obliged to refer to the effects of quitting as 'cessation' rather than withdrawal but it was much harder for me to stop taking these SSRI drugs than it was to quit any illegal drug I've ever taken; and that includes crack cocaine.

This only served to uncover various other problems. For example, when I stopped drinking in 2008 I started taking large daily doses of ibuprofen in order to deal with the terrible headaches I developed. I became dimly aware after three or four years of this that my headaches were now caused solely by me forgetting to take enough painkillers during the course of the day. So when the withdrawal from SSRIs really started to kick in with headaches, memory loss, stunningly harsh and psychedelic levels of arachnophobia, night terrors, fatigue, depression and brain zaps galore, I took what I felt was the only option open to me and added codeine-based medication to my daily dose of analgesia.

By autumn I was stressed, sick, depressed, suicidal and in a lot of pain so I went to see my doctor who seemed pretty appalled. I don't know for sure if she said, "For fuck's sake John!" But she certainly muttered something that sounded very similar under her breath.

She made me promise to stop taking all pain relief immediately and reassured me that if I got that and my stress under control then the SSRI trouble would right itself as well.

During the three months I'd taken off work I had been trying to write every day but the little I'd committed to paper was garbage and I had to seriously consider the idea that the entire project had been a waste of time. In fact, at that very moment it was hard to see my entire six-year project of self-improvement as anything but a waste of time as well. I felt much worse at the end of 2014 than I had done at any point when I was drinking or using drugs heavily.

And things got worse before they got better. I had a serious conversation with my doctor about the pros and cons of spending some time in a psychiatric facility as a voluntary inmate. Luckily before I came to any firm conclusions on that score – after three months of being so low I could barely operate – things suddenly started improving rapidly.

In a last ditch attempt to break the deadlock of feeling so awful during every waking moment of every single day, I did the unthinkable and joined a gym. And true enough the experience was abominable, barbaric and gauche… but only aesthetically speaking. My paranoia made me convinced that there was something unpleasant about the way these facilities were set up: twenty rowing machines, twenty treadmills, twenty cross trainers and twenty exercise bikes all facing a row of five large TV screens showing rolling news about people getting beheaded in Syria; a continuous loop of a slightly overweight Meghan Trainor dancing away; a continuous loop of a slightly underweight Taylor Swift dancing away; some reality TV show picturing terrified looking pensioners trying to buy a knackered old house; and a seemingly never ending celebrity cookery show. But even by the end of my first week I had to begrudgingly admit that daily heavy aerobic exercise made me feel much better both physically and mentally, in no time at all.

I started taking instruction in Dhyana meditation care of London's Theosophical Society; and while I found some of the spiritual and philosophical concepts I was being presented with slightly outlandish, I benefitted almost immediately from the practice of attempting to still and clear my mind of all thought.

I finally got to see a dietician at Homerton Hospital in Hackney and she placed me on a super conservative food regime in a last ditch attempt to find out why problems with my digestive system were spiralling out of control. The Spartan food programme was very boring and made eating outside of my own flat next to impossible but the improvement in how I felt – especially as regards headaches – was remarkable.

The combination of exercise and ultra-healthy eating also meant that kilograms started dropping off me and within a few months I started approaching the ideal weight for my height for the first time since the early 90s.

So during the winter I started writing again and this time managed to produce something that didn't resemble the manifesto of the Unabomber written on homebrew cider and magic mushrooms. Swept up in the excitement I started planning the reading tour in earnest.

My good friend Kjetil, a Norwegian musician who records under the name of Årabrot, himself recuperating from a serious illness, signed up for the project. No matter where the tour went – no matter how large or small the venue, whether it was in someone's front room or in a large concert venue, whether in a bookshop or in a church, he would provide musical accompaniment to my readings and double up as my driver and tour manager.

When people asked why I was doing the tour, I stammered that it was important for me as a music writer to have a clearer understanding of the lot of an independent musician in 2015. I wanted to know how difficult it was to book a tour, to find the money, to plan the route, to come up with merch to sell on the way, to find suitable support acts.

I told my preternaturally cosmic and relaxed publisher Mark Pilkington that I was undertaking the 31-date jaunt in order to generate material for my next book – a snapshot of my country in 2015 based loosely on the JB Priestly book *English Journey*. I was going to call the tour and the book – *An English Trip*.

But while both of these reasons were true to a certain degree they didn't represent the fundamental reason for why I wanted to undertake such an odd project

So as I looked at the large road map on my living room floor, covered liberally with star stickers, wondering where the idea had come from, I thought back to my trip to Dungeness with Jonny Mugwump. About my night spent in his camper van parked in Hastings in a storm a decade earlier and how I'd come up with an idea of undertaking a secular pilgrimage. I hadn't realised it at the time – or hadn't wanted to – but the idea of walking round the coast of the UK was a cypher for all of the things I would never be able to achieve while I was chained to the bottle, the pill and the wrap. But now, after six and a half years of sobriety and a year or so drug free, I was beginning to understand that this hare-brained scheme to walk twice round the coast of Great Britain without break had been a sublimation of my desire to be free... not to be constantly beholden to cravings.

My book ends here simply because it's time to send the manuscript to my publishers. I'd like to personally apologise to anyone who feels it's fizzled out slightly without much in the way of closure. If I'd been writing a novel, this would have been the stage at which I would have introduced a bird into proceedings to symbolise the chance of future resolution or the idea of hope at least. I would have had a seagull fly into the room, necessitating capture and release by the protagonist, symbolising one chapter ending and another hope-filled chapter just beginning.

But real life isn't a novel and I hate birds. Stupid flapping things with their ghastly little eyes. Always eyeing up your chips. If a bird flew into my flat now – as long as Maria and John were out and I wasn't on deadline – I can guarantee you that I'd hit it with my shoe, fry it and eat it.

And, when all is said and done, is there really such a thing as closure? I'm unconvinced.

This is the problem with attempting to portray life as far as I'm concerned; there is no resolution or closure as such. It just rattles along at its own pace with no symbolic seagull to signify one chapter ending and another starting. It just keeps on rattling along. And then, one day, it suddenly doesn't even rattle along any more.

It's up to me to form a narrative out of the chaos, to choose a terminus point for this particular story and I choose here and now. This is not because I'm cured of depression or because I've beaten my addictions (there is no complete recovery from these things and never will be). It's not because my project, to sort out all of the damage done while I was drinking and drugging, is complete. It isn't and I have a sneaking suspicion I will be working on these things for the rest of my life. It is because simply, for the first time ever, some of the time I can see clearly that illness and addiction are no longer my defining characteristics. Sometimes I go for weeks without thinking about drugs. Sometimes I go for months without thinking about drink. Sometimes I go for a week or two without suffering depression, anxiety or rage. And now, from time to time, I have periods where I feel free, whether it's an illusion or not. And I used some of this freedom to write a book, simply to show people who know me that I could. And I used some of this freedom to plan a weird music and spoken word tour round England, simply to show them that I could. And now, from time to time, I have periods – lengthy periods – where I feel some hope for the future, whether this is an illusion or not.

But sometimes when I feel this way I don't plan any grand schemes, I simply take my son down the park for an ice cream.

And if you'll excuse me, that's what I'm going to do right now

An English Trip (2015)

"What's the point?" asks Charlie Harpoon, The Man With The Van.

Charlie, a handsome rock & roller with a moustache and a quiff, is driving me to my rendezvous at a petrol station near Gatwick. I'm meeting my good friend, driver and musical collaborator Kjetil Nernes. He and his van Doris are my primary collaborators for the next month.

Kjetil, is, for all intents and purposes, the Norwegian rock group, Årabrot. And it is his fault I'm undertaking this ridiculous excursion. 31 shows over 31 dates collaborating with a whole bunch of different poets, writers, filmmakers, musicians, a group of ethical undertakers, Hull's second most famous mountain climber, a member of Nurse With Wound, half of Factory Floor, two thirds of The Eccentronic Research Council, all of GNOD, a robotic mannequin head called Hugo and a counter cultural research group. The shows are being delivered to a community poetry group in Sunderland; bohemian acoustic instrument designers in a village hall in Worcestershire; a cinema in Nottingham; a bookshop in Norwich; a Victorian cotton mill in Salford; a former police station in Newcastle; a unitarian church in Cambridge.

But what is the point? I'm not sure.

My creative activities with Kjetil have been building for some time. Back in 2011 he asked me to provide some sleeve notes for the Årabrot EP, *Murder As Art*. I wrote him a short story called 'Gun Lore' and it ended up being reprinted in full on the inner sleeve.

I was so made up. It was the first piece of fiction I'd written since leaving school and the first I'd ever had published. I couldn't wait to show my mum. I counted down the days until I got a copy of the record sent through the post from Norway. The first thing I saw on opening the heavy card packaging was Johannes Høie's striking artwork which featured a group of dead terrorist women in heaven. At least I think they were women because their faces were obscured by paramilitary balaclavas but they had holes cut in their blouses to expose their breasts. However, at least three of them had erect penises, which muddied the water somewhat. They were also carrying AK-47s and goose stepping across clouds. There was a lot to unpack in the artwork and I decided that it would be best if I showed Mum my second piece of published fiction instead.

There was no plan for us to work together again as such, but chance forced our hand. In 2014, Kjetil became seriously ill with cancer and nearly died. He underwent a very invasive and intensive treatment which put him out of action for half a year. Like me, he's a workaholic and during this time he switched from regular studio use to making music from home – a deconsecrated church in the Swedish countryside. He encouraged me to record myself reading 'Gun Lore' and then started adding ambient music to it with his girlfriend, the musician Karin Park; the results were intense and dark. They transformed my relatively static reading into something altogether more dynamic. This was one of two ways in which the groundwork for a spoken word and music project and an extensive live tour was laid, with me barely registering the fact.

May Day is beautiful as we set off from Stamford Hill. I try to explain what the point is to Charlie as best I can. I will have to do this many, many times over the next month: "I have this book about alcoholism, depression and mental illness called Jolly Lad. I'm touring it around. Doing readings. Doing collaborations. The thing is, I have a common or garden variety of bipolar disorder. I come up with these ideas all the time – militant beekeeping in Hackney, building a pirate radio station in the flat, walking twice round the coast of Britain in a loop until thousands of people follow me on a pilgrimage – but after an intense period of obsessing about them, I snap out of it (usually after I've been prescribed medication) and never think about them again.

"But this time I applied for an Arts Council grant and then by the time I'd come to my senses I couldn't back out of it.

"I guess because of my day job as a music writer I want to know what it's like for a young artist or writer or musician to go on a small, self-booked, independent tour of England, and I want to know what problems and pitfalls they face. And I want to write about stuff that's going on outside of London during election month.

"But what's the point? I don't know. I'm hoping to find out en route."

At Gatwick we meet Kjetil. He is dressed in tight fitting black suit, chains, shades and a wide brimmed hat. He looks like Asa Hawks, the "blind" preacher played by Harry Dean Stanton in John Huston's 1979 adaptation of Flannery O'Connor's *Wise Blood*. He tips his big wide-brimmed hat hello. This is not his stage hat but his everyday hat. His stage hat, the kind of prairie Stetson you can see in the opening scenes of *The Holy Mountain* is massive and kept in the type of box that suggests it's an essential part of a drum kit. It has its own carefully allotted slot in the back of the van with the tons of amplifiers, speaker cabinets, guitars, synthesizers, boxes of books, suitcases full of clothes and bags and bags of oranges we are taking with us. There is only one correct way to fit all of this stuff into the back of Doris, like 3-D Tetris, and all it takes is one giant hat in the wrong place and then everything has to be taken out again and reloaded in the correct position.

Kjetil has just spent the previous month on tour, driving Karin all over Europe. Without taking a day off he's now ready to do the same for me.

Karin's band take their stuff out of the van and I load mine in. The process takes less than an hour and then we're ready to go. Kjetil seems to enjoy the ten minute break he has between month long tours.

Karin looks more like she's stepped off the set of *Blade Runner* than a Jodorowsky or John Huston movie. They make a very striking couple. She is joining us for part of An English Trip to play synthesizer, something I'm very pleased about.

From the outset Kjetil is knackered. He eschewed the comfort of a hotel room to spend the previous night in a squat with his new touring band, Ghold. "I love those guys but all they want to do is stay up all night drinking beer and listening to Elvis in their squat with no water.

"I need to go on more tours with old guys like you."

He's talking to me. I'm 43. There will be no late night drinking of beer. I'm a recovering alcoholic. There will be no powders and potions. I have a near 30-year history of substance abuse and have to practice abstinence for all kinds of reasons. There will be no Elvis. The King is dead. Long live the Black President – Fela Kuti.

The scars on Kjetil's pale neck are less angry than they were when I saw him at Christmas but he's still thin as a rake and clearly hasn't entirely regained his full strength. After this tour he and Karin are heading back home to remote rural Sweden so they can get married during the Summer solstice weekend; but then instead of a honeymoon, Årabrot are heading out on the first of maybe three American tours they're going to undertake in the next 12 months. They won't make that much money – in fact there's every chance they could lose some if anything goes wrong – and it will be an arduous task.

What indeed is the point of going on tour? I am hopefully about to find out.

The second we hit the M25 we immediately get stuck in May Day traffic. I realise immediately that most of the next month is going to be spent looking at slow moving traffic on motorways.

The journey from London to Brighton takes considerably more time than my 40 minute set does that evening. Once we load in at the venue, a converted coaching house, I am dismayed to realise that I'm absolutely terrified. My hands are shaking so much I can barely see what it says in my book. Because Kjetil and I live in different countries we've only had one four hour rehearsal in a hotel room in Oslo. I complained at the time that this just wasn't enough but he insisted: "If you read out what you have written with absolute conviction in a manner that suggests that what you have to say is of the utmost importance then it will be exemplary." At the time this short but passionately delivered sermon seemed very reasonable so we stopped rehearsing early and went out to eat Turkish food instead, but now I can't help but wish we'd prepared a little bit more thoroughly.

The audience are lovely and there are some familiar faces which helps a little but I still spend more time nervously wittering between pieces than I actually do reading. I make a terrible Sir Mix-A-Lot joke which no one laughs at ("Oh my God Becky, would you look at John's book") but otherwise it's fine, I guess, and I get to share the stage with the fantastic Kemper Norton and his blood spattered zither.

The following day on the motorway, time stretches and contracts simultaneously in a temporal Doppler effect. The days seem longer but time blisters, pops and breaks apart pleasantly as the brain switches down a few gears into a near pure experiential mode. There's little to worry about. Just count the pylons and pretend you've got a flamethrower to aim at UKIP billboards. Luxuriate in motorway sign typography and listen to Funkadelic's *Maggot Brain* as loud as it will go. *Agharta* by Miles Davis is the soundtrack to us speeding out of the South up the M1 towards the Rainy City. Al Foster's ringing, open hi-hat is our fuel. And then it's nothing but John

Coltrane, Electric Wizard and NOMEANSNO until we reach our destination.

It starts raining the second we hit Stoke. And then before long we're on the Mancunian Way heading for Piccadilly in torrential rain.

It would be a lie to say that the Star And Garter on Fairfield Street is a ghost of its former self because it's always looked ravaged. This is certainly how it was when I drank here regularly 21 years ago. Perhaps it's always been here. The rupturing effects of Gondwanaland breaking apart several millions of years ago split the colossal Piccadilly boulder in half and there, at its centre, was the Star, complete with laminated posters for punk all-dayers, scratched plastic pint pots and dour Morrissey-themed discos.

Everyone I speak to says the venue's on its last legs, that it won't survive much longer – not just threatened by regeneration but by fans of live music no longer wandering down to this end of town. However, for now, it remains a glorious carbuncle, a cultural outpost, a piece of structural intransigence. I hope it doesn't close, but if it does, in one last act of violence against the architectural homogenisation of Manchester, I hope it splits the wrecker's ball in half and shatters their vehicles to scrap.

As soon as I get out of the van, I learn a very important lesson about on-the-road hygiene. And that is, you must never think to yourself: "Ah, my deodorant is packed away in my suitcase; I'll just load into the venue and then dig it out and put some on before the show, after all I've just put clean clothes on and had a shower. How bad could I possibly get?" The answer to this is, after you've helped carry a Moog Taurus Bass V3, a baritone, an electric guitar and a bass all made by the Electrical Guitar Company out of solid metal, a Hiwatt PA 100, a Hiwatt Custom 100 and a Hiwatt Custom 200 amp, a Hiwatt 412 cabinet and a 15/410 bass cabinet and several boxes of your stupid fucking vanity project memoir up two flights of stairs you will smell like a kebab that a rhino has used as a butt plug. And a liberal spraying of Right Guard after this point will not improve matters.

My pal John Robb would never have made this mistake. This well-dressed gentleman of punk rock and tireless champion of the musical underdog has been playing live music with The Membranes on and off for the last four decades. He bursts into a cackle when I explain that we were in Brighton last night, we're in Manchester tonight and then back in Eastbourne tomorrow.

I sigh and explain: "When I planned An English Trip, it was this perfect thing. We were going to drive all the way round the outside of England and then spiral inwards toward the centre. "But what happens is this: after you plan your perfect tour, then promoters start phoning you up or emailing you... 'We've double booked you with a Stereophonics tribute act'; 'There's actually a bar mitzvah on that day'; 'It's Record Shop Day...' And then the careful plan falls to pieces."

(By the end of May, the distance we actually cover in the van is just shy of 5,000 miles – the same as if we'd done a tour across America.)

I continue: "So our original tour route was this amazing pattern and now it looks like that terrifying film of a spider on LSD trying to spin a web."

"There's only one thing worse than a spider on LSD trying to spin a web", says Brother John with a serious look on his face. "And that's a spider on caffeine trying to spin a web."

We have a very long conversation about artificial arachnid consciousness expansion and how much of a good idea this is and how different drugs would affect spiders and scorpions.

It's a rum do. I mean, it must be bad enough being a spider and realising you are without anyone spiking you with a massive dose of LSD.

It becomes clear early on that the Travelodge is our friend. Every Travelodge room Kjetil and I share is identical. Twin beds, minimal decoration, very interesting mass produced art, a chair, tea making facilities and a portable telly, often chained to the wall. The Travelodge may have less furniture in it than the average bail hostel, and may sometimes smell like a suburban pet shop circa 1984, but it is totally fine as we're low ranking touring musicians/ writers, not visiting dignitaries from Saudi Arabia.

Our first Travelodge is situated in a motorway retail park so the following morning we only have to walk just a few hundred yards to the Toby Carvery for breakfast. Pushing open the double swing doors we are confronted by a man in stained chef's whites, with hair pushed under a light blue plastic turban crowning a jowly and crimson face. He is methodically and noisily applying a large cleaver to a foot long cylindrical sharpening steel with a schnick-schnick sound.

"Hello!" says Kjetil cheerfully. "Are you Toby?"

He looks up slowly and a pendulous and translucent bead of sweat sways under his nose. His eyes are like drill holes in gammon, bruised udders of flesh hanging below each nicotine stained ocular orb. He is possibly the most hungover man I have ever seen. He jaws away silently, his eyes flickering dully with rage as he starts straightening up. The BPM of metal on metal increases. We both circle round him gingerly and head rapidly for the breakfast counter past tables rammed full of people who look like they're about to die. I have never seen so many morbidly obese people in one place at one time. It's like God's waiting room flanked by pyramids of fried egg.

It is only £5 per head and you can eat as much as you want but the choice is only bacon, sausages, roast potatoes, black pudding, fried egg, fried bread, beans and mushrooms. This is the life! The thrill of the open road. Unlimited roast potatoes and bacon for breakfast.

Later on in the tour we spend one night at the supposedly more upmarket Premier Inn, and it is relatively more luxurious but due to its incomprehensible and automated entry machine, it takes us an hour-long conversation with two angry receptionists to gain access to our room. "Getting into this hotel was like the opening scene from an episode of *Black Mirror*", says Kjetil, a recent convert to the show. "There's nothing like waking up in some shitty English town, before eating some shitty English breakfast, before driving slowly down some shitty English motorway for 12 hours, before loading into some shitty English venue and playing a shitty gig to ten people before going to some shitty English motel on a shitty English retail park just to watch a really well made English TV series which explains to you exactly why everything is so fucked", he tells me gleefully.

Plus any hotel room is actually very much like home as long as you have a laptop, a handful of Nick Cave CDs, some Right Guard and a copy of *Threads* on DVD, which is exactly what I do have in my overnight hotel bag.

The trip up to Sunderland the next day is beautiful. Fields of golden rapeseed glow under a blue sky. But I give up counting the UKIP billboards. There are just too many. The purple pound signs zip past in a blur. We've been on the road for five days now. I haven't seen a single sign for Labour. It is almost a relief when we pass a huge hoarding in an arable field next to a broken tractor which proclaims: "Prepare to meet your Lord!" We pull in soon after to stretch our legs in front of a petrol station that shares a forecourt with a sex shop, which is wrapped in a large tarpaulin hoarding that reads: "Under new management!" We get back in and drive past a garden centre flying a row of ten Confederate flags and two Union Jacks before stopping at a knackered and rusty Jetstream caravan serving up cups of tea.

The original idea for this trip was mad, in a very literal sense. It was going to be two months on the road, playing two shows every day, one matinee and one main, each in a different English location over two months. That would essentially have meant visiting 120 different places in England alone. It was based loosely on JB Priestley's *English Journey* (1934). I wasn't well when I planned the trip. I was having a hypomanic episode. So I turned down the idea of doing shows in Scotland or Wales.

We could have gone to the Hay-On-Wye literary festival but I said no, because the venue was half a mile over the border into Wales. And now I can't even remember why this was important. Likewise we could have done some really good shows in places like Glasgow but my mania prevented it. The original plan was so wrong-headed it had to be abandoned after a week of trying to organise performances in several Category A prisons, three lighthouses, an abandoned WWII pillbox, a psychiatric hospital and on a sandbank jutting out into the North Sea. I couldn't abandon the idea altogether as I had committed to doing the tour and even raised some funding but I called time on the utter insanity of doing 120 gigs in 60 days and reduced it to the only just tolerable idea of doing 31 shows in 31 days. With me booking and promoting the whole thing.

But remnants of mania remain. Like why are we playing in community centres, village halls and churches rather than book shops? Why aren't we having a day off? I can no longer remember.

Pop Recs Ltd is a second hand record shop, a gig venue, a rehearsal space and a cafe but more than anything it is a community centre along a street that doesn't have much going for it beyond pound shops, an all you can eat Chinese buffet and a massive Wetherspoons. We've been tagged on to the end of the King Ink poetry night run by the dapper Brian.

It's an open mic event featuring many readers, from a precocious and slightly cosmic teenager (who is dressed exactly like Sylvester McCoy's incarnation of Dr Who) to Chris, a 72 year old in a baseball cap who has only taken up writing and performing poetry within the last year.

Rhys, the venue's sound person, tells me that the pensioner has come on in leaps and bounds: "When he started he was influenced by The Beats and he would be doing these really provocative readings punctuated by Nazi salutes. We had to ask him to rein it in a little but he's showing a real flair for writing verse."

As soon as we start though we run into trouble. There is a 20-something man pacing up and down at the back of the room, swigging from an oversized bottle of Becks. I start talking to the group about getting beaten by soldiers when I was 21 and an "amusing" incident that happened when I was having my nose rebuilt in hospital as a result. The young man cheers at some of the things I'm saying and boos at others.

Finally his patience snaps and he barks at me: "Come with me now to Wetherspoons! Come with me and let's do a real reading together over the road in the pub where the real people are."

I slump inside because I recognise this thinking intimately. I try and tell him that I can see more real people – pensioners, mums, children, teenagers – in this poetry group than I would find in any Wetherspoons.

He shouts: "Fuck King Ink! Let's go to Wetherspoons!"

One of the women in the audience chimes in: "You can't go to Wetherspoons Mark! Not since you knocked all those tables over."

I try and carry on with my story about my nose but I'm completely upstaged as Mark tears his shirt off and shouts: "Can you see my scar?!"

It's impossible to miss – right up the centre of his chest like a fucking axe wound.

"I had open heart surgery when I was 25. I had a massive heart attack. It nearly finished me off."

I have to abandon the reading and let him talk. He tells me about the flashes of insight alcohol gives him. How he is a true poet. I believe him.

I try to explain to him that I get more inspiration myself from swimming and meditating and that while I used to feel very inspired by alcohol as a young man, nothing ever came from it other than pipe dreams and a rich interior life; and then eventually even the daydreams began to shrivel up faster than my liver. And all of the novels, all of the poems, all of the screenplays, all of the bands... none of them came to anything. He spits scornfully on the floor and interrupts sarcastically: "Rimbaud would have been proud of you. Do you know who Rimbaud is?"

It's no word of a lie to say I've been waiting over three decades to make the Rimbaud/ Rambo confusion joke.

I look at Mark brandishing his gigantic bottle of Pilsner, his eyes sparkling with madness and the precursor to tears and I realise sadly that my time hasn't yet arrived: "I have heard of Rimbaud yes but I haven't really read that much French poetry..."

"Ah well FUCK OFF!" he shouts and storms through the door.

Dr Who's mum, a pretty poet with purple hair called Lesley, tells me that Mark is a sensitive guy, a great visual artist and talented writer, who is perhaps a touch too highly strung for local pubs and is banned from nearly all of them. I take down his address so I can write to him. Mark and I are like peas in a pod – bar the massive chest scar – I hope he doesn't spend as long making the same mistake I made, in only being able to discern reality at the bottom of a Wetherspoons pint glass.

We do a show and it's good. I mean, it's really good, I can feel the air between Kjetil and I crackling as if it's about to take on physical form. There is a doorway to a new place standing ajar. It's opening and light is spilling out. The performances we are doing change slightly every night and usually without us having to discuss it. There is no analog to this in the static world of writing. The feedback loop from performance is dynamic and stimulating. But despite all this, I feel deflated as we head to the Travelodge. When I set out to write this book, Mark was exactly the person I was trying to reach, and now he thinks I'm just some appalling cunt. Some London faker who has no idea how he feels.

Waking up in another identical Travelodge on another identical motorway retail park the next day I realise that this is literally the worst place for a writer to be during General Election month. Nowhere has wifi that works. It's like being in a bubble of ignorance for 31 days. We have to choose these parks to minimise the chances of Doris getting stolen with all of our gear inside it. Every Travelodge we stay in is essentially the same, surrounded by a handful of other outlets – a Toby Carvery or a Harvester or, if we're really unlucky, both of them, a Costa, a Boots and a BP petrol station. And all accessible from a motorway roundabout that isn't really near anything other than either an airport, a power station, a prison or an industrial estate. A hangover from reading a lot of JG Ballard as a schoolboy led me to believe that there would be some kind of brutal but mind-expanding beauty to be had from this aspect of the venture, but these cloned motorway retail parks are the most co-opted and least free spaces of all.

Outside, sitting on a wall drinking a cup of tea in the sunshine, I look intently at a semi-circle of black-coloured birds, rooks maybe, surrounding a single bird of their kind. They are slowly advancing towards it. The bird in the middle is stock still and not moving. It doesn't look like a friendly encounter. Kjetil comes out and joins me. It looks as if the parliament are just about to attack the solitary bird, to peck it to death. But just as the corvine jury are about to bear down on the accused, they are disturbed by a loud noise in the sky. The red arrows fly over the Travelodge in formation. It's almost as if Kjetil exists in a bubble of uncanny, apocalyptic events that moves with him wherever he goes. He doesn't notice the striking red planes flying in a triangle formation bifurcating the sky. I stand pointing upwards. "The Red Arrows... The Silver Jubilee... 1977..." Then I point at where the birds had been: "The crows... The punishment..."

"Yes, yes" he snaps irritably, as if he's sick of life constantly throwing symbols in his face. "Let's get in the van and get off otherwise we won't get to Digbeth in time for tonight's show."

That night I dream that the solid iron and nickel core of the Earth is set to slough us all off until the planet rolls raw and bleeding in space, just vast plains of roiling magma with no dirty crust to contain it. Suffering the utter indignity of being born between waves on a flat, unmagical land, the scions of a pusillanimous age, we will all be cast into the void with this filthy scab of a country we call England.

When I open my eyes Toby is stood in the corner of the room, sharpening his cleaver, schnick-schnick, schnick-schnick. Empty eye sockets carved out of rancid, fly-blown gammon.

"We have to stop eating lunch at the Harvester!" I spring out of bed shouting, waking Kjetil from his sleep. "The unlimited Pepsi refill is fucking killing me!"

Fuck the Harvester. Fuck Toby Carvery. All of the clothes that were hanging off me on May Day are now snug, and it's only the twelfth... My ears are ringing with precognitive dread; the tinnitus omen of some imminent blue cheese dressing related pulmonary catastrophe.

It had to happen eventually but on the thirteenth I hit a wall. It's been too many days trying to get by on five hours sleep, powered only by Coca-Cola and Harvester 83 Combos of ribs and roast chicken. Energy and spirit desert me entirely and something that I've been trying to ignore bubbles up to the surface. We roll into Totnes and I can see it's a beautiful town and that the venue we're playing at, Drift, is a really cool, independent record shop, but all I want to do is to crawl into a Travelodge room, shut the curtains and sleep for two days.

Today an absent friend is weighing heavy on my mind as Kjetil and I head over the road to an Indian restaurant. I am hoping that the hottest dish on the Cafe Mumbai menu will somehow revive me. The food is astoundingly good. The endorphin rush created by the phaal and the fact that the waiters are playing gabba speed bhangra at full volume resets some of my dials. It's easy to see how ruinous life on the road can be, even when you don't drink or do drugs. I feel sorry for younger bands who feel they have to go out partying every night after shows. After a couple of weeks it must end up hellish.

Back at the shop I have just enough time to say hello to a bohemian couple called Ru and Claire, who introduce themselves as the undertakers. When my publisher Mark said that his friends from Totnes, The Undertakers, should support Årabrot, I presumed he was talking about some psych rock group. It didn't occur to me for a second that they were actually undertakers. I'm glad I didn't know, because I would have turned the idea down flat. I don't want to seem closed minded but I would have found the idea risible and would have vetoed it immediately. I remain eternally grateful that this misunderstanding happened.

I don't want to state the obvious, but I've taken a lot of drugs in the past and had more "visionary" experiences than I'll ever remember, but most of them pale next to what the straight life has thrown at me. The birth of my son is probably the most genuinely psychedelic thing that's ever happened to me, in the sense that it altered my perception of the world irrevocably. (And I was as straight as it's possible to be – I even refused a sneaky go on the gas and air when no one was looking.) And by the same token, undergoing this ritual, presided over by a pair of youthfully middle-aged countercultural funeral directors in a record shop in Devon, surrounded by people I don't know, ends up being one of the most mind-altering experiences I will ever have.

When I originally planned the tour, this was the date, halfway through the month, that Nick Talbot, aka Gravenhurst, was supposed to join us on the road, playing acoustic sets as our support. He was also involved in helping me make the CD that accompanied the first edition of this book. After some discussion I sent him a reading of 'Slaughter In The Air', the final chapter, to which he was going to add music. And then all of the discussions about gigs and readings and recordings stopped. I sent a couple of emails saying I was worried – that normally I wouldn't go so long without hearing from him when we were working on something, that it didn't seem usual – but didn't hear back from him. A week later a friend phoned me up to tell me that he had been found dead at his flat.

In the shop Ru and Claire press play on a Technics turntable so a plastic skull with a smiley badge in one eye socket, a rose crystal on its forehead and a cigar clamped between its teeth starts spinning round. The skull, I later find out, represents Papa Gede, part of the Haitian Vodun pantheon, the guardian of the graveyard and representative of the corpse of the first man to die.

Ru begins in a pleasant burr: "We are going to bless this book tour, well underway as it is, with a little light Devon Voodoo, bring attention and recognition to this brave self revealing, from other possible worlds. And in doing so, we hope to convey important things. Well, one important thing, actually, and it comes down to this: don't ever be afraid, of anything, ever, because you are already dead. This moment, here, now, this is the moment between the click and the bang.

"You are already dead...

"The truth is the glass of life, it is not half full, or half empty; it's smashed on the floor, and every drop of experience that passes your lips is sucked from the lip of non-existence.

"We are all absent friends in waiting, ancestors already, peering out through the fabric of our burial shroud, the soil of our graves filling our mouths, the flames from our funeral pyres scorching the inside of our greasy, cracked skulls.

"Your solid certainties line the inside of your coffin. Your grand plans for tomorrow, just stains and scratches on the lid. Your voice, your touch, your name, just memories and stories, soon to be forgotten forever. We are motes of dust in a sunbeam, fragments of experience, echoes of atoms dispersing into endless night, radio signals becoming fainter and fainter and fainter. Our homes are tombs, our towns and cities, boneyards. We are lonely piles of calcium carbonate becoming dust.

"We are already dead."

Without missing a beat Claire adds: "By the way we're available for children's parties, christenings, summer barbecues, out of town superstore blessings, whatever. Usual rates apply, plus forty pence per mile if it's any further than Exeter.

"We are undertakers, and we run a burial ground. That's how we know we're all already dead. We buried you, shortly before we buried each other. Every day we take the dead, the grateful and the reluctant, the snatched and the driven, the too-soon and the not-soon-enough, and we dress them, and lift them into their coffins, bring their families in to sit with them and cry and kiss them one last time.

"We pace out their graves, we book the crematorium, we dig the hole, carry them and their kin to the edge of the known world. We stand around them and tell the story of their life. We bury or we burn them, we shove them out and off across that dark river, where the mist closes behind us all.

"We are not Death, but we are on the payroll, and it's okay for that to make you feel a little uncomfortable; it sits oddly with us too. We did not expect to become this. And in becoming this we get no staff discount, we have no special offers today. And we don't approve of death either, we do not love it like goths, or ISIS, but daily, it grips our faces in a bony vice, and turns us toward this truth: Love is the law, there is only now, we are our own ancestors."

To a soundtrack that includes Cyclobe, the pair carry out a humanist funeral celebration – pretty much what they would actually do if they were burying someone, they inform me later. They talk candidly about death and about what it means, lighting candles for the rock writer Lester Bangs, Amy Winehouse and John Balance of Coil – talismanic figures representing those who have fallen early in the music industry. But really it's as if I can just see a postcard of Nick propped up on the counter of this record shop, in between all of the piles of CDs, novelty mugs and flyers for local gigs, with a tealight candle flickering in front of him.

They finish reading with Claire joking that they rubbed liquid acid on the door handle to the shop which would explain why we are now feeling so strange, but I can actually hear someone gasping for breath and it does feel as if someone has pumped DMT into the room via air vents. I can hear a woman muttering, "Oh my God..." under her breath.

The short ceremony ends and I'm about to start crying so I head quickly over the road to the toilets of the restaurant where I can get my shit together before starting our set. Everything about my readings, which I chose days ago, chimes perfectly with the ritual that Ru and Claire performed. Everything they said was prescient and beautiful. What great people... I've never thought about it before but I know who I want to bury me now when my time comes. I don't really like thinking about death, but I can now visualise my own funeral and it suddenly seems a lot less awful.

The drive that night to London – to Maria and Little John – is perfect, but the next day I creak with anxiety. Anxiety is a tyrant and it bears its cudgels and maces at me with unrelenting ferocity. Drink? I'm done with it. Drugs? Tempting but no thanks. Depression? A worthy opponent but one I'm sometimes in better shape than. Anxiety though? It beats me savagely to my knees every single day. As soon as more than three things start going wrong at the same time, I am flooded with an abundance of adrenaline which I struggle to convert to anything useful. I wish I had a tap on the side of my head, so I could pour this evil stuff out of me and watch it burn straight through the floor like the Alien's blood.

By the time we're ready to go on stage at The Lexington near Kings Cross I've reached some kind of fugue state of terror and it's by far and away the biggest crowd we've had so far, around 150 people. I remember Kjetil's words about delivering my reading as if it means everything and as soon as I start, I slip into the hypnotic pulse of his industrial noise and the words start flowing out more smoothly. I'm in a trance and for a split second – or maybe a minute or two, or maybe a day or two – I step outside myself. I'm no longer the hypersensitive, over-stressed, irritable, bipolar, traumatised, moody, middle-aged journalist – momentarily I become what I was chasing for all of those years of utter dissolution. And it isn't drink or drugs that gets me there. The show is great. Rough around the edges but great. As I walk off stage I'm dimly aware that people are cheering. And I mean, really cheering at the top of their lungs. And it sounds like the singing of one thousand chilled cans of Stella Artois – not the British cans mind but the ones you get from a European booze run – hissing as the rings are pulled back. There is a chill on my skin like I've just placed my hand into an ice cold rock pond on the beach at Tenby without disturbing a single grain of sand.

And everything is just so. What a perfect night this restless day ended up being. Performance hinges on the vanity of self-belief. If you are unshakable in your belief in what you are doing then you will blow the walls out.

I have an all too short ten minutes standing with my girlfriend and then I'm out in the rain, soaked to the skin walking to the van. I totally understand why people do this now. Nothing beats this feeling!

After driving for hours we get all the way to Stevenage before I realise that I've left my coat, my money, my books, my phone and my records at the venue and that we'll have to go back the next day to pick them up before we can drive to Hull. For fuck's sake, Doran you massive iron-clad dobber!

There are some poor dates on the tour for various reasons. Hull is, for me at least, tough. It's my first night sober in the city, despite the fact I lived there for five years. It's dark as we drive into town and ghosts line Ferensway waiting to greet me. The cinema where I had my first date in town, the pair of us just turned 18 – watching *Shirley Valentine*, saying, "Imagine being that old…" about Pauline Collins and Bernard Hill – is now a Mecca Bingo; the war memorial that I regularly drank sherry in front of on a bench; the Welly nightclub where I saw a punter swan dive off a balcony and go headfirst through the corner of a formica-topped table. When they took him out on a stretcher there was a blanket pulled up over his face. And then down past my old house on De Grey Street and into the car park of the Adelphi. I know nearly everyone in the audience back from when I was constantly drunk. Suddenly nothing I've written seems that funny. As a knock on effect, I fear that I do not manage to deliver my words with absolute conviction in a manner that suggests that what I have to say is of the utmost importance.

Only five people turn up in Leicester to watch us and the wonderful Lone Taxidermist – and two of them are friends. But at least the capacity of the room is only 28 at a push. Liverpool is much more of a conspicuous disaster. After being talked out of playing the relatively compact Leaf bar on Bold Street with Jane Weaver – an artist who could comfortably fill the space several times over – we end up playing The Kazimier, a 700 capacity venue, where I don't think we get more than 30 people through the door. And given that the lineup ends up being Årabrot, the double drumming, body-stocking-wearing prog trio Barberos, Jay Binary and Cosmic Kenichi Iwasa's Krautrock Karaoke, this is a bit of a disaster. At one point there are more people on stage than there are in the cavernous venue. I'd always wondered how bands cope with this. "Why aren't they mortified playing to a near empty room?" I would always think to myself. But really everything is about the performance itself and tonight we're on fire. It's the opposite to Hull which was quite busy but where I gave a stuttering, stilted performance. Tonight I almost feel like I'm tripping when I come off stage. Ex-Easter Island Head, one of the bands who were supposed to be joining us, send word that they can't make it because they've gone to watch *Mad Max: Fury Road* instead. You can't fault their priorities really but it was their loss. When I get off stage I see that two very old mates are in the 'crowd'. One of them says to me: "That was great Doran. I'm off to the bar. What shall I get you? It's Stella isn't it?"

But the really good nights outnumber the shaky ones by a large margin. The dreamlike B-Arts warehouse in Stoke and the beautiful volunteers who run it. An oasis of DIY culture that everyone should visit. Playing the Picture House Social, a former cinema, in Sheffield with a rambunctious Eccentronic Research Council and harmonium player Hayley Forsyth, then staying with hip young couple Daniel Dylan Wray and Tash Bright and their large collection of *Twin Peaks*-themed wooden spoons. Trading prose in Northampton with the experimental writer Ali Fruish and the poet Roger Robinson. Sharing verses in Leeds with the poet Rick Holland and analog techno maniacs Chrononautz. Being joined by Andrew Liles of

Nurse With Wound and Current 93 in Bradford where we're supporting Richard Dawson. (Liles, who is wearing bright pink espadrilles, enhances our performance violently and vividly by shredding on a B.C. Rich all the way through the set. Before the final whistles of metallic feedback have even fled the venue he unplugs his guitar and says: "Nandos?") Årabrot and ANTA joining forces to play 'I Rove' as we summon a black hole to swallow up all of Bristol. Being joined by Nik Void of Factory Floor when we play at the Broadway Cinema in Nottingham. Sharing a stage with English Heretic. Sharing a stage with Bronze Teeth. Sharing a stage with ILL and Ten Mouth Electron. Sharing a stage with Henry Blacker. Sharing a stage with Sarah Angliss. But it's too much work for just two people to organise and complete in one month and inevitably things start to fray.

No one tours non-stop for 31 days without taking a day off and by day 29 we're dangerously close to coming off the rails. And if it wasn't for the miraculous reappearance of Karin, this is exactly what would have happened. The drive to Great Yarmouth is gruelling and 13-hours long because of traffic – we get stuck behind no less than three serious road accidents. But luckily Karin is there to stop us murdering each other (or anyone else) and we have plenty of long albums to listen to. Just like a mattress in a shared student house or the narrative flow of the Bayeux Tapestry – Kendrick Lamar's *To Pimp A Butterfly* sags in the middle but it is very, very long, making it ideal for the van. We load into the town's only metal venue, sound-check and nip out to get a takeaway before the gig. While waiting for food, I grab a copy of the local listings mag to flip through, and scan that month's gig diary for the venue we are playing. We're nestled in among all the local bands with names like Led Henge, Siege Machine and Kurgen. I notice with some irritation that we've been billed as John Doran and Arab Rot, as if I'm fronting some kind of EDL-friendly NSBM band. And then, just below that, listed for the following night at the same venue, I see the words Marie Antoinette.

Sometimes – just once or twice in a lifetime, by my reckoning – things happen that are so terrifying, so utterly anxiety-generating, that they propel you into a sweet spot of horror so complete that it is an analogue of total zen calm.

I view the rest of my evening as if from outside of my own body. I see myself traipsing back to the venue to perform on a stage where a man who sent me multiple death threats after being locked up because of me is due to appear in less than 24 hours' time. I see myself clutching sweatily onto a copy of the listings mag that he clearly reads. I see myself glancing at the advert over and over again, as if somehow, magically, my name will no longer be next to that of Marie Antoinette. I see myself asking the venue owner if Great Yarmouth is home to two different bands of that name and then I see myself slump slightly when the answer comes back that no, there are not; that Sauron V had recently formed a new version of the band with local teenagers on release from hospital.

I wonder what the likelihood of him growing calmer and happier, while locked up in hospital for a decade is. And I realise that it's not likely at all.

It turns out that the word 'indefinitely' when applied to people detained in psychiatric hospitals doesn't actually mean what I thought it did, and that a year or so beforehand he had been judged to be well again and was released.

It is on stage in this fugue state, beyond fight or flight, that I read the passage from my book about Sauron V. "Whatever happens tonight," I reason to myself, "will either end very badly or provide me with something else to write about."

As Årabrot's doom-ridden riffs clang round the basement – as we fill the venue with controlled feedback and machine noise – I can feel a presence in the room, a hulking solidity to the shadows at the rear of the venue by the cigarette machine where the purple pools of light give way to voids of black. But when the house lights come up there is no one there – either I'd imagined it or whoever was stood there has left. We load out of the venue in record time and hit the road immediately, despite the fact the main act of the night, the mighty Sly and the Family Drone, are one of my favourite live bands in the whole world and I've been looking forward to watching them play all week.

We fly down the A47 like we are clinging to a rocket, listening to Slayer albums at full volume, gabbling like a bunch of four year olds.

When you have a history of alcohol and drug abuse then there is a very good chance that you are the sort of person who acts impulsively; not just in the fields of intoxication but in all aspects of your life. This is the sort of person you are. It is interesting to observe to what extent this impulsivity remains when the drink and drugs have gone. For me, acting on impulse has been a double edged sword over the years. It's got me into some trouble for sure but also perhaps if I had the ability to properly sit down and work out how much stress and pain a future project is going to cause me then I wouldn't have started a website, I wouldn't have started a record label and I definitely wouldn't have written this book.

At the start of the tour I was convinced that I had wasted about 23 years of my life but now, on the penultimate day, I'm not so sure. All of these sureties reveal themselves to be little more than subjective feelings, sensations... hunches. They depend entirely on my position and state of motion at the time the observations are made.

We return for the fifth and, this time, final, stay at the beautiful and stridently utopian Islington Mill in Salford, and tomorrow we will be performing here as well.

Sam Weaver, the modular synth player and auxiliary member of GNOD, swings open the giant iron door to the Mill's courtyard and we drive inside to what feels like sanctuary. Inside the artists Bill Campbell, Michael Holland and Maurice Carlin are beavering away in the kitchen making big vats of fine-smelling food despite it being 1am because they have their Sounds From The Other City festival kicking off tomorrow.

My room is a vision of minimalist perfection. I wish all hotel rooms were as comfortable and well designed as this. I want to read but fall immediately into a very deep sleep. The people at the Mill are the best. They are fellow travellers.

I've been a fan of GNOD for about a decade and I was at their first London show, where they ended up signed to Rocket Recordings. Some time later I went to see them play live at the extreme music festival Supersonic in Birmingham. On the first day of the long weekend I ran into Jimmy The Saint, my procurer friend with the gold tooth and the embellished Honda Civic. I asked him if he was carrying and, to no one's surprise, it turned out he was. He handed me a baggie but told me to be careful as it was "very strong". I ignored him and tipped the whole lot into my mouth. I said, "Urgh, disgusting. What is it? MDMA?"

And he replied with the most frightening sentence that I have ever heard: "No. My mate Steve makes it in his caravan."

There were several experiential peaks and troughs over the next three days that I was awake. I did spend several hours believing I was trapped in a pinball machine. And I saw a terrifyingly caustic show by Scorn. But certainly the highlight was watching GNOD play live on the Sunday afternoon. All the band looked like characters from *Mad Max 2* and behind them was a huge black hole. As they powered through 'Genocider' I could see the massive, super-dense astral phenomenon sucking all matter into its catastrophically heavy core, beyond the event horizon from where nothing, not even light, could escape. They looked like clerics; the leaders of a post-apocalyptic cult, ensuring that the remnants of humanity gave praise to the giant gravity events at the core of all galaxies.

Of course, in reality there was no supermassive black hole behind the band, just the brick wall of the warehouse they were playing in on a drizzly Sunday afternoon in Digbeth. But the hallucination made a great impact on me.

After the show I was introduced to Paddy Shine from the band. And bearing in mind it's usually considered bad form for anyone to speak to a musician like this – let alone if they're the middle-aged editor of a music magazine – I started gibbering at him about how I needed to move up to Salford and join their band to read out poetry about the worship of black holes. Now, usually at this point any musician hearing this drivel would look embarrassed and walk away as quickly as possible but Paddy just said, "Yeah man. Just do it. Come up to Salford and stay with us for a bit at the Mill…"

It only took me a couple of days and a conversation with my girlfriend to come to the realisation that I wasn't going to give away all of my worldly possessions and go and live in a Victorian cotton mill with a renegade psychedelic band and read poetry about black holes, but the experience made a deep impression on me.

Over the years I'd go on to meet GNOD several times and we'd occasionally laugh about the time I was totally off my nut and I asked if I could become their interstellar poet. But then, one time, and I can't remember why, it actually came up, the idea: "Why don't we actually do it?"

When I was drinking, every single morning I'd wake up with this incredible feeling of shame and guilt. I didn't want a hole in the ground to open up and swallow me; I wanted a hole in the sky to appear and to swallow everything that had ever existed and to crush all of it down to a single point that would be too small to see. I sent them a recording of me reading this out in the form of an invocation.

I'm not sure if the audio I sent to GNOD conveyed what I felt adequately but what they did with the piece was incredible. I was in tears when I first heard it. I was so moved that finally, something creative had come out of all of this ugliness and nihilism. My recording with GNOD called 'Lacerated Sky' symbolised a move from doing something impulsive but potentially destructive into the realms of doing something impulsive but creative. This was the second way in which the groundwork for a spoken word and music project was laid.

GNOD's equipment is set up on a table, a giant network of synthesizer modules, delays, reverbs, guitar pedals – a throbbing cityscape of electronic gateways, from which they slowly summon creaks, groans and clanks which echo around the Burrow venue of Islington Mill. When the unreasonably handsome and dapper David Mclean, of Tombed Visions, another Mill resident, starts teasing noirish licks out of his saxophone it's my queue to start reading.

In 1994 I lived in Manchester in a succession of grim shared houses that were either always being burgled or full of insects. During this period I'd take drugs when I could get hold of them and spend most of the nights upset and awake in a state of terror praying for morning to come, swearing to myself that I would never take drugs again. Only to repeat the process the very next night. One of the few things that would calm me down was a cassette I had made of the reassuring sounds of the Radio 4 Shipping Forecast. Outside I imagined ghosts roving the streets and bus routes of Greater Manchester, while inside I cowered under the blankets, wreathed in sweat, listening to talk of North Utsire, German Bight and Fastnet. My reading with GNOD, 'Area Forecast Manchester', is the shipping forecast but reimagined for the regularity and intensity of ghost sightings on public transport.

The noise GNOD are making is glorious. After reading I sit down on the edge of the stage, hoping to remove myself totally from the eyes of those in the band, to not distract from their industriousness and heads down concentration. I close my eyes, clear my head of all thought and vaporous hands take mine, leading me away from the stage, out of the double swing doors, down the main corridor and into an adjacent room. I know, thanks to mental degradation and age, tonight's experience will inevitably fade, like a Tibetan sand mandala exposed to the elements. The sharpness of line and vividness of colour will become blotched and mixed till nothing but a few scant facts remain. But it is enough just to be here, to participate, to be creating rather than destroying, so I try and be in the moment as much as possible, to be flatter, to open myself up to receive... for once not wrapped up in regret over something I did in the past or worrying about things that I'll have to do in the future, but empty and inside music. I'm now merely the outline of a human being with matter and energy streaming right through me.

I roll out flat and float through swing doors, across a corridor, through more doors and into a stairwell of glazed bricks. And then I start to ascend. One storey, two storeys, three storeys, four storeys, five storeys and into the spacious attic. I flatten further still, I narrow, I lengthen, becoming light enough to be carried by the air, out through a ventilation brick and into the sharp Salford twilight. Eddies carry me up above the now receding red brick mill. I pass silently through a cloud of particulates and ozone, on a swell of birch tree pollen, ryegrass and timothygrass, on the threat of lime tree particles, above the stone flagged courtyards, above the tarmac'd avenues, above the tangle of flyovers, above the rain slick parking lots, above Ordsall Hall. Above the blood spattered flags outside the Lass O'Gowrie. Above Gladstone hailing a cab imperiously. Above Alan Turing sitting on a bench contemplating his final apple. Above the giant steel bicycle of Deansgate. Above the pavements oil-decorated with rainbows outside Piccadilly Records. Above the Whitworth and above Popeyes kebabs and pizza. Above the spider teeming towpaths of the Rochdale Canal. Above the decorative tuba bolted above the doorway of Johnny Roadhouse. Above Blackfriar's bridge and the black water of the Irwell. Above the football fields of Kersal. Above Crumpsall Cemetery. Above Prestwich. Above Stretford. Above Failsworth. Above Stockport. I spread thinner and thinner until I create a dome one atom thick over all of Greater Manchester. Even Wigan. No longer afraid, I can afford psychic protection for the whole metropolitan county tonight. Solar radiation bounces off me, reflected back into the void. We harness energy, trap it and reflect it back outwards toward the nothingness, saying, temporarily: "We are here."

I started May 2015 terrified of standing up and reading in front of any group of people no matter how small, and ended the month falling asleep onstage while performing with my favourite psychedelic rock band.

A strong boot to the shin brings me back to the room. Marlene, GNOD's bassist glares and nods at the microphone centrestage. The nod says: "Get up there you melt." The last whistles of electronic noise are slowly completing circuits round their chained equipment, echoing out into nothingness as I begin to read: "It's funny how you can pick up ideas without even noticing it and have them stay with you for the longest of times. In 1977, during Queen Elizabeth II's Silver Jubilee celebrations, I was six years old. I saw The Red Arrows performing aerobatics..."

Acknowledgements And Notes

First of all I need to thank Maria, the best girlfriend and mother in the world, and John, the best son in the world. Without wanting to state the obvious, there have been some ups and downs over the years and they continue to give me the strength and love I need to keep on keeping on. Because of them I am blessed – without them I would be nothing.

I'd like to thank my Mum, Dad and sister and the rest of my family for love and support over the years. I'd specifically like to thank my parents for the extremely understanding way they reacted when I filled them in about my history and told them about this book project, despite some of this information being presumably distressing for them to learn.

I'd like to thank all of my friends. I am blessed with good pals, to the extent that there isn't room to mention everyone here, but a hearty cheers to each and every one of you.

As regards to this book, first and foremost I need to mention my dear friend Natasha Soobramanien – without her gentle prodding over the last 25 years I almost certainly would never have contemplated actually writing a book. I already knew that she was an amazing writer but now I can attest she is a fantastic editor as well. Thank you.

Again, this whole thing would never have happened without

my initial invitation to become a contributor to *VICE* from Alex Miller and the continued encouragement and support I received from my commissioning editor Kev Kharas. Jah bless, you good people. And many thanks also to my other editors past and present at *VICE* – Andy Capper, Piers Martin, Lauren Martin and Alex Hoffman.

Another key player in this project is my esteemed Quietus co-pilot and dear friend Luke Turner. Without his patience, support and advice this project would have flown into the side of a mountain. Thanks to all Quietus staff, all contributors and friends of the site past and present – especially Laurie, Sophie, Mat, Anna, Aug, Karl, Giles, MANHEIM, Rory, Ben, Mitch, Ian, Sean, Moatsy and Charles.

May satori and universal consciousness be bestowed via the brow chakra to my very cosmic and very agreeable publisher, Mr Mark Pilkington, whose only concern during this whole process has been to support whatever hare-brained creative ideas that I've had. And thanks to the equally agreeable and dapper Travis Elborough for being the first to suggest Strange Attractor to me.

Thanks to everyone I mention in the book, especially Martin, Mike, Debbie, Brother Manish, Brother John Robb, Brother Jeremy, Natalie, Sister Anthea, Simon, Phil Hebblethwaite, Mickey, Rich, Stimmy, Conn, Riki, Frank, Jonny, Bob, Chris, Tim, Ken, Gabe, Vince, Richard, Tom W, Tom B, Kelly, Jeanie and Damien.

Thanks to Stu Green for his excellent advice and for four decades of friendship and still counting. Big shout out to Paula and Seth as well.

Some people call it writing; I recognise it for what it truly is – noting down funny things that my good friend John Tatlock says.

Thanks to Pete McIntyre [RIP], Melvyn Hoyle [RIP] and Stephen Sunderland. Giants among mere mortals.

Massive praise be heaped 'pon the heads of Chris Bye, Alison Boyle and everyone else at ACE North West, without whom this entire project would have been a much more modest affair. Thanks also to Shelley Warren and everyone at the Arts Foundation.

Thanks to everyone at *Metal Hammer* past and present – especially Jon Selzer, Alex Milas, Alex Burrows and Dom Lawson.

Thanks to Becca Gaskell and Stuart Maconie at BBC Radio 6. Thanks to Michael Hann and Harriet Gibsone at the *Guardian*. Thanks to Lucy O'Brien and Gareth Thomas at UCA Epsom.

Special thanks to Helen for her love and friendship over the decades.

Thanks to my fantastic mother-in-law Judy for helping out with childcare on such a regular basis during the writing of this book. Thanks also to Emma and Sophia.

It is highly unlikely that anyone remembers bar me but I only agreed to write MENK on the understanding that it would one day feature a photograph of me and London's best dressed man, Tony Sylvester, smoking pipes. I haven't forgotten. Roll on pipe day because valar morghulis &c.

Some of this material originated in an attempt to impress Jack Seale over at the old When Saturday Comes OTF message board, while other bits of it came from a three-part article about alcoholism and mountain climbing called Disco Legs, originally published on the Quietus. Plenty of this material was road tested at East London's Red Army Fiction night – jah bless Alison and Raven.

Thanks to everyone who has had me as a reader – especially all of my pals at Incubate Festival in Tilburg, Festival No. 6 in Port Merion, Lisa and everyone at Supersonic, the Supernormal team, Bad Language in Manchester and Sensoria in Sheffield. Thanks to the good havefolket at Traena, Sam and everyone at Foyles and Andy and everyone at Threadfest, Dave at Pop Recs, everyone at King Ink, Richard at HMP Franklin for inviting to speak later in the year.

Thanks also to Andy K, Mandy, Lucy, Phil Ramsden, Wyndham, Phil Mount, Fiona, Lee, Dan, David, SOMA, Julian, Andy C, Jane, Andy V, Gillian P and James P, Lilith W, Ben M and Juno, Mike Doran and everyone at National News, Paul, Gill, Ade, Jake, Ian, Nicci, Clive, Chris, Rhydd, Daniel, Barry, Sam, Melissa, Caroline, Eleanor, Rupert, Teacher Jon, Lawrence, Craig and Chris at Bido Lito, Peter Guy/GIT, Vez, Philly Kev, Mark AP, Richard, Noreen and everyone at RTE and Spencer.

Praise be to all of the musicians who have contributed to the *Jolly Lad* CD and *Hubris* LP – Arabrot, Bronze Teeth, Mark Dicker, English Heretic, Adrian Flanagan, Abi Fry, GNOD, Grumbling Fur, Dean Honer, Loz, Karin Park, Teeth Of The Sea, Nik Void, Ali Wells, Neil Hamilton Wilkinson and Nicky Wire. Thanks also to the musicians, poets, writers and artists who are contributing to An English Trip tour which currently stands at – ANTA, Chrononautz, The Counter Culture Research Group, Falling From Cloud 9, Adrian Flanagan, Neil Francis, Alistair Fruish, Ben Graham, Henry Blacker, Rick Holland, Dean Honer, If Wet, Ill, King Ink Spoken Word, Krautrock Karaoke, Richard H Kirk, The Lone Taxidermist, The Membranes, Martin Newell, The Undertakers, Roger Robinson, Natasha Soobramanien, Stargazer's Assistant, Ten Mouth Electron, Wyndham Wallace, Luke Williams and Louise Woodcock. Thanks also to Craig and Chris at PIAS and Milan Adamik at Masterworks Audio.

Many thanks to Simon Fowler and Krent Able for their excellent art. More power to Al Overdrive and Barry The Barber for taking on the unenviable job of trying to make me look good. Thanks also to readers Jonathan Meades, Rick Holland and Caitlin Moran.

Thanks to Richard Bancroft for his superhuman proof reading skills.

Finally, thanks to everyone who has encouraged me to write my column and this book; if I've forgotten to thank you by name here, it was a genuine oversight and I'm sorry.

Some of this book was written in the comfortable study room above Stamford Hill Library. Please support your local library.

At one point in this book a character refers to me as Scouse – I would like to apologise to any true Liverpudlians upset by this reference. I am, of course, a bad wool or a placcy Scouser at best but I can't be held responsible for other people's perceptions.

Second Edition Acknowledgements

All my love as always goes to Maria and John, who continue to be the best mother and best son in the world, respectively.

My warmest thanks to my publisher (and, in this instance, second edition editor) Mark Pilkington and likewise to my two excellent readers, Adelle Stripe and Benjamin Myers.

Thanks once more to Krent Able for the additional gnarly illustration.

A big shout out to Lesley and George Cooperwaite, Mark Murphy and everyone else who has read at King Ink.

I tried to thank everyone who was part of An English Trip in the first edition but it was such a huge, chaotic affair that quite a few names didn't quite make it as far as the printers. In an attempt to correct that rude oversight I'd also like to thank Charlie Harpoon, Verity Spot, Kemper Norton, Andrew Liles, Cosmic Kenichi Iwasa, Sexton Ming, Ru and Claire, Papa Gede, Michael Atkin, Henry Layte, Tom Butchart and everyone at Sound It Out, Dan Dylan Wray and Tash Bright, Keeley Forsyth, Simon Wright, Josephine Dickinson, Sarah Angliss, Hugo, Sam Underwood, David Morton and everyone at If Wet, Rupert Morrison and everyone at Drift/Seachange, Stacey Thomas, Matty Hall, Delia Sparrow, Andy Kirkpatrick, Conn O'Grady and The Patron Saints, Philip Harding and everyone from Black Cat Records [RIP], Barberos, Jay Binary, Bob Collins, Punching Swans, Barry

Fentiman Hall, Thomas Kelly, Stuart Turner And The Reactor Core, Lawrence Montgomery and everyone at Rise Bristol, Emily Andrews and everyone at B-Arts, Moscow, Dog Ruff, Trent Vale Poet, Adam Dentone, Nev Clay, Dawn Bothwell, Mariam Rezaei, Ant Macari, Dean McPhee, Jooklo Duo, Andy Abbott and everyone at Threadfest, Joe and everyone at Outlaws Yacht Club, Declan Allen, Cad Taylor and everyone at Ipswich CSV, Dingus Khan, James Riley and Evie Salmon, Richard Dawson, Sly And The Family Drone, Knifed Out Of Existence, Steve Strong & Richard Thomas, Richard Onslow and everyone at South, Bill Campbell, Michael Holland, Maurice Carlin and everyone at Islington Mill, Emma Thompson, Verity Gardner and everyone at Fat Out, Sam Weaver, Jamie Robinson and David McLean.

Mighty praise as always goes to my second wife Luke Turner and everyone at *The Quietus* – whose number currently includes Anna Wood, Paddy Clarke, Christian Eede, Bobby Barry, Seb White and Todd The Dog.

Thanks to everyone currently at *VICE* including my editors/producers Alex Hoffman, Tshepo Mokoena and Jamie Clifton. Thanks to everyone currently at *The Guardian* including my editors Ben Beaumont-Thomas and Laura Snapes. Thanks to everyone at Bandcamp Daily. Thanks to everyone at Huck. Thanks to everyone at Reduced Listening, especially Alannah Chance and Barney Rowntree. Thanks to everyone at the BBC especially Stuart Maconie, Max Reinhardt and Nick Luscombe.

I know I thanked them in the first edition but wanted to restate my ongoing debt to Kjetil Nernes and Karin Park – true friends and brilliant people. And a shout out to their young daughter, Lydia. Likewise much love to the GNOD family.

Finally and most shamefully, I need to get two things off my chest. The most frequent questions I'm asked regarding this book are as follows. Was writing the book cathartic? And is everything in it 100% true? To which the answers are as follows: No, it wasn't, it was fucking horrible and, yes completely true apart from one outright lie and one unintentional but notable distortion of the truth.

First of all, the distortion. I left a lot of incidents out of the book, mainly for reasons of space; and likewise, to tidy up what otherwise would have made for a messy and confusing narrative, I compounded and condensed some other disparate incidents to save on a lot of space and boring exposition. In retrospect though there was one such incident where I clearly shouldn't have done this. At the end of the 'A Sound Like A Tiger Thrashing In The Water (1997)' chapter, I outline a temporary switch of gears down from constant cocaine use into crack smoking. This is all true except that (bar for one or possibly two incidents - my memory is pretty unclear on the subject if I'm being truthful) they happened in two separate locations, with a mainly different group of people. With this in mind, in the unlikely event that they've ended up reading this book, I'd like to apologise to Mr MC, R&R, Snow Queen, Slice, B McB, Snakeskin and anyone else that I've inadvertently labelled a crackhead when they were simply, y'know, having a bit of a laugh. More power to your chess playing elbows.

And the outright lie? I loved 'Don't You (Forget About Me)' by Simply Minds when it first came out. Fucking sue me.